UNARMED INSURRECTIONS

Social Movements, Protest, and Contention

Series Editor: Bert Klandermans, Free University, Amsterdam

Associate Editors: Ron R. Aminzade, University of Minnesota
David S. Meyer, University of California, Irvine
Verta A. Taylor, University of California, Santa Barbara

For more books in the series, see page 230.

UNARMED INSURRECTIONS

People Power Movements
in Nondemocracies

Kurt Schock

Social Movements, Protest, and Contention
Volume 22

University of Minnesota Press
Minneapolis • London

Published by the University of Minnesota Press
111 Third Avenue South, Suite 290
Minneapolis, MN 55401-2520
http://www.upress.umn.edu

Library of Congress Cataloging-in-Publication Data

Schock, Kurt, 1963–
    Unarmed insurrections : people power movements in nondemocracies /
Kurt Schock.
        p.   cm. — (Social movements, protest, and contention ; v. 22)
    Includes bibliographical references and index.
    ISBN 978-0-8166-4192-5 (hc : alk. paper) – ISBN 978-0-8166-4193-2 (pb : alk. paper)
    1. Nonviolence. 2. Social movements. I. Title. II. Series.
    HM1281.S36 2004

                                                                2004015059

Printed in the United States of America on acid-free paper

The University of Minnesota is an equal-opportunity educator and employer.

12 11   10 9 8 7

To my parents,
Paula and Jacob Schock

Contents

Acknowledgments

I gratefully acknowledge the Albert Einstein Institution for providing me with funding to work on this project. (The views expressed in this work are not necessarily those of the Albert Einstein Institution.) I am especially grateful to Ronald McCarthy and Bruce Jenkins of the Albert Einstein Institution for their enthusiastic support of this research project and their even greater patience as this project underwent mutation and dragged on for a few years past its originally projected date of completion.

Thanks go to Craig Jenkins and Brian Martin for penetrating comments and criticisms of the manuscript. Thanks also go to Ed Amenta, Jeff Goodwin, Ed Lehman, and participants in the workshop on Politics, Power, and Protest, Department of Sociology, New York University, and to Andy Andrews, Irene Bloemraad, Marshall Ganz, Ziad Munson, and participants in the Meaning and Mobilization workshop, Department of Sociology, Harvard University, for insightful comments and criticisms of various papers that were later to become parts of this book.

The Weatherhead Center for International Affairs at Harvard University provided an environment conducive for working on this book while I was a visiting scholar there in 1998–99. This book also benefited from my participation in the summer institute on contentious politics at the Center for Advanced Study in the Behavioral Sciences in Stanford, California, during the summer of 2000. Thanks go to the directors of the institute, Doug McAdam and Charles Tilly, as well as the wonderful group of participants for providing a stimulating environment. I would also like to acknowledge David Hosford, former dean of the Faculty of Arts and Sciences, Rutgers

University, Newark, for his promotion of faculty research and his support for my competitive fellowship leave, and Clay Hartjen, chair of the Department of Sociology and Anthropology, Rutgers University, Newark, and his wife, Prya, for their support as well. A Rutgers University research council grant in 1998 helped get this project off the ground.

Thanks go to Carrie Mullen, the acquisitions editor at the University of Minnesota Press, and the editors of the series Social Movements, Protest, and Contention, Ronald Aminzade, Bert Klandermans, David Meyers, and Verta Taylor. Especially useful were the constructive criticisms by two readers, Lester Kurtz and Sarah Soule.

Finally, thanks go to the Chakkappan sisters, Roopa and Elizabeth, for their friendship and support.

Needless to say, all problems with the finished project are entirely of my own creation.

Abbreviations

South Africa

ANC	African National Congress
AZAPO	Azanian Peoples' Organization
BCM	Black Consciousness Movement
BPC	Black People's Convention
COSATU	Congress of South African Trade Unions
FOSATU	Federation of South African Trade Unions
MDM	Mass Democratic Movement
MK	Umkhonto we Sizwe (Spear of the Nation)
NECC	National Education Crisis Committee
NUWCC	National Unemployed Workers' Coordinating Committee
Oassa	Organisation for Appropriate Social Services in South Africa
PAC	Pan African Congress
SASO	South African Students Organization
SAWCO	Sarmcol Workers' Co-operative
UDF	United Democratic Front

The Philippines

Bayan	Bagong Alyansang Makabayan (New Nationalist Alliance)
BCC	Basic Christian Communities

CBCP	Catholic Bishops' Conference of the Philippines
CNL	Christians for National Liberation
COMELEC	Commission on Elections
CORD	Coalition for the Restoration of Democracy
CPP	Communist Party of the Philippines
EDSA	Epifanio de los Santos Avenue
JAJA	Justice for Aquino, Justice for All
KBL	Kilusang Bagong Lipunan (New Society Movement)
KMP	Kilusang Magbubukid ng Pilipinas (National Farmers' Movement)
KMU	Kilusang May Uno (May First Movement)
LABAN	Lakas ng Bayan (Strength of the Nation)
NAMFREL	National Movement for Free Elections
NDF	National Democratic Front
NPA	New People's Army
PDP	Pilipino Democratic Party
PKP	Partido Komunistang Pilipinas (Philippine Communist Party)
RAM	Reform the Armed Forces Movement
TUCP	Trade Union Congress of the Philippines
UNIDO	United Democratic Opposition

Burma

ABFSU	All Burma Federation of Students' Unions
ABSDF	All Burma Students Democratic Front
ABYMU	All Burma Young Monks' Union
BSPP	Burma Socialist Program Party
DAB	Democratic Alliance
GSC	General Strike Committee
MIS	Military Intelligence Service
NCGUB	National Coalition Government of the Union of Burma
NLD	National League for Democracy
NUP	National Unity Party
SLORC	State Law and Order Restoration Council

China

BSAF	Beijing Students' Autonomous Federation
BWAF	Beijing Workers' Autonomous Federation
CCP	Chinese Communist Party

Nepal

NC	Nepali Congress Party
ULF	United Left Front
UNPM	United National People's Movement

Thailand

CPD	Campaign for Popular Democracy
NPKC	National Peace-Keeping Council
SF	Students' Federation of Thailand

Introduction

Nonviolence is a paradox. Although its promise as a method for challenging oppression is a recurrent theme throughout history, as exemplified by Jesus of Nazareth, Mohandas Gandhi, and Martin Luther King Jr., contentious politics continues to be characterized by armed rebellion, terrorism, and civil war, especially in less-developed areas of the world. Furthermore, nonviolent action is often viewed in a paradoxical manner. While proponents of nonviolent action claim that it is a panacea for the world's problems, detractors claim that it is a futile strategy for promoting change in repressive contexts, that violence is the ultimate form of power, or that structural relations determine the direction and pace of political change. Nonviolent action must not be romanticized, but neither should it be underestimated. In this study I note the potential of nonviolent action as a method for challenging oppression and injustice, and empirically examine both "positive" cases, where it promoted political change, and "negative" cases, where struggles waged primarily through nonviolent action were suppressed. Rather than focusing on the moral force of nonviolent action, I view nonviolent action as "politics by other means" and focus on its pragmatic force. In doing so, I hope to contribute to a more nuanced and empirically grounded understanding of nonviolent action.

At the end of the twentieth century, undoubtedly the bloodiest century in human history, a wave of unarmed insurrections swept across the globe, whereby mass protest demonstrations, strikes, boycotts, civil disobedience, and other methods of nonviolent action were implemented to promote political transformations in the "second" and "third" worlds. The "people power" movement in the Philippines, the Solidarity movement in Poland, the fall of the Berlin wall in Germany, and the collapse of the apartheid system in South Africa captured the popular imagination and motivated challengers in their struggles against oppression throughout the world. Yet these jubilant scenes were contrasted with the brutal suppression of unarmed insurrections in Niger, Palestine, Pakistan, Tibet, East Timor, Burma, China, and elsewhere. Is it possible to make sense of the divergent outcomes of unarmed insurrections? While case studies of particular struggles abound, there is a lack of explicitly comparative and analytical examinations of how nonviolent methods of struggle contribute to political transformations in some nondemocratic contexts but not in others. I attempt to address this gap by examining six unarmed insurrections that occurred in late twentieth-century nondemocracies: the anti-apartheid movement in South Africa (1983–90), the people power movement in the Philippines (1983–86), and pro-democracy movements in Burma (1988), China (1989), Nepal (1990), and Thailand (1991–92).

Following Stephen Zunes, I define *unarmed insurrections* as organized popular challenges to government authority that depend primarily on methods of nonviolent action rather than on armed methods (Zunes 1994).[1] They are "popular" in the sense that they are civilian-based and carried out through widespread popular participation. That is, civilians, rather than being relegated to the position of providing support for an armed vanguard, are the main actors in the struggle. Thus the term *people power* is often used to describe these struggles. They are "nonviolent" in the sense that their primary challenge to state power and legitimacy occurs through methods of nonviolent action rather than through methods of violence. Of course unarmed insurrections are almost always met with violence by authorities. That is to be expected. And of course unarmed insurrections are rarely completely nonviolent, as riots, arson, and murders of opponents or government collaborators may occur during the course of these highly charged struggles. Yet, as Zunes notes, when violence does occur in an unarmed insurrection, it usually results from the activities of fringe elements who defy the leaders of the opposition movement or from the actions of agents provocateurs, and the violence that is implemented by these elements often takes the form of responding to state violence with nonlethal weapons such as stones or Molotov cocktails (Zunes 1994).[2] Unarmed insurrections are examples of what Ralph Summy refers to as "non-idealised nonviolence." He states, "In its non-idealised form a nonviolent campaign may extend into other political categories. Though remaining predominantly nonviolent, it may contain some actions that are conducted in the conventional sphere, and perhaps even lapse into the violent sphere" (Summy 1993, 16).[3] Thus, like many episodes of political contention, unarmed insurrections may be transgressive, yet the main thrust of the challenge comes through civilians engaged in methods of nonviolent action rather than through military cadres engaged in armed rebellion or youths hurling stones at armed agents of the state.

Moreover, unarmed insurrections typically involve pragmatic rather than principled nonviolence. Pragmatic nonviolence is characterized by a commitment to methods of nonviolent action due to their perceived effectiveness, a view of means and ends as potentially separable, a perception of the conflict as a struggle of incompatible interests, an attempt to inflict nonphysical pressure on the opponent during the course of the struggle to undermine the opponent's power, and an absence of nonviolence as a way of life. Alternatively, principled nonviolence is characterized by a commitment to methods of nonviolent action for ethical reasons, a view of means and ends as inseparable, a perception of the conflict as a problem shared with the opponent, an acceptance of suffering during the struggle in order to convert the views of the opponent, and a holistic view of nonviolence as a way of life (Burrowes 1996, 98–101).[4] More generally, a distinction can be made between nonviolent action as a method of struggle and nonviolent action as a lifestyle. The focus of this study is on the former; that is, on pragmatic nonviolent action and on nonviolent action as a method of struggle.

Each of the six cases examined in this study qualify as "unarmed insurrections" and as episodes of "non-idealized" and "pragmatic" nonviolent action. In the cases where political transitions occurred, arguments can and have been made that it was the power of nonviolent action rather than violence or the threat of violence that most directly contributed to political change. Of course violence occurred along with the nonviolent struggles in these six cases, most directly in South Africa, more tangentially in the Philippines and Burma, where peripheral guerrilla struggles occurred contemporaneously with the unarmed insurrections, and in isolated incidents of violence in China, Nepal, and Thailand. However, just as it would be a grave mistake for social scientists to idealize nonviolence, it would also be a grave mistake for social scientists to limit their analysis of nonviolent action to only those rare struggles that were completely nonviolent or to overlook or dismiss the power of nonviolent action in struggles where violence occurred. Much is to be learned about the operation of nonviolent action, and it should be examined when and where it occurs. The violence that may occur in addition to the implementation of methods of nonviolent action is one of many variables that should be considered when examining the dynamics of unarmed insurrections.

What contributions do I hope to make? I hope to contribute to a movement-oriented approach to democratization. While the cases examined in this study fall squarely within the "third wave" of democratization (Huntington 1991; Markoff 1996), the literature on democratization is problematic, given its traditional emphasis either on the structural requisites of democratization or on the negotiations among elites that occur on the verge of a democratic transition. This leaves a tremendous gap in our understanding of the processes of mass political contention that almost always precede democratization. This can be addressed by more movement-oriented studies of political change.

More central to the purpose of this study, I hope to contribute to the increasing application of the political process approach to explanations of political contention in nondemocracies, and I hope to demonstrate how social movement scholarship would benefit from a serious consideration of the nonviolent action literature. The following suggestion, I believe, is just as appropriate today as when it was originally stated decades ago: "Integrating these separate bodies of theory, that of nonviolent action and that concerning political protest, would substantially add to the understanding of both phenomena" (Lipsitz and Kritzer 1975, 729).[5] The strength of each theoretical perspective addresses the weakness of the other. Political process scholarship is strong on explaining the emergence of social movements, but less so on explaining their trajectories and outcomes. Political process scholarship is strong on identifying aspects of the political context that facilitate or constrain social movements, but less so on identifying movement strategies and tactics that contribute to a recasting of the political context. On the other hand, the nonviolent action scholarship has focused on the trajectories of social movements rather than on their origins, and has emphasized the role of agency, especially strategy, in promoting political change. I hope to illustrate how the nonviolent action literature addresses some of the underspecified aspects of the political process approach and how a judicious use of the nonviolent action literature can yield useful insights for scholars of social movements.

Methodologically, the study of social movements is overwhelmingly characterized by case studies by movement or area specialists. Although undoubtedly necessary and useful—this study could not have been undertaken without such a body of literature—single case studies are less suited for identifying patterns, mechanisms, and dynamics that recur across diverse episodes of contention. While recognizing that all countries are the unique products of their own histories and circumstances, I also recognize that their uniqueness does not vitiate appropriate comparison, and that cross-national comparisons may uncover insights that may not emerge from holistic case studies. Thus, I draw on a methodological approach that attempts to identify similar mechanisms and dynamics that operate in diverse cases of contention and that produce different movement trajectories and outcomes based on different initial conditions, sequences, or combinations (McAdam, Tarrow, and Tilly 2001; Tilly 1995b, 1997, 2001). I hope that the benefits of this methodological approach outweigh its drawbacks. Movement or country specialists looking for thick descriptions, new primary data, or holistic historical explanations of each episode of contention will undoubtedly be disappointed by this study. So, too, will macrocomparative theoreticians looking for a Millian isolation of the "necessary and sufficient" conditions for a particular outcome across cases of unarmed insurrection. Unabashedly, the approach taken in this study does neither.

The modest goal of this study is to shed some light on the cross-national variation in the trajectories of unarmed insurrections in late twentieth-century nondemocracies. Rather than attempting to construct definitive accounts of these six episodes of contention or a general theory of unarmed insurrections in nondemocracies, I merely attempt to sketch a framework that may be useful to scholars studying unarmed insurrections in nondemocracies. I attempt to do so by assessing the extent to which each of the challenges examined was characterized by attributes and actions, specified in the literatures on nonviolent action and social movements, that should enhance their ability to remain resilient in repressive contexts and increase their leverage relative to their opponents. I also attempt to illustrate how movement characteristics and the political context interact to influence the trajectories of unarmed insurrections. Given the lack of comparative analyses of unarmed insurrections, I view this study as a first draft of an explanatory sketch. I hope this study is at least provocative enough to motivate others to undertake comparative analyses of the dynamics of nonviolent action and unarmed insurrections—by either elaborating on or criticizing my findings.

The comparative study of the role of nonviolent action in struggles in nondemocratic contexts is beginning to draw scholarly attention. Three excellent books have been published on the subject: *Nonviolent Social Movements: A Geographical Perspective,* edited by Stephen Zunes, Lester Kurtz, and Sarah Beth Asher (1999), *A Force More Powerful: A Century of Nonviolent Conflict,* by Peter Ackerman and Jack DuVall (2000), and *Strategic Nonviolent Conflict: The Dynamics of People Power in the Twentieth Century,* by Peter Ackerman and Christopher Kruegler (1994). The volume edited by Zunes, Kurtz, and Asher surveys a broad range of episodes of nonviolent action across the globe in the last three decades of the twentieth century, including nonviolent protest against the military dictatorship in Brazil, challenges to communist rule in Eastern Europe and the Soviet Union, Palestinian resistance to Israeli occupation, the people power movement in the Philippines, pro-democracy movements in Burma and Thailand, the Ogoni struggle for human rights in Nigeria, and the anti-apartheid movement in South Africa. While their survey illustrates the extent to which nonviolent action became a global and modular method of contention by the end of the twentieth century, the volume lacks a coherent analytical framework. Certain themes recur in many of the chapters, such as the paradox of repression, the efficacy of nonviolent discipline, the role of third parties, and the diffusion of nonviolent action across time and space, but an analytical framework is not developed that draws on these to account for the trajectories or outcomes of the various movements.

The study by Ackerman and DuVall also surveys a broad range of struggles in which nonviolent action has been implemented, chronicling the historical development of unarmed insurrections across the twentieth century, from Russia in 1905 to Burma and Yugoslavia in the 1990s. It, too, is useful for documenting the increasing use of nonviolent action across the globe and the power of nonviolent action in struggles against oppression and injustice, but it lacks an explicit analytical framework for explaining the trajectories and outcomes of the diverse challenges.

The study by Ackerman and Kruegler differs from these books in that it develops an explicit analytical framework to explain the trajectories and outcomes of struggles prosecuted primarily through nonviolent action. Ackerman and Kruegler specify twelve "principles of strategic nonviolent conflict" and assess the extent to which the principles operated in six diverse campaigns of nonviolent action across the twentieth century, including four from Europe (the first Russian Revolution from 1904 to 1906, the German struggle against French and Belgian occupation of the Ruhr in 1923, the Danish struggle against Nazi occupation from 1940 to 1945, and the Solidarity movement in Poland in 1980 and 1981), one from South Asia (the national liberation movement in India in 1930–31), and one from Central America (the civic strike in El Salvador in 1944). They conclude that the implementation of the principles of strategic nonviolent conflict increases the likelihood that campaigns of nonviolence will succeed. While providing an analytical framework not provided in the other works, Ackerman and Kruegler, however, do not adequately engage the relevant literature on social movements and undertheorize the political contexts of the struggles. Moreover, their cases include unarmed insurrections against foreign occupation as well as struggles by people against their own governments—conflicts that may involve different logics.

My study differs from these works and adds to the emerging literature on the comparative study of nonviolent action in two ways. First, I sketch an analytical framework to shed light on the trajectories of unarmed insurrections, and I do so by directly engaging the scholarly literature on social movements and identifying points of synthesis across the political process and nonviolent action theoretical approaches. Second, the cases examined in this study are more delimited across time and global context. The Zunes, Kurtz, and Asher volume usefully illustrates the extent of nonviolent action across the globe in the late twentieth century, in both democracies and nondemocracies, and the studies by Ackerman and DuVall and by Ackerman and Kruegler usefully illustrate the recurrence of primarily nonviolent struggles over the course of the twentieth century, but for analytical purposes it is more useful to examine a set of cases more closely bounded by time and context.

While Asian studies scholars may be bewildered by my inclusion of an African case among Asian ones, and experts on South Africa may be similarly perplexed by my inclusion of a South African case with Asian cases, I find comparisons that transcend the divisions constructed by area studies scholars intriguing. I examine two cases of unarmed insurrections in the third wave of democratization that pivoted around the mid-1980s (in South Africa and the Philippines), two cases from the late 1980s (in Burma and China), and two cases from the early 1990s (in Nepal and Thailand). Moreover, the six cases provide substantial variation with regard to their organization, tactics, regime type, and movement outcomes. Their organization varied from relatively spontaneous in Burma to pre-planned and highly coordinated in Nepal. Their tactics ranged from primarily protest and persuasion and disruptive nonviolent intervention in China to tactics in South Africa that spanned the range of methods of nonviolent action, with an emphasis on noncooperation and creative nonviolent intervention, and also included an armed wing that engaged in acts of sabotage in support of the unarmed insurrection. With regard to regime type, the six episodes occurred in a racially exclusive oligarchy in South Africa, a personal dictatorship in the Philippines, a military regime in Burma, a communist one-party state in China, a kingdom in Nepal, and a constitutional monarchy/"semi-democracy" in Thailand.[6] With regard to outcomes, the people power movements facilitated democratization in South Africa, the Philippines, Nepal, and Thailand, while they were suppressed without promoting democratization in Burma and China. No claims are made about how well the six cases represent the population of unarmed insurrections in late twentieth-century nondemocracies, but given their variation in terms of organization, array of actions implemented, regime type, and outcomes, the findings from them may be generalizable beyond the six cases at hand.

In chapter 1 I define nonviolent action and compare it to other strategies for responding to oppression and injustice, such as exit, everyday forms of resistance, institutional political action, and violent resistance. One factor prohibiting the development of an accurate understanding of the dynamics of nonviolent action is the degree to which nonviolent action is characterized by misconceptions. In my opening chapter I attempt to debunk some of the bountiful popular and scholarly misconceptions about nonviolent action, including the beliefs that nonviolent action is "passive resistance," that nonviolent action consists of anything that is not violent, that nonviolent action is a form of institutional politics, that nonviolent action is a form of negotiation or compromise, that those implementing nonviolent action are pacifists, that nonviolent action is based on moral pressure and works by converting the views of opponents through suffering, that nonviolent action is a failure if the state responds with violence and that nonviolent action may be dismissed because it results in the deaths of activists, that nonviolent action is a method of last resort that is used when the means of violence are not available, that nonviolent action is a method of the middle class whose use is limited to the pursuit of moderate or reformist goals, that nonviolent action is inherently slow in producing political change, that nonviolent action can be effective only in or against democracies or "benign" oppressors, and that the outcomes of nonviolent challenges are determined solely by the views of the oppressor or by the oppressor's capacity and willingness to counter with violent repression.

In chapter 1 I also briefly discuss broad trends in political contention in the third world across the second half of the twentieth century. And I suggest that a confluence of structural and normative processes contributed to a global upsurge in successful unarmed insurrections and a decline in successful armed guerrilla insurgencies in the late twentieth century. The structural processes of state making and state expansion and states' increased monopolies on the technologies of violence contributed, in many places, to a shift in the balance of power away from armed insurgents to state forces. Simultaneously, advances in communication technologies increased the transnational flow of ideas, facilitated the monitoring of state activities, and made it more difficult for states to completely censor their citizens. Crosscutting these structural transformations were growing normative concerns about human rights in the international community and increasing reservations by activists about the effectiveness and consequences of violent resistance. These structural and normative processes contributed to the development of nonviolent action as a global and modular form of contention in the late twentieth century. Rather than assuming that these developments were linear, I merely assert that a number of factors converged in the late twentieth century to promote unarmed insurrections in nondemocracies.

Despite the global wave of unarmed insurrections identified in chapter 1, social scientists understand very little about their dynamics. In chapter 2 I discuss two theoretical approaches that may be useful in accounting for the trajectories and outcomes of unarmed insurrections: the political process and nonviolent action approaches. For unarmed insurrections to promote political change in nondemocracies they must remain resilient in the face of repression, undermine state power, and in many cases attract the support of third parties. Drawing on the literatures of political process and nonviolent action, I specify attributes of nonviolent struggles that facilitate these actions and attempt to specify the mechanisms that link movement attributes and the political contexts outside of the movements to the trajectories of struggle.

Chapter 3 consists of an examination of the challenge to apartheid in South Africa from 1983 to 1990 and the challenge to the Marcos dictatorship in the Philippines from 1983 to 1986. Both the anti-apartheid movement in South Africa and the anti-Marcos struggle in the Philippines were dispersed struggles aggregated and united by federations or umbrella organizations. Both movements implemented a broad range of methods of nonviolent action, and in both cases the states suffered from a loss of legitimacy—in South Africa due to the rejection of political reform by nonwhites, and in the Philippines due to the opposition of the Catholic Church. In both cases, internal pressure combined with external pressure to promote political change—in the case of South Africa capital flight and the imposition of sanctions by the international community, and in the case of the Philippines capital flight and diplomatic pressure by the United States.

In addition, in chapter 3 I consider why armed resistance movements by themselves were incapable of ending oppressive rule in South Africa and the Philippines. In South Africa, the military might of the apartheid regime far exceeded the military capacities of the African National Congress (ANC), and the ANC lacked bases from which to launch guerrilla operations within the country. In the Philippines, the communist insurgency carried out by the New People's Army (NPA) was growing, but the Philippine military had the full backing of the United States, which was unlikely to let a violent communist insurgency succeed given U.S. economic and strategic interests in the Philippines. While recognizing that the cultures of resistance forged by the ANC and the NPA facilitated mobilization, I also recognize that the implementation of nonviolent action contributed to the cultivation of support that the challengers might not have received if the struggles had been primarily violent. In the case of South Africa, it is less likely that the anti-apartheid movement would have received crucial support from South African churches or Western countries if the challenge had been made primarily through armed methods. In the Philippines, it is unlikely that the Catholic Church would have thrown its institutional weight behind the anti-Marcos struggle if it had been primarily violent.

In chapter 4 I examine the pro-democracy movements in Burma in 1988 and in China in 1989. Whereas the challenges in South Africa and the Philippines gained momentum over a period of years, the challenges in Burma and China were each violently suppressed after a few months of sustained collective action. While the pro-democracy movement in Burma was surprisingly effective in implementing diverse methods of nonviolent action, the pro-democracy movement in China was based almost exclusively on methods of protest and persuasion and on disruptive nonviolent intervention. While these methods indicated the extent of opposition to the regime and the commitment of the Chinese activists to their cause, by themselves they did not provide the challengers with sufficient leverage against the communist regime to promote political change. Crucial factors inhibiting the challenges in both cases were disorganization, the lack of autonomous infrastructures, and a lack of effective pressure on the regimes from abroad during the course of the struggles.

Despite the outcomes of the struggles, both challenges contributed to the development of "cultures of nonviolent resistance"—indications of the emergence of an oppositional civil society—and international networks of activists that will most certainly be invoked in future struggles.

In chapter 5 I examine the pro-democracy movement in Nepal in 1990 and the anti-military movement in Thailand in 1991–92. The challenge to the monarchy in Nepal and the challenge to military rule in Thailand were both prosecuted by broad-based movements that drew on the coordinated action of diverse opposition groups. Both movements were adept at implementing a variety of methods of nonviolent action. In contrast to the challenges in Burma and China, which lacked crucial support from abroad, the challenges in Nepal and Thailand were both facilitated by external pressures, albeit in different ways. In Nepal the leverage of the regime was undermined due to pressure from India and the international donor community, while in Thailand international pressure reached the regime through networks of nongovernmental organizations and neoliberal capitalists.

The success of the unarmed insurrections in Nepal and Thailand contrasted with the failure of earlier attempts to topple the state through armed force. In the early 1960s, the Maoist Communist Party of Thailand declared that armed struggle was the proper strategy for revolution, and it began engaging government forces in battle in 1965. The insurgency was kept at bay during the 1960s and 1970s, and the guerrilla movement crumbled during the early 1980s for a variety of reasons, including the expansion of democratic procedures, the granting of amnesty to those who defected from the guerrilla forces, and the popular mobilization of extreme right-wing political organizations and militia to counter the guerrillas in the countryside, as well as greater government attention to development in rural areas. In Nepal a guerrilla uprising occurred in the early 1970s in the Terai, the Nepalese lowlands adjacent to the Indian states of Bihar and West Bengal, but failed due to lack of broad-based support and state counterinsurgency operations.

In the final chapter I draw conclusions about how and why unarmed insurrections may or may not contribute to political transformations in nondemocracies. The dynamics of contention in the six cases are highlighted with reference to each other, and the role of violence and the possibility of the operation of radical flank effects are addressed.[7] I also identify general lessons that activists may want to consider with regard to their struggles.

In conclusion, let me be perfectly clear about a few points. First, I never idealize nonviolence or make any moral claims concerning violence or nonviolence. It is a worthwhile endeavor, I think, to attempt to understand the potential and the limitations of pragmatic nonviolent action, and the best method for doing so is by examining nonviolent action in a dispassionate social scientific manner. Moreover, I never claim that violence is ineffective in promoting political change. Certainly there are instances where violence may be justified, and the most cursory glance through history texts will uncover a plethora of episodes of successful violent insurrection. Furthermore, I make no claims about the "end of history" or the idea that the world is evolving to a point where there will be an inevitable decline in violent struggles. I merely assert that there was a global wave of unarmed insurrections in the late twentieth century and that it would behoove social scientists to understand why this occurred and the role that nonviolent action played in contributing to political transitions in some cases but not in others.

Finally, I do not idealize representative democracy. What I refer to in this study as movement "outcomes"—that is, whether or not a challenge contributed to democratization, the process whereby an authoritarian polity becomes more democratic—is in many ways merely the beginning of the struggle. Undoubtedly, respect for civil rights and political liberties, freedom of speech, separation of powers, institutionalized electoral competition, and constitutional rule—however imperfectly they are implemented—have real consequences for the lives of human beings. Yet representative democracy is not the promised land of political development. The process of democratization is often coopted into programs of polyarchy (i.e., bourgeois democracy) and neoliberalism by the United States and international financial institutions so as to prevent popular democracy from taking root (e.g., see Robinson 1996). Thus, democratic transitions are merely the first steps in ongoing struggles for participatory democracy. Far from representing a sharp dichotomy, democracy and authoritarianism are terrains in which ongoing struggles between domination and resistance are played out. The transition to democracy may diminish overt political authoritarianism, but struggles against covert authoritarianism, statism, militarism, patriarchy, racism, political corruption, environmental degradation, and capitalist economic exploitation continue. If anything, a transition to a formal democratic system is significant because it may provide a context in which these struggles are more effectively waged.

1

From "People's War" to "People Power"?

On January 7, 1978, exactly one week after Mohammed Reza Pahlavi, the shah of Iran, hosted a New Year's Eve party where the president of the United States, Jimmy Carter, toasted to the shah's health and long life, *Ettelaat,* a national newspaper in Iran, published an article critical of Ayotallah Ruhollah Khomeini, accusing him of being connected with a foreign power.[1] Khomeini, a longtime critic of the shah who had lived in exile since 1964, mostly in Iraq, after speaking out against the shah's Westernization policies, continued to criticize the shah from abroad, thus provoking the government's attempt to decertify its most vocal critic. The juxtaposition of the shah's strong ties to the United States with the *Ettelaat* attack on Khomeini was not lost on Iranian citizens, inciting demonstrations against the shah on January 8, 1978. Hundreds of people were killed or injured during demonstrations in Qom, Khomeini's hometown, when security forces responded with violence. Protest funerals occurred precisely forty days later, in the Islamic tradition of public mourning forty days after a death. As the state continued to respond with force to public displays of mourning and support for Khomeini, the cycles of forty-day protest funerals imbricated and the pace of resistance accelerated. Anti-regime protests spread to Tehran, Tebriz, Kazerun, Mashad, and Isfahan. By July, people had been killed or injured by security forces in thirteen cities across Iran.

Cross-cutting the cycles of protest funerals was an incident in Abadan, where 410 people died in a suspicious fire at a movie theater on August 20, 1978. It was widely believed that the fire was set by government officials, and by September protest marches and demonstrations against the government were being held regularly in Tehran and other cities. On Friday, September 7, 1978, on what came to be known as "Black Friday," approximately fifty thousand people gathered at Jaleh Square in Tehran, apparently unaware of the recent imposition of martial law in Tehran and eleven other cities. The shah's forces responded with tear gas to disperse the crowd of unarmed demonstrators, and in the confusion that followed, military forces opened fire, killing hundreds of people. Throughout Tehran protestors and soldiers engaged in battle, and by the end of the day many hundreds of people, mostly unarmed civilians, had been killed.

As the iterative process of demonstrations and repression continued, mass mobilization was framed in an explicitly anti-shah manner. Khomeini, now in France after being forced to leave Iraq in 1978, encouraged resistance, calling for nonviolent civil disobedience. Tapes of Khomeini's instructions for boycotts, strikes, and noncooperation were circulated throughout Iran. On October 7, 1978, public employees went on strike. Soon thereafter, two major newspapers were shut down by workers who walked out in protest of the imposition of censorship. A general strike was called in Mashad, and by late October major anti-shah demonstrations were occurring throughout Iran. On October 31 oil workers went on strike, depriving the regime of tens of million of dollars per day. The government imposed martial law nationwide on November 5, and the next day citizens responded with a nationwide one-day general strike. On December 4 thousands of oil workers renewed their strike. Khomeini called for a day of mourning for those killed by the state and a general strike in support of the striking oil workers. By December 28 the oil industry was completely shut down. On December 29 the general strike escalated and the central bank was shut down as well. The lifeblood of the shah's regime was drained by mass civil disobedience.

On December 30, 1978, the shah appointed Shapur Bakhtiar to form a civilian government. Khomeini denounced Bakhtiar and proclaimed the formation of a parallel government, the Revolutionary Council. On January 16, 1979, the shah left Iran for Egypt, while demonstrations continued against the Bakhtiar government. On February 1, 1979, Khomeini, cheered on by crowds five million strong, returned to Iran from exile. Bakhtiar resigned on February 11, ushering in a revolutionary transfer of power.

The revolutionary outcome in Iran was significant in that it did not fit neatly into popular or scholarly conceptions of revolution, nor did it rely on the prevailing revolutionary repertoires of armed rebellion.[2] The insurrection that toppled the shah was unexpected given the military might and extensive internal security apparatus of the regime and the absence of a powerful armed guerrilla movement. The two underground armed guerrilla movements in Iran, the Fedayeen and the Mujahhadin, were small and ineffective in challenging the state. Their membership did not surpass three hundred at their peak, and they were infiltrated by the SAVAK (Sazeman-i Ettelaat va Amniyat-i Keshvar, or National Organization for Intelligence and Security), the shah's infamous internal security apparatus. While there were armed battles between military forces loyal to the shah and soldiers who deserted the regime immediately prior to the transfer of power,[3] the shah was toppled not by an armed insurgency, but rather by an unarmed insurrection whereby ordinary citizens engaged in methods of nonviolent action, such as protests, demonstrations, strikes, boycotts, and civil disobedience. Moreover, Khomeini encouraged nonviolent discipline and urged people to treat soldiers as brothers rather than as enemies. Soldiers who deserted from the military were treated as heroes and carried atop people's shoulders in mass marches.

As one expert on revolutions, and on the Iranian Revolution in particular, correctly stated, "The relative absence of armed force and the strategies of general strike and massive, peaceful demonstrations fit almost no one's conception of how revolutions succeed" (Foran 1994, 162). This statement reflects the fact that prior to what transpired in Iran, the events defined by social scientists as revolutions had involved armed rebellion, and it also reflects the fact that the violent components of revolution have typically been emphasized, if not glorified, while the importance of unarmed components, which have also characterized events defined by social scientists as revolutions, have often been downplayed, overlooked, or forgotten.

The toppling of the shah of Iran was also significant because it was one of the first in a wave of unarmed insurrections throughout the "second" and "third" worlds that occurred from the late 1970s through the 1990s whereby authoritarian regimes, most with a monopoly on military force, were seriously challenged by their own citizens, who relied primarily on unarmed rather than armed methods of resistance (see Table 1). Of course unarmed insurrections are not a new phenomena, as they have occurred sporadically throughout history. There have even been waves of unarmed insurrections in the past, such as the transnational wave that swept through Europe in 1848 and the 1968 wave that included unarmed insurrections in a number of developed countries, most notably France. Nevertheless, methods of nonviolent action have typically been associated with political contention in countries that are more politically developed rather than being used as pivotal actions in underdeveloped and nondemocratic countries. Regime change in nondemocracies occurring through unarmed methods did not fit into the prevailing conceptions of how political change occurred in less-developed or

Table 1. Major Unarmed Insurrections in the Second and Third Worlds, 1978–2001

Country	Peak year(s) of struggle	Direct contribution to political transition
Iran	1978–79	+
Bolivia	1978–82	+
El Salvador	1979–81	-
Poland	1980–89	+
Pakistan	1983	-
The Philippines	1983–86	+
Chile	1983–89	+
South Africa	1983–90	+
Haiti	1985	+
The Sudan	1985	+
South Korea	1987	+
Tibet	1987–89	-
Palestine (West Bank and Gaza Strip)	1987–90	-
Burma	1988	-
Bulgaria	1989	+
China	1989	-
Czechoslovakia	1989	+
East Germany	1989	+
Hungary	1989	+
Kenya	1989	-
Bangladesh	1989–90	+
Mongolia	1989–90	+
Mali	1989–92	+
Nepal	1990	+
Niger	1991–92	-
Thailand	1991–92	+
Madagascar	1991–93	+
Indonesia	1997–98	+
Nigeria	1998–99	+
Yugoslavia	2000	+
The Philippines	2001	+

Note: Dates are approximate. See Goodwin (2001a, 295) and Zunes (1994) for similar tables.

nondemocratic contexts. Hence the surprise of social scientists at the events in Iran in 1978–79 as well as the events in Eastern Europe a decade later.

In addition to Iran, the late twentieth-century wave of unarmed insurrections in nondemocracies included insurrections against military juntas in Bolivia in the late 1970s and the early 1980s; uprisings against the Duvalier regime in Haiti and the Nimiery regime in the Sudan in 1985; the "people power" movement in the Philippines in 1986; pro-democracy movements in Chile, South Africa, and South Korea in the 1980s; and pro-democracy movements in Bangladesh, Nepal, Mali, Madagascar, and Thailand between 1989 and 1993, in Indonesia in 1997–98, and in Nigeria in 1998–99. The communist world was rocked by unarmed insurrections as well, beginning with the Solidarity movement in Poland in the 1980s. Between 1989 and 1991 unarmed insurrections spread to most Eurasian communist regimes within the Soviet sphere, from East Germany to Mongolia. These unwonted challenges, along with a wave of primarily nonviolent secessions occurring from the Baltic States to Central Asia, contributed to the disintegration of the Soviet Union as well.[4] Although months of NATO bombing failed to topple the dictatorship of Slobodan Milosevic in Yugoslavia, an unarmed insurrection toppled him in 2000. Yet while all of the above-mentioned unarmed insurrections contributed to substantial political transformations, comparable episodes of contention in other countries did not. Unarmed insurrections in El Salvador,[5] Niger, Palestine, Pakistan, Burma, Tibet, and China were brutally crushed in the 1980s, and unarmed uprisings in Kenya and East Timor in the early to mid-1990s made only marginal inroads in challenging authoritarian political relations.[6] While the outcomes differed, the common denominator of all of these challenges was their predominant reliance on methods of nonviolent action to challenge repressive nondemocratic regimes.

What is nonviolent action? What factors contributed to an apparent global wave of unarmed insurrections from the late 1970s through the 1990s? Why did some of the unarmed insurrections in the 1980s and the 1990s contribute to political transformation and democratization, while others did not? The first two questions are addressed in this chapter, while the third question is addressed in subsequent chapters.

Nonviolent Action

As noted in the introduction, political contention often transgresses institutional boundaries and may involve a spectrum of methods across the continuum from nonviolent to violent. Nevertheless, while recognizing that empirical cases of political contention are frequently transgressive and often involve both violent and nonviolent action, it is nevertheless necessary to make conceptual distinctions between different types of resistance in order to more clearly understand the role of strategy and tactics in the dynamics of contention.

What is nonviolent action? As the name implies, nonviolent action is nonviolent—it does not involve physical violence or the threat of physical violence against human beings—and it is active—it involves activity in the collective pursuit of social or political objectives. More specifically, nonviolent action involves an active process of bringing political, economic, social, emotional, or moral pressure to bear in the wielding of power in contentious interactions between collective actors (McCarthy 1990, 1997; Sharp 1973, 1990, 1999). Nonviolent action is noninstitutional, that is, it operates outside the bounds of institutionalized political channels, and it is indeterminate, that is, the procedures for determining the outcome of the conflict are not specified in advance (Bond 1994). Nonviolent action occurs through (1) acts of omission, whereby people refuse to perform acts expected by norms, custom, law, or decree; (2) acts of commission, whereby people perform acts that they do not usually perform, are not expected by norms or customs to perform, or are forbidden by law, regulation, or decree to perform; or (3) a combination of acts of omission and commission (Sharp 1973). Rather than being viewed as half of a rigid violent-nonviolent dichotomy, nonviolent action may be better understood as a set of methods with special features that are different from those of both violent resistance and institutional politics (McCarthy 1990).

Misconceptions about Nonviolent Action

The social scientific analysis of nonviolent action has been inhibited by the numerous misconceptions that people have about what nonviolent action is, how it works, when it is used, and by whom it is implemented.[7] A major factor contributing to these misconceptions is that the history of nonviolent action has been marginalized or misinterpreted, while the history of violence has been emphasized, if not glorified. Although there is abundant historical material on violent struggles, there is far less material on nonviolent struggles (see Burrowes 1996; Sharp 1973; Wink 1992, chapter 13). Nineteen of the most common misconceptions are discussed below.[8]

1. Nonviolent action is not inaction (although it may involve the refusal to carry out an action that is expected, that is, an act of omission), it is not submissiveness, it is not the avoidance of conflict, and it is not passive resistance. In fact, nonviolent action is a direct means for prosecuting conflicts

with opponents and is an explicit rejection of inaction, submission, and passivity (Sharp 1973).

The term *passive resistance* is a misnomer when used to describe nonviolent action. There is nothing passive or evasive about nonviolent resistance, as it is an active and overt means for prosecuting conflicts with opponents. Although Mohandas Gandhi at first used the term *passive resistance,* he subsequently rejected the term due to its inaccurate connotations. Similarly, Martin Luther King Jr. rejected the term *passive resistance* and used words such as *aggressive, militant, confrontational,* and *coercive* to describe his campaigns of nonviolent action. Likewise, social scientists would benefit from abandoning the term *passive resistance* and using the more accurate and precise term *nonviolent action.* This is not a mere semantic distinction, but rather is crucial to the understanding of nonviolent resistance.

2. Not everything that is not violent is considered nonviolent action. *Nonviolent action* refers to specific actions that involve risk and invoke nonviolent pressure or nonviolent coercion in contentious interactions between opposing groups.

3. Nonviolent action is not limited to state-sanctioned political activities. Nonviolent action may be legal or illegal. Civil disobedience, that is, the open and deliberate violation of the law for a collective social or political purpose, is a fundamental type of nonviolent action.

4. Nonviolent action is not composed of regular or institutionalized techniques of political action such as litigation, letter writing, lobbying, voting, or the passage of laws.[9] Although institutional methods of political action often accompany nonviolent struggles, nonviolent action occurs outside the bounds of institutional politics. Contrary to what is the case for those engaging in regular and institutionalized political activity, there is always an element of risk involved for those implementing nonviolent action, since it presents a direct challenge to authorities. Thus nonviolent action is context-specific. Displaying anti-regime posters in democracies would be considered a low-risk and regular form of political action, whereas the same activity in nondemocracies would be considered irregular, would involve a substantial amount of risk, and would therefore be considered a method of nonviolent action. Similarly, strikes that occur within the bounds of institutionalized labor relations in democracies would not be considered nonviolent action, since they are not noninstitutional or indeterminate. However, a wildcat strike in a democracy and most strikes in nondemocracies would be instances of nonviolent action given their noninstitutionalized, indeterminate, and high-risk features.

5. Nonviolent action is not a form of negotiation or compromise.

Negotiation and compromise may or may not accompany conflicts prosecuted through nonviolent action, just as they may or may not accompany conflicts prosecuted through violent action. In other words, nonviolent action is a means for prosecuting a conflict and should be distinguished from means of conflict resolution (Ackerman and Kruegler 1994, 5).

6. Nonviolent action does not depend on moral authority, the "mobilization of shame," or the conversion of the views of the opponent in order to promote political change. While conversion of the opponent's views sometimes occurs, more often than not nonviolent action promotes political change through nonviolent coercion, that is, it forces the opponent to make changes by undermining the opponent's power.[10] Of course moral pressure may be mobilized, but in the absence of political and economic pressure it is unlikely to produce change.

7. Those who implement nonviolent action do not assume that the state will not react with violence. Violence is to be expected from governments, especially nondemocratic governments. The violent reaction of governments is not an indication of the failure of nonviolent action. In fact, governments respond with violence precisely because nonviolent action presents a serious threat to their power. To dismiss the use of nonviolent action because people are killed is no more logical than dismissing armed resistance for the same reasons (Zunes 1999a, 130). Nonviolent struggle does not mean the absence of violence.

8. That said, suffering is not an essential part of nonviolent resistance. The view that suffering is central to nonviolent resistance is based on the misguided assumption that nonviolent action is passive resistance and that nonviolent action is intended to produce change through the conversion of the oppressor's views (Martin 1997). While those implementing challenges that incorporate nonviolent action should expect a violent response by the government, they should also prepare to mute the impact of the opponent's violence. That is, they should, in the words of Peter Ackerman and Christopher Kruegler, "get out of harm's way, take the sting out of the agents of violence, disable the weapons, prepare people for the worst effects of violence, and reduce the strategic importance of what may be lost to violence" (Ackerman and Kruegler 1994, 38). Nonviolent resistance is much more sophisticated than the widespread (mis)conception that it is characterized by activists meekly accepting physical attacks by the agents of their oppressors in the hope that their suffering will convert the opponents or make publics sympathetic to their cause.

9. Nonviolent action is not a method of contention that is used only as a last resort, when the means of violence are unavailable. Although non-

violent action may be used when no weapons are available, it may also be used instead of violent methods.

10. Nonviolent action is not a method of the "middle class" or a "bourgeois" approach to political contention. Nonviolent action can be and has been implemented by groups from any and all classes and castes, from slaves to members of the upper class (McCarthy and Kruegler 1993). For obvious reasons, though, it is used by the less powerful, that is, those without regular access to power holders, more frequently than by the powerful.

11. The use of nonviolent action is not limited to the pursuit of "moderate" or "reformist" goals. It may also be implemented in the pursuit of "radical" goals. Anders Corr, for example, has documented the extensive use of nonviolent action in land and housing struggles across the developed and underdeveloped worlds (Corr 1999). Challenges to private property relations can hardly be considered reformist, moderate, or bourgeois. Similarly, the feminist movement has radically challenged patriarchal gender relations—almost entirely through methods that do not involve violence. Challenges can be militant, radical, *and* nonviolent.

12. While nonviolent action by its very nature requires patience, it is not inherently slow in producing political change compared to violent action (Shepard 2002). Armed insurgencies that served as models for a generation of revolutionaries took decades to succeed: the communists in China were engaged in armed combat for over twenty years before they assumed power in 1949, and the Vietnamese were engaged in armed combat against French, Japanese, and American imperialists for over three decades before they achieved national liberation. Similarly, numerous campaigns of terror, such as those waged by the Euskadi Ta Akatasuna (ETA, Basque Homeland and Freedom) in Spain, the Irish Republican Army (IRA) in Northern Ireland, and the Liberation Tigers of Tamil Eelam (LTTE) in Sri Lanka have operated for decades without meeting their objectives.[11] By contrast, leaders of the nonviolent Solidarity movement in Poland took office about a decade after its emergence, and it took a mere thirty months following the assassination of Benigno Aquino in August 1983 for the "people power" movement in the Philippines to topple Ferdinand Marcos—something the Filipino communists had been trying to do through armed methods since 1969.

13. The occurrence of nonviolent action is not structurally determined. While there are empirical relationships in geographically and temporally bound places and time periods between the political context and the use of a given strategy for responding to grievances,[12] the methods used to challenge unjust or oppressive political relations are not determined by the political

context. Processes of learning, diffusion, and social change may result in the implementation of nonviolent action in contexts or situations historically characterized by violent contention. Conflicts involving land, separatism, or autonomy, for example, are generally assumed to be—and have historically been—violent. However, nonviolent strategies are increasingly being used in such conflicts. Certainly the context of the conflict and the issues at stake influence the strategies of resistance, but not in a deterministic manner.

14. The effectiveness of nonviolent action is not a function of the ideology of the oppressors. It is often claimed that nonviolent action can succeed only in democracies or only when it is used against "benign" or "universalist" oppressors. The beliefs of the oppressors may influence the dynamics of contention, but they are not the sole determinants of the outcomes of struggles prosecuted through methods of nonviolent action.

15. Similarly, the effectiveness of nonviolent action is not a function of the repressiveness of the oppressors. In fact, campaigns of nonviolent action have been effective in brutally repressive contexts, and ineffective in open democratic polities. Repression, of course, constrains the ability of challengers to organize, communicate, mobilize, and engage in collective action, and magnifies the risk of participation in collective action. Nevertheless, repression is only one of many factors that influence the trajectories of struggles relying on nonviolent action. It is not the sole determinant of their trajectories or outcomes.

16. The mass mobilization of people into campaigns of nonviolent action in nondemocracies does not depend on coercion. While some campaigns of nonviolent action in nondemocracies have involved coercion to promote mass mobilization, coercion is not a necessary feature of mass mobilization in nondemocracies. Coercion is not inherent to campaigns of noncooperation, but rather is something that varies, depending on contextual factors such as the consensus within the community, the extent to which there is knowledge about the campaign throughout the community, and the type of noncooperation implemented. With regard to consumer boycotts in South Africa, for example, when the political loyalties of a community were sharply divided or when the campaigns were not adequately publicized, coercion was more likely to be used to enforce the consumer boycotts. However, when there was solidarity within the community and people were well aware that a consumer boycott was to be implemented and how long it was supposed to last, coercion was less likely to occur. Moreover, the use of coercion to promote participation in mass campaigns in South Africa varied across the types of noncooperation that were implemented. Although consumer boycotts sometimes involved coercion in order to pro-

mote mass mobilization, mass participation in rent boycotts were less likely to involve coercive mobilization (Seekings 2000, 179).

17. Participation in campaigns of nonviolent action does not require that activists hold any sort of ideological, religious, or metaphysical beliefs. Contrary to popular and scholarly assumptions, those who engage in nonviolent action are rarely pacifists. Those who engage in nonviolent action hold a variety of different beliefs, one of which may be pacifism, but pacifism is not prevalent among those engaged in nonviolent action. As George Lakey notes, "Most pacifists do not practice nonviolent resistance, and most people who do practice nonviolent resistance are not pacifists" (Lakey 1973, 57).

18. Similarly, those who implement nonviolent action do not have to be aware that they are implementing a particular class of methods. An American theologian, Walter Wink, interviewed participants in the anti-apartheid movement in South Africa in 1986. He writes, "What we found most surprising is that a great many of the people simply do not know how to name their actual experiences with nonviolence" (Wink 1987, 4). When asked about methods of nonviolent action, a common response was "'We tried that [nonviolent action] for fifty years and it didn't work. Sharpeville in 1960 proved to us that violence is the only way left'" (Wink 1987, 4). Yet when Wink pressed them to identify the methods that were most effective in challenging the state over the past two years,

> they produced a remarkably long list of nonviolent actions: labor strikes, slow-downs, sit-downs, stoppages, and stay-aways; bus boycotts, consumer boycotts, and school boycotts; funeral demonstrations; noncooperation with government appointed functionaries; non-payment of rent; violation of government bans on peaceful meetings; defiance of segregation orders on beaches and restaurants, theaters, and hotels; and the shunning of black police and soldiers. This amounts to what is probably the largest grassroots eruption of diverse nonviolent strategies in a single struggle in human history! Yet these students, and many others we interviewed, both black and white, failed to identify these tactics as nonviolent and even bridled at the word. (Wink 1987, 4)

The point is that those who implement methods of nonviolent action may not recognize them as "methods of nonviolent action," and they certainly do not have to adhere to a theory of nonviolence or a moral code to successfully implement them. Furthermore, whether or not "nonviolence" is identified by name as a method of struggle by activists, social scientists should be able to operationalize nonviolent action and differentiate between nonviolent and violent action. Certainly social scientists should be capable of distinguishing between violent rhetoric and nonviolent action.

19. Campaigns of nonviolent action do not need a charismatic leader in order to succeed. Popular conceptions of nonviolent action often invoke images of Mohandas Gandhi or Martin Luther King Jr. inspiring mass campaigns of nonviolent struggle. Yet in many successful campaigns of non-violent action the leader or leaders lacked charismatic attributes, and some struggles have even lacked identifiable leaders (Sharp 1999, 570).

Different Standards

Related to the misconceptions about nonviolent action are the different log-ics used to compare the effectiveness of violent and nonviolent action and the extreme standards that are often invoked to judge the effectiveness of nonviolent action. Take, for example, the failure of the United States gov-ernment to impose its will on Vietnam through the use of violence during the Vietnam War. The military defeat of the United States did not lead to a fundamental questioning of the efficacy of the strategy of military violence. That is, people did not conclude that military violence as a strategy was fundamentally flawed. Instead, characteristics of that particular military campaign were identified to explain its failure, such as that the military did not have clear goals, it was unprepared for asymmetric battles, it failed to identify the Vietnamese center of gravity, the war was losing support at home, and so on. Perhaps more to the point, a single failed guerrilla insur-gency is not taken as "proof" that engaging in armed guerrilla struggles is a futile strategy for promoting political change.

On the other hand, when a particular campaign of nonviolent action fails to produce change, rather than identifying the characteristics of that particular campaign that contributed to its failure, the entire strategy of nonviolent action is often questioned. A logic that assumes that a particular failed occurrence of nonviolent struggle proves its futility as a strategy (a logic not applied to violent struggles) is fundamentally flawed.

Along these lines, some tend to dismiss the power of nonviolent ac-tion by invoking some extreme case to "prove" its futility. For example, critics maintain that campaigns of nonviolent action undertaken by Jews in Nazi Germany would not have succeeded. This may be correct, but it is also unlikely that violent resistance by Jews would have succeeded in Nazi Germany. Or, for example, critics of nonviolent action maintain that it would not have worked against Stalin in the Soviet Union. This, too, may be correct. Nevertheless, these are extreme cases, and in reality most con-texts are not so extreme. Using extreme cases to dismiss an entire strategy of resistance is illogical. Let me emphasize that I do not raise these issues to idealize nonviolent action; instead I raise them so that we can more clearly understand the limits and potential of nonviolent action.

Responding to Grievances

Nonviolent action is one of many possible responses to situations of oppression or injustice. Figure 1 identifies a number of hypothetical responses to such situations. These responses are differentiated for conceptual purposes to facilitate clearer insights into the dynamics of political contention. We need to keep in mind that struggles do not fit into neat categories and often transgress categories.

Before action can be taken to transform an oppressive or unjust situation, people must recognize, name, and construe the situation as unacceptable

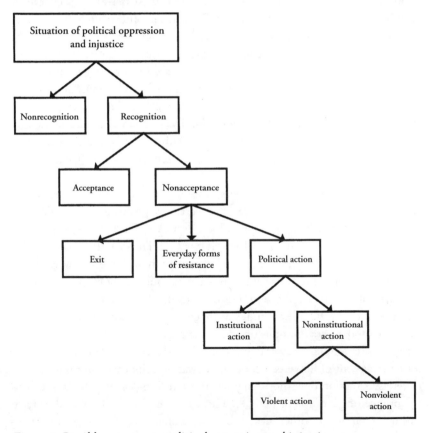

Figure 1. Possible responses to political oppression and injustice.

through cultural processes, and they must overcome obstacles such as fear, ideological hegemony, apathy, fatalism, and grudging acceptance. This typically involves processes of identity formation, solidarity, consciousness raising, and the construction of counterhegemonic cultural frames.[13] Once the oppressive or unjust situation is recognized and viewed as unacceptable, it may be acted upon in a variety of ways. One response is for members of the aggrieved group to *exit* the situation. Situations of oppression, injustice, political exclusion, and economic exploitation have fueled emigration from less-developed countries to more-developed ones, where polities are often more inclusive and economic exploitation is often more tolerable. After the Second World War notable exits occurred in Europe across the "iron curtain." Each year during the 1950s and into the 1960s, hundreds of thousands of East Germans left their country to settle in the West, leading to the construction of the Berlin Wall by the East German government in 1961 to stop the flow of emigration from East Berlin to West Berlin. This effectively eliminated the exit response until 1989, when the official emigration policy in East Germany was relaxed. In addition to emigration encouraged by the official relaxation of policies, illegal emigration increased in 1989 as well. The West German diplomatic missions in East Berlin, Prague, Budapest, and Warsaw were closed after being inundated with thousands of East German citizens attempting to exit their country. East German exits intensified during the summer of 1989, when Hungary began dismantling the iron curtain by opening its border with Austria. Subsequently, thousands of East Germans fled to the West through Hungary each day (Bleiker 1993, 10–13; Hirschman 1993).[14]

A second response by members of an aggrieved group is to engage in *everyday forms of resistance*. These are covert, low-profile actions against the powerful by subordinate groups in local contexts (Dirks 1994; J. C. Scott 1985, 1989, 1990; Scott and Kerkvleit 1986; Thaxton 1997). Everyday forms of resistance are typically implemented when the less powerful have no institutionalized recourse and fear the consequences of engaging in overt noninstitutional political action. Historically, this form of resistance emerged in opposition to the rule of landlords in agrarian societies and has continued into the modern era in opposition to processes of state making and capitalist intrusion. Examples of everyday forms of resistance include underreporting or concealment of harvests, tax evasion, evading military conscription, character assassination of authority figures, the spreading of rumors, and feigned ignorance of government policies. These acts tend to be local and isolated from similar acts in other locales, but occasionally local struggles may connect with one another, resulting in more overt political movements.

Third, members of aggrieved groups may engage in *political action,* which, in addition to solidarity and framing, also involves surpassing some minimum threshold of organization and mobilization in order to be sustained.[15] Political action may occur within or outside institutional political channels. *Institutional political action,* the study of which comprises a substantive domain of political science, includes acts such as voting, holding referenda, circulating petitions, lobbying, and engaging in litigation.[16] However, even in the most democratic countries, disparities exist between groups with regard to political access and resources, resulting in biased political systems. G. William Domhoff, for example, has illustrated how the American polity, one of the most open in the world, is dominated by a power elite (Domhoff 2002).[17] When people want perceived grievances to be redressed, but cannot satisfactorily do so through institutionalized political action, they may turn to methods of *noninstitutional political action.*

While the outcome of institutional political action is determinate, that is, prescribed by some procedure, practice, or norm, noninstitutional political action is indeterminate, that is, it is not prescribed by any such existing rules or regulations, and its outcome is a function of contentious interactions between opposing forces (Bond 1994). The power of noninstitutional politics inheres in its indeterminateness and disruptiveness. When noninstitutional political action loses its uncertainty and disruptiveness and becomes institutionalized, as in highly choreographed and regulated protest demonstrations at the Mall in Washington, DC, its effectiveness in promoting political change decreases. Two types of noninstitutional politics are violent and nonviolent action.

Violent political action involves the use of physical force or the threat of physical force against human beings in pursuit of political objectives. Violent action includes techniques such as imprisonment, kidnaping, assault, rape, torture, arson, murder, assassination, bombing, air strikes, and armed attacks. *Coercion* refers to intimidation backed up by the threat of force. Of course throughout history states rather than challengers have incorporated violence in an overwhelming proportion (Rummel 1994; Tilly 1985, 1992). In this study I refer to the state's use of violence or coercion as a form of repression, and an aggrieved group's use of violence to challenge the state as violent political action.[18]

Nonviolent political action is another way for responding to situations perceived to be oppressive, unjust, exclusionary, or exploitive. Like violent action, it occurs outside of institutional political channels and is indeterminate; however, it does not involve the use of violent force or the threat of violent force against human beings. In *The Politics of Nonviolent Action*

Gene Sharp identifies 198 methods of nonviolent action that have been used throughout history. Since its publication in 1973, numerous additional methods have been implemented and identified. The number of methods of nonviolent action is unlimited, since the development and application of novel methods is a constantly unfolding process. Sharp aggregates the methods of nonviolent action into three broad categories: methods of protest and persuasion, methods of noncooperation, and methods of nonviolent intervention. Methods of protest and persuasion are used to reveal a problem, illustrate the extent of dissatisfaction, rouse public support or the support of third parties, overcome fear and acquiescence, and expose the state's illegitimacy. They include methods such as protest demonstrations, marches, rallies, public speeches, declarations, the collective display of symbols, and vigils. Methods of noncooperation are used to disrupt the status quo and undermine the state's power, resources, and legitimacy. They include methods such as boycotts, strikes, open refusal to pay taxes or enter the military, and other forms of civil disobedience. Methods of nonviolent intervention are used to disrupt attempts at continued subjugation. They include methods such as sit-ins, nonviolent sabotage, pickets, blockades, hunger strikes, land occupations, and the development of parallel or alternative institutions.

Although exit, everyday forms of resistance, institutional political action, and noninstitutional political action have been distinguished for conceptual purposes, empirically they tend to occur together. Everyday forms of resistance often constitute the prior social practices and actions from which overt political action arises. Institutional political action spills into the noninstitutional sphere. Violent and nonviolent action are often used in tandem, and typically struggles fall somewhere along a continuum from more to less violent. Nevertheless, as stated previously, in order to more clearly understand the dynamics of contention, it is necessary to make analytical distinctions between these various forms of resistance.

Political Contention in the Third World

Taking a broad look at political contention in the third world over the course of the second half of the twentieth century, one can discern a shift in the prevailing repertoires of contention used to challenge states. From the Chinese Revolution in 1949 through the 1970s, Marxist-Leninist-Maoist–inspired rebellions and other forms of violence were the modal methods for challenging regimes in the third world (Colburn 1994). The Marxist-Leninist-Maoist strategy involved the political organization of peasants into a viable military apparatus and the prosecution of a protracted "people's war" against the state. Local guerrilla operations would eliminate government control in specific areas and build autonomous political infrastructures. Armed force was used to expand the territory controlled by the guerrillas. This strategy had an enormous impact on revolutionary movements throughout the third world, and was implemented and elaborated upon by such revolutionaries as Ho Chi Minh in Vietnam, Fidel Castro and Che Guevara in Latin America, and Amilcar Cabral in Africa. However, since the late 1970s revolutionary movements successfully incorporating strategies of guerrilla warfare have become less common. This does not suggest that there have not been any successful guerrilla insurgencies since the late 1970s; witness the success of the Taliban in Afghanistan in the mid-1990s. Nor does this suggest that there are no longer Marxist-Leninist-Maoist–inspired armed revolutionary movements; witness the ongoing struggles of the Sendero Luminoso (Shining Path) in Peru, the Fuerzas Armadas Revolucionarias de Columbia (FARC, or Revolutionary Armed Forces of Columbia) in Columbia, the New People's Army in the Philippines, and the Maoist insurgents in Nepal. This does not suggest that the "mythology of violence" has been eclipsed; witness the tactics of the Irish Republican Army, the Basque ETA, the Palestinian Liberation Organization, and the Tamil Tigers.[19] Nor does this suggest that violent political conflict has generally declined in the underdeveloped world.[20] Nevertheless, there was a notable change in the *modal* manner in which regimes in the third world were successfully challenged in the late twentieth century: armed guerrilla insurgencies and violent rebellion as methods for successfully challenging the state declined, while nonviolent strategies for successfully challenging regimes increased.[21]

A confluence of structural and normative processes in the late twentieth century contributed to this trend. The structural processes of state making and state expansion, as well as increased monopolies on the technologies of violence by states, contributed to a shift in the balance of power away from armed insurgents and toward state forces in many places. In the West a discernable change in the repertoires of contention from violent to nonviolent resulted from the increased capacities of nation-states to suppress private violence and monopolize organized violence within their territories (Tilly 1985, 1992). A parallel process in the expansion of state power has occurred more recently in the third world, although, as in the West, it has been highly uneven. In order for an armed guerilla insurgency to succeed, guerrilla forces need sanctuaries for bases of operation, rest from combat, the provision of food, rearmament, and military training. When a state controls all of its territory, the insurgency's likelihood of finding sanctuaries, and therefore the likelihood of a successful armed revolutionary movement, decreases (Debray 1967; Goodwin and

Skocpol 1989; Zunes 1994). Of course there are still places in the world outside of state control, such as the jungles of Colombia and Burma, the mountains of Peru and Afghanistan, and the archipelagos of the Philippines and Papua New Guinea. And states may break down, as occurred, for example, during the 1990s in Liberia, Zaire, and Somalia.[22] Nevertheless, the ability of states to completely penetrate and control their territories generally increased throughout the third world during the second half of the twentieth century.

Advances in the technologies of violence and the development and training of counterinsurgency forces also contributed to tipping the balance of power in violent struggles from rebels to states. The development of "low-intensity warfare" by states to combat violent challenges produced experts in propaganda and disinformation, assassination, torture, forced relocations of potentially sympathetic populations, and selective but precise air strikes and limited military incursions.[23] The emergence of death squads, that is, paramilitary units with ties to state security services, also increased the costs of violent challenges. In sum, when challengers employ armed violence in their conflicts with modern states, they tend to become trapped in an escalating spiral of violence that they are unlikely to win (Tarrow 1998, 96; Zunes 1994, 1999a; Zunes and Kurtz 1999).

Technologies have multiple uses, but they are more easily used for some purposes than for others. While modern technologies of violence and war may be more useful to states than to challengers, newer communications technologies may be more useful to nonstate actors than to their oppressors (Ackerman and DuVall 2000, chapter 14; Martin 1996, 1999; Martin and Varney 2003). Traditional centralized mass media, such as television, radio, and newspapers, promote collective passivity, since they are one-directional and a small number of people (leaders of states or corporations) can influence or control what is transmitted to a large number of people. Newer decentralized communications technologies, on the other hand, are more independent of centralized control and more difficult for states or corporations to censor, and they permit direct communication among citizens, both within and between countries. The ability of states to control communications has diminished as communications technologies have become decentralized, cheaper, and more accessible. Short-wave radios, cassette tapes, video recordings, fax machines, mobile phones, the Internet, and electronic mail (e-mail) were used by activists during the course of many unarmed insurrections or by outsiders to publicize unarmed insurrections in the late twentieth century.[24] Of course these technologies are not necessary for unarmed insurrections to occur, but they facilitate their mobilization and the cultivation of third-party support.

Late twentieth-century transformations in communications technologies have seemingly compressed time and space through acceleration of the velocity of information sent around the globe (Giddens 1990; Harvey 1989; Held 1995). The possibilities of rapid transnational flows of information and the identification of people across borders are undoubtedly much greater now than a few decades ago. This, in turn, has facilitated the development of international audiences, transnational advocacy networks, transnational social movements, and a global civil society. These developments are significant given the crucial role that influential allies and third parties from abroad may play in the trajectories of unarmed insurrections.

The transnational social movement sector that mushroomed in the late twentieth century represents the development and deepening of a global civil society. The emergence of a global civil society is significant in that it provides an organizational infrastructure that permits nonstate and noncorporate actors to routinely interact with counterparts in other countries. While there are tremendous disparities between the power of states and corporations on the one hand and that of civil society actors on the other, the emergence of a global civil society at least increases the likelihood of providing a voice to the oppressed and is potentially a source of empowerment. While highly uneven, the expanding reach of transnational networks increases the likelihood that local or national challenges will become global, that is, involve actors that are geographically removed from the site of contention, and that frames, organizational templates, and methods of contention will become modular, that is, transferable to distant locations for various causes over short periods of time. Of course there are deep divisions between people based on their experience, education, language, nationality, gender, class, race, and religion. Nevertheless, the emergence of a global civil society provides, at the very least, a mechanism for people to articulate, recognize, and confront these differences and to discover their commonalities (Smith 1997, 1998).[25]

While a global civil society provides spaces through which ideas and activities may be debated and diffused, transnational advocacy networks and social movement organizations provide the relational links through which oppressed groups may receive tangible support from abroad. Transnational advocacy networks are actors working internationally on an issue who are bound together by shared values, common discourses, and a dense exchange of information and services (Keck and Sikkink 1998). Transnational advocacy networks, and especially transnational social movement organizations, that is, organizations with active members in two or more countries that promote social change through institutional and noninstitutional channels (Smith et al. 1997), amplify the ability of challengers within states to frame their grievances in terms that resonate transnationally, thereby increasing the likelihood of obtaining resources and support from abroad. Challenges by oppressed groups may also be facilitated through the "boomerang pattern," whereby challenging movements within nondemocracies exert pressure on their own states indirectly through ties to transnational social movements that mobilize international pressure against the target state to help them achieve political change at home (Keck and Sikkink 1998, 12–13). When repression increases at home, activism may be directed to international media, international conferences, Internet campaigns, and protest actions abroad. Transnational social movements and the transnational networks in which they are embedded are significant, since third-party support is often crucial in tipping the balance of power in favor of challengers in nonviolent struggles.

Cross-cutting structural transformations in the late twentieth century were growing normative concerns with human rights by the international community and increased reservations about the negative consequences of violence as a strategy for social change. While widespread international concern with human rights can be traced back to the Universal Declaration of Human Rights in 1948, prior to the 1970s the idea that the human rights of citizens in one country are the legitimate concern of the people and governments of other countries was considered radical (Keck and Sikkink 1998, 79).[26] Significantly, many transnational advocacy networks and international social movements are concerned with human rights issues. From 1973 to 1993 the number of international nongovernmental social change organizations concerned with human rights increased from 41 to 168 (Smith 1997, 47). Not only do international human rights organizations work to expose and prevent state violence; they also promote nonviolent resistance to oppression.

One of the first and most influential transnational human rights organizations was Amnesty International (AI), which was formed in 1961 and contributed to making the people in one country aware of human rights abuses in others. In contrast to the mass media's coverage of human rights violations, if they were covered at all, AI developed a tactic of emphasizing the human side of state violence, that is, making it clear that victims of human rights violations were human beings with names, faces, histories, and family members. Thus, they focused on promoting the cases of individual victims of human rights abuses to increase the identification between the victim and the public. To protect itself from accusations that it was using human rights abuses to pursue a broader ideological agenda, AI selected one urgent case each month from a country in the first world, one case from the second world, and one from the third world. Significantly, AI promotes only dissidents who use nonviolent rather than violent methods to advance political change (Keck and Sikkink 1998; Scoble and Wiseberg 1974).

Another human rights group, Peace Brigades International (PBI), founded in 1981, pioneered the tactic of "accompanying," whereby activists threatened by state repression are shadowed by a team of international volunteers. PBI's accompaniment takes many forms, including escorting activists twenty-four hours a day, being present at the offices of threatened political organizations, accompanying refugees or political dissidents returning to their home countries, and serving as international observers at collective action events. The logic of the tactic of accompaniment is based on the notion that governments and death squads do not want their activities exposed to the outside world, since it would adversely effect their foreign aid and international legitimacy. The physical presence of PBI volunteers prevents violence from occurring, and if it does occur, exposes it to the international community. Significantly, the PBI volunteers are unarmed, and they promote nonviolent resistance to oppression by providing training in nonviolent action to people involved in conflicts with their states (Mahony and Eguren 1997).

The Unrepresented Peoples Organization (UNPO) was founded in 1991 to promote the interests of people unrepresented in major international organizations, such as the United Nations. Typically these include oppressed peoples without states, such as indigenous peoples and minorities, who are struggling against human rights abuses and for political or cultural autonomy. The UNPO provides professional services, education, and training in diplomacy, international and human rights law, building democratic institutions, and protecting the environment. Moreover, one of the principles of the organization's charter is the promotion of nonviolent action and the rejection of violence and terrorism as methods for promoting change. For peoples to become members of the UNPO, they must adhere to the principle of nonviolent discipline. Thus, for issues concerning autonomy or self-rule, issues that have historically involved violent strategies and terrorism, UNPO is forging a nonviolent strategy for social change.

Thus, human rights organizations like these do not merely document state violence and provide protection to victims of human rights abuses, but they also promote nonviolent rather than violent struggles against political oppression throughout the world. Along with an increased recognition by the international community of human rights abuses, there has been an increased recognition by scholars and activists in the third world of the power of nonviolent action and a desire to break vicious cycles of violence.[27] An awareness has grown that armed struggles often result in an ethos of violence and an elite vanguard, and that what is won through violence must be defended with violence. An awareness has also developed that violent struggles often produce major social and environmental dislocations, the loss of life among innocent bystanders as well as parties to the conflict, and long-term negative consequences such as social distrust, economic decline, and increased militarization. Moreover, more people have become aware of the power of nonviolent action and some of its virtues, such as diffusing power and maximizing the segments of the population that can participate in a challenge, and the idea has developed that a people can create a new political order *through* struggle rather than hoping to create a new political order *after* the destruction of the old one (Sharp 1990, 38; Zunes 1994; Zunes and Kurtz 1999).

While the guerrilla and counterinsurgency cycle of violent contention was largely state driven, with revolutionaries supported by the Soviet Bloc or China and counterinsurgencies supported by the United States, post–Cold War challenges in the third world have tended to receive support and funding from more dispersed and decentralized transnational sources. If states, transnational corporations, and capitalist international organizations such as the International Monetary Fund, the World Bank, and the World Trade Organization represent globalization from above, transnational social movements that have arisen in response to them represent globalization from below. While responses to globalization from above are not inherently nonviolent, globalization from below has provided a predominantly nonviolent counterforce to the exploitive and often violent engines of globalization from above. As Richard Falk has noted, "Much of the energy of globalization from below is directed against violence and militarism, and more fundamentally, refrains from tactics that rely on counter violence" (Falk 1995, 219).[28]

Whether or not the theory and project of Marxist-inspired violent revolutionary change has run its course, the problems that motivated it remain, including political oppression, capitalist economic exploitation, patriarchy, and inequalities between the North and the South. In response to these problems, over the past few decades there has been an expansion of challenges via nonviolent collective action on the part of the oppressed in the less-developed and nondemocratic world. These challenges address a range of issues, such as human rights, women's rights, indigenous people's rights, workers' rights, sustainable development, and environmentalism, and they have arisen for the most part beyond the control of the state. Whereas the goals of violent challenges are often to capture state power or gain control over territory, in the late twentieth century the goals of many of the challenging movements in the third world were not to capture state power or exercise a monopoly of power over a piece of territory, but rather to roll back the frontiers of the authoritarian state, make the polity more inclusive, and promote sociopolitical empowerment. It is possible that these goals may be more readily realized through civilian-based nonviolent action than through armed violence.

Terrorism as a Strategy for Political Change

In addition to "people power," the ability to engage in transnational terrorism[29] as a method of political contention also seems to have benefited from advances in communications technologies and the growth of transnational networks that are not dominated by states or corporations. Nevertheless, terrorism has an abysmal track record in promoting change unless it is combined with forms of mass political contention. Of course terrorism can have a symbolic value in forging identities and promoting mass collective action; however, when a challenge occurs primarily through acts of terrorism or when challengers turn to terrorism because they lack popular support, they are not likely to succeed. In fact, a major difference between a "people's war" and "people power," on the one hand, and terrorism, on the other, is that the former depend on mass collective action and support, while the latter does not.

Conclusion

In conclusion, in the late twentieth century, as nonviolent action became a modular and global phenomenon there was a shift in the modal manner in which successful struggles against states in underdeveloped and nondemocratic countries were prosecuted. Nevertheless, it would be a mistake to view this trend as part of a linear history, since factors that converged in the late twentieth century to facilitate nonviolent action may diverge in the future.

Moreover, despite the profound political transformations that were facilitated by unarmed insurrections in the late twentieth century, nonviolent action is not a panacea, nor is it always effective in promoting political change. In order to understand why unarmed insurrections contribute to political transformations and regime change in some instances but not in others, we need to make sense of how challengers, states, and third parties interact during episodes of contention. To this end, in chapter 2, I examine theoretical perspectives on nonviolent action and social movements. Then in chapters 3–5 I consider six episodes of unarmed insurrection.

2

Political Process and Nonviolent Action Approaches to Political Contention

Three transnational waves of democratization have occurred over the past few centuries (Huntington 1991; Markoff 1996).[1] The first occurred in Western Europe across the nineteenth century as the deepening of market exchange and the intensification of the industrial revolution gave birth to new class relations and empowered the bourgeoisie relative to the ancien régime. The second wave occurred in the aftermath of the Second World War, when the North Atlantic Allies implemented democracy in the vanquished Axis countries and the process of decolonization led, at least initially, to the emergence of democratic polities. The third wave began in the mid-1970s, spurred on by contradictions between global capitalist market relations and closed polities. Originating in Southern Europe, where dictatorships in Portugal, Spain, and Greece fell to liberalizing movements, the third wave spread to Latin America, where a number of military regimes gave way to civilian rule in the 1980s. By the late 1980s and early 1990s, Eastern European countries in the Soviet Bloc and then the Soviet Union experienced democratization, and by the 1990s the wave of democratization reached Africa. Peppered throughout the 1980s and 1990s were democratic transitions in Asia.

Explanations of democratization fall into four broad theoretical approaches: modernization, world polity, transition, and structural approaches.[2] The modernization approach focuses on the relation between formal political institutions and social and economic characteristics of countries. Economic development, cultural homogeneity or pluralism, and a legacy of British rule are among the factors thought to promote democratization. While useful in identifying the correlates of institutionalized democratic structures, this approach tell us little about the process of democratization or about why democratization may occur in countries with "low probabilities" of democratization or not occur in countries with "high probabilities" of democratization.

The world polity approach assumes that nations exhibit convergent structural similarities due to the diffusion of a world culture of rationalized modernity. Countries across the globe have increasingly similar educational systems, forms of scientific investigation, and state structures. Moreover, norms concerning citizenship, human rights, and political liberties are part of the prevailing world culture; thus democratization results from the isomorphism of political systems. While providing extensive empirical data to support its propositions, the world polity approach has been criticized for assuming that the spread of global structures and norms, such as those concerning political rule, is an inexorable process. The spread is not necessarily inevitable, as indicated by failed movements for democratization and transitions from democratic to authoritarian rule, and when democratization does occur, it is often the result of specific change agents, that is, popular uprisings against authoritarian regimes or elite pacts.

The transition approach brings agency into explanations of democratization, focusing on the more proximate processes of elite negotiation, compromise, and pacting that characterize political transitions and consolidation. According to this approach, three conditions are necessary for a successful democratic transition. First, an agreement must be reached between reformers in the regime and moderate opponents to establish institutions under which the social forces they represent would have significant power in a democratic system. Second, the reformers must be able either to deliver the consent of regime hard-liners or to neutralize them. Third, the moderates must be able to control the more progressive mass-based elements in the opposition, isolate the so-called radicals, and prevent the occurrence of protest demonstrations, strikes, and other forms of noninstitutional political action. If the moderates do not control the more progressive or radical elements of the opposition, hard-liners may gain the upper hand and crush the democratic forces (Przeworski 1991). This approach is useful in accounting for the role of political elites in democratic transitions and consolidation, but it overlooks the initial pressures put on the system through mass political contention, and views noninstitutional political action as a threat rather than a contributor to democratization. However, in most contexts popular insurrection, rather than being an obstacle to democratization, is the only realistic method for attaining it.

The structural approach to democratization is concerned with the relation between large-scale social change, changing structures of class and state, and types of political regimes. Democratization is assumed to result from a favorable coalition of class forces and transnational relations. Where workers and capitalists are aligned against large landowners, which have historically been anti-democratic, and are not suppressed by a powerful autonomous state, the prospects for democratization increase. While the long-term perspective of the structural approach is useful in accounting for how changing social, economic, and political structures provide opportunities for or constraints on the formation of certain class coalitions and state relations favorable to democratization, it misses the more proximate agency-driven aspects of democratization. That is, it underspecifies the role of agency, particularly the impact of mass contention on elite coherence and state power.

More recently a more movement-oriented perspective on democratization has emerged that applies social movement theory to challenges in nondemocratic and democratizing contexts (Adler and Webster 1995; Bermeo 1997; Bratton and van der Walle 1992, 1997; Collier and Mahoney 1997; Giugni et al. 1998; Markoff 1997; Tarrow 1995; Wood 2000). While this approach does not necessarily contradict the modernization, world polity, or transition approaches to democratization and is not unrelated to the structural approach, it provides an alternative perspective that is agency-oriented and recognizes, rather than neglects or dismisses, the transformative power of mass noninstitutional political action. This approach emphasizes the relationship between mass contention, transition cycles, and political change. According to Sidney Tarrow, "Most scholars of democratization have either ignored movements altogether or regarded them with suspicion as dangers to democracy, while most students of social movements have focused on fully mature democratic systems and ignored the *transition cycles* that place the question of democratization on the agenda and work it through to either democratic consolidation or defeat. When they do turn to movements in less developed systems, it is frequently only to catalogue and condemn ethnic and nationalist movements" (Tarrow 1995, 221–22). *Transition cycles* refers to how changing political relations produce—and are altered by—popular collective action. In this study I outline a theoretical framework that contributes to the movement-oriented approach to political change.[3] More important, I attempt to do so by drawing on and pulling together two separate theoretical approaches to contentious politics: the political process and nonviolent action approaches.

The Political Process Approach

The political process approach elaborates upon the resource mobilization critique of classical theories of social movements, which characterized noninstitutional political action as an irrational product of various forms of structural and psychological strain. The political process approach expands the theoretical focus of resource mobilization theory from the resources at the disposal of social movement organizations to account for the structures through which people and resources are mobilized, their representations of the social world, and the political context in which movements occur. The political process approach also transcends resource mobilization theory's limited application to the American context of the 1960s and 1970s.[4] Although it was originally developed to explain social movements in democratic Western contexts as parallels in the dynamics of contention across diverse polities were becoming evident, the political process approach has been increasingly incorporated into explanations of contentious politics in the second and third worlds as well.[5] Three central components of the political process approach are collective action frames, mobilizing structures, and political opportunities and constraints. I discuss these in the following sections, paying attention to how they may differ across democratic and nondemocratic contexts.

Collective Action Frames

For the oppressed to engage in collective action, there must first be cognitive liberation, that is, a diminution of fatalism coupled with a perception that conditions are unjust, yet subject to change through collective action (Gamson et al. 1982; McAdam 1999, 48–51; Moore 1978; Piven and Cloward 1979b, 3–4). Cognitive liberation is facilitated by the development of collective action frames, which "underscore and embellish the seriousness and injustice of a social condition or redefine as unjust and immoral what was previously seen as unfortunate but perhaps tolerable" (Snow and Benford 1992, 137). To motivate collective action, collective action frames must successfully critique the dominant belief system that legitimizes the status quo and provide alternative belief systems that legitimate noninstitutional political action. Successful collective action frames must strike a responsive chord with individuals in the oppressed population and must overcome the symbolic dilemma of mediating between inherited symbols that are familiar but lead to acceptance of the status quo and new ones that promote collective action but may be too unfamiliar to result in action (Gamson et al. 1982, 15; Tarrow 1998, 107).[6]

The process through which movements link individual interests and orientations with their activities, goals, and ideologies is called frame alignment, of which there are four types: frame bridging, frame amplification, frame extension, and frame transformation. Frame bridging involves linking a social movement organization with unmobilized sentiment pools. Frame extension involves extending the boundaries of the movement's primary frames to encompass interests that are incidental to its primary goals but are salient to potential adherents. Frame amplification involves activating latent values or beliefs that inhere in oppressed populations but have heretofore not inspired collective political action. Frame transformation occurs when a new set of beliefs gains ascendence over the previous ones, functioning as a new kind of master frame (Snow et al. 1986).

Although these frame alignment processes may operate in democratic or nondemocratic contexts, frame bridging and frame extension seem to be more suited to democratic contexts, where dissent is tolerated and there is a relatively freer flow of information. In democracies frame bridging is facilitated by less constrained information flows whereby the mass media, direct mailings, telephones, and e-mail are commonly used to spread frames. Frame extension is facilitated by the tolerance of dissent in democracies, where social movements may gradually expand their frames to encompass tangential pools of support. In nondemocracies frame amplification and frame transformation are more likely to be the frame alignment processes through which people come to adhere to a movement's cause. Frame amplification, for example, draws on existing but latent values and beliefs that may have been suppressed by authorities. As discussed later, however, a regime's capacity and propensity for repression varies over time, so opportunities may arise for latent values and beliefs to be amplified thereby facilitating collective mobilization. If populations in nondemocracies have been thoroughly indoctrinated with the regime's political ideology, frame transformation may be necessary to promote collective action. Central to frame transformation are redefining injustice as intolerable rather than tolerable and attributing the injustices to the regime's policies or structure. Given the relatively high levels of injustice and oppression in nondemocracies, the potential always exists that the hegemonic ideology will be questioned and that the state may lose legitimacy through frame transformation (Havel et al. 1985).

Although collective action entails risks in democracies, it involves substantially more risk in nondemocracies. Given the greater risk associated with acts of dissent in nondemocracies, fear is a potent obstacle that must be overcome (Aung SanSuu Kyi 1991, 183–85). Violent repression by itself does not induce obedience and cooperation; it must induce fear in order to promote compliance. Nondemocratic regimes have developed elaborate methods to invoke fear and acquiescence in their populations. Thus, whatever the process of frame alignment used in nondemocracies, fear and acquiescence must be diminished through framing.

Mobilizing Structures

While collective action frames represent a form of symbolic mobilization, mobilizing structures are the networks through which the mobilization of tangible resources, people, and organized collective action occurs. The central dilemma of movement organization, according to Sidney Tarrow, is how to create organizations that are sufficiently robust to structure sustained relations with authorities, yet flexible enough to permit informal connections that link people to one another in order to aggregate and coordinate political action (Tarrow 1998). Tarrow maintains that the best way to address this problem is through partly autonomous and contextually rooted local organizations that are linked by connective structures and coordinated by formal organizations (Tarrow 1998; see also Gerlach and Hine 1970). Connective structures are links between leaders and followers and among different organizations within the movement sector, permitting coordination and aggregation and allowing movements to persist without hierarchical organization (Diani 1995; Tarrow 1998). This type of organization facilitates mesomobilization, that is, mobilization characterized by joint campaigning by coalitions of organizations through temporary umbrella organizations (Gerhards and Rucht 1992). While these characteristics may be the mobilizing strategy of choice by challengers in democracies because they inhibit institutionalization and cooptation, they may be the mobilizing strategy of necessity for movements relying on nonviolent action in nondemocratic contexts, where centralized organizations are easy targets for repression.

In addition to using social movement organizations, challengers may mobilize resources, people, and collective action through allied organizations, such as religious organizations, cultural organizations, and universities, whose primary purpose is not collective action (Gould 1995; Klandermans 1997, chapter 6; McAdam 1988, 1999; Morris 1984; Osa 1997, 2001; Tarrow 1998, chapter 8). Related to the mobilization through allied organizations is social appropriation, whereby the identities and networks of inactive or marginally active social groups are accroached by a movement (McAdam et al. 2001, chapter 4). In addition to social appropriation, challengers may forge organizational structures through creating autonomous networks. Indeed, in nondemocratic contexts this process may be crucial if society lacks autonomous organizations and is unable to appropriate state-dominated organizations. In nondemocratic contexts, the forging of oppositional networks is vital to successfully challenging the state and developing civil society and democratic relations.

Political Opportunities and Constraints

Political opportunities and constraints encompass aspects of the political environment external to social movements that facilitate or inhibit their mobilization and shape their trajectories. While individual case studies of social movements have referred to just about anything external to movements as a political opportunity or constraint, the central dimensions are political openness, elite divisions/realignments, influential allies, and the state's capacity and propensity for repression (see Goodwin 2001b; McAdam 1996; Tarrow 1998).[7]

Although the political opportunity framework developed largely from studies of social movements in democracies, it is applicable to explanations of challenges in nondemocracies as well (see note 5). In fact, political opportunities may be even more important for challenges in nondemocracies than in democracies, since opportunities for dissent are less common and therefore any signs of political opportunity are likely to generate opposition. Moreover, since noninstitutional political action is riskier in nondemocracies, it is likely that there must be definite and significant political opportunities that lower the costs of collective action for it to occur. In his analysis of the influence of political opportunities in one hundred political challenges from 1786 to 1996, Jeff Goodwin found that political opportunities are more likely to facilitate the emergence of political contention in nondemocracies than in democracies (Goodwin 2001b). Political opportunities and constraints can be divided into two broad types: responses by authorities to noninstitutional challenges and challengers' relations to political elites and third parties.

Responses by Authorities

Similar to the repertoires of contention available to dissidents are the repertoires of social control that states have to respond to challenges. As indicated in Figure 2, authorities have four broad options with which to respond to noninstitutional political action: they can ignore, conciliate, reform, or repress (Piven and Cloward 1979b, 27–30).[8] Of course these, too, are transgressive, as states often answer with a combination of responses, such as reform and repression. First, challenges may simply be ignored. In democracies, where dissent is tolerated, ignoring a challenge is an option as long as the challenge does not disrupt central institutions or directly threaten elite interests. In nondemocracies, by contrast, almost any noninstitutional political action may be construed as regime-threatening; therefore, ignoring a challenge is a less likely response. When authorities are unable to ignore

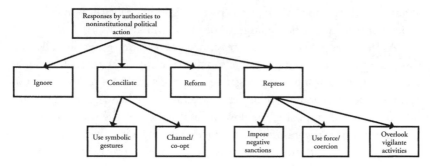

Figure 2. Possible responses by authorities to noninstitutional political challenges.

a challenge and unwilling to risk the uncertain repercussions of repression, efforts may be directed towards conciliation. Conciliation may entail the use of symbolic gestures, whereby the authorities acknowledge that "something should be done," channeling, whereby the authorities attempt to direct the energies and anger of the aggrieved into institutionalized and less disruptive forms of political action, or co-optation, whereby incentives are offered to movement leaders or aggrieved populations to participate in institutionalized political channels.

Political reform involves making concrete concessions whereby actual changes in policies or political relations are made. When concessions are made by authorities, mobilization is usually encouraged. Recognizing that even larger concessions might be wrought with larger numbers of participants in collective action, more people are mobilized, and with each new concession mobilization increases. This process is referred to as the bandwagon or threshold effect (Francisco 2000; Lichbach 1995, 114–18; Tocqueville 1998). Although democracies may be better equipped to deal with the consequences of increased mobilization resulting from reform, the situation tends to be more problematic for nondemocratic regimes, since reform is more likely to undermine the formula for political rule.

A fourth response, repression, is "behavior applied by governments in an effort to bring about political quiescence and facilitate the continuity of the regime through some form of restrictions or violation of political and civil liberties" (Davenport 2000, 6). Thus, *repression* refers to actions by governments against people that are above and beyond ideological hegemony, which is also central to maintaining the status quo. Since repression is applied to perceived threats to the regime, it is likely that ideological hegemony has already been overcome by the challengers through the process of frame alignment. Repression may be overt or covert, legal or illegal, nonviolent or violent, as well as specifically targeted or indiscriminate.

As indicated in Figure 2, repression by authorities generally falls into three categories: imposing negative sanctions, using force or coercion, and violence by proxy. Imposing negative sanctions includes actions such as curtailing political and civil liberties, imposing martial law, censoring public or private media, impeding the flow of information or the travel of people, banning political organizations and meetings, engaging in discriminatory legal practices, infiltrating movements, using agents provocateurs, spying, using psychological warfare or harassment, imposing fines, and confiscating resources. Using force entails using physical force against human beings through means such as imprisonment, beatings, rape, torture, disappearances, assassinations, executions, bombings, armed attacks, air strikes, and physical retaliation against colleagues or relatives, while using coercion entails intimidation or the threatened use of force against human beings. A third form of repression occurs when authorities overlook or encourage the actions of third parties that raise the costs of collective action, such as actions by vigilante groups, lynch mobs, death squads, paramilitary forces, and the like (Churchill and Vander Wall 1990; Glick 1989; Gurr 1986; Lopez and Stohl 1989; Marx 1974, 1979; Rummel 1994; Stohl and Lopez 1983). From the state's point of view, repression works either by raising the costs of organization and mobilization or by suppressing collective action (Tilly 1978, 100–102). Whereas in democracies repression is more likely to be used against movements that are disruptive, use violence, or directly threaten elites (Gamson 1990, chapter 4), repression is far more pervasive in nondemocracies, since most overt challenges present a direct threat to the regimes.[9]

What effect does repression have on dissent? Studies have found support for negative relationships whereby repression decreases dissent, positive relationships whereby repression increases dissent, and an inverted U-shaped relationship whereby dissent is likely to be lowest at low and high levels of repression and highest at middle levels of repression. Generally the political opportunity approach assumes that increasing repression is a constraint that is likely to inhibit mobilization, while declining repression or the inability of authorities to apply repression facilitates mobilization; however, this generalization is based primarily on case studies of social movements in democracies. Others argue that declining opportunities or threats to a group's interests serve as catalysts to mobilization (Goldstone and Tilly 2001; Tilly 1978). In his analysis of one hundred cases of political contention, Jeff Goodwin found that only eleven of the one hundred cases emerged in response to declining repression (Goodwin 2001b). Studies incorporating quantitative methodologies have tended to find support for the positive and inverted U-shaped relationships between repression and dissent.[10] Most likely the impact of repression on dissent is influenced by the political context in which it occurs, so repression may increase or decrease mobilization depending on the presence or absence of other dimensions in the opportunity structure (e.g., Brysk 1994; della Porta 1995; Gupta et al. 1993; Lichbach 1987; Schock 1999; and Tilly 1978).

In addition to the degree of repression, the targeting of repression and its relationship to dissent has been examined. Repression that is specifically targeted is more likely to suppress dissent than indiscriminate repression, since indiscriminate repression may backfire and incite increased protest behavior (Lichbach 1987; Mason and Krame 1989; Moore 1995). Similarly, extreme or indiscriminate repression may suppress challenges in the short run, but undermine regime legitimacy and produce intensified challenges over time (Dix 1984; Kurzman 1996; Lichbach 1987; Opp and Roehl 1990; Rasler 1996).

A major problem with the repression-dissent literature is that challengers are generally assumed to be passive objects and powerless in the face of regime repression. Thus, the literature neglects to consider how characteristics of challengers affect the relationship between repression and dissent.[11] As discussed later, the nonviolent action approach suggests that characteristics of challengers, such as the strategy implemented (violent or nonviolent), the range of methods employed (limited or diverse, concentrated or dispersed), the targets of protest (security forces versus other agents of the state), and the level of organization of the challenge (disorganized or organized, centralized or decentralized), are of central importance in determining how repression influences mobilization. Whether repression crushes dissent or propels the mobilization of collective action depends on a variety of conditions other than the level of repression, some of which may be within the control of challenging groups. In addition to the intensity and targeting of repression and challenger attributes, moreover, the strategic or dialectic interaction between challengers and authorities must be considered in accounting for the relationship between repression and dissent (Lyng and Kurtz 1985; McAdam 1983, 1999).

Relations to Elites and Third Parties

Elite divisions provide opportunities for challengers by increasing the incentives to risk engaging in collective action. Moreover, segments of the elite that are threatened with the loss of power relative to other elites may be more likely to align themselves with challengers if doing so will enhance their position. In democracies, for example, closely divided ruling coalitions may increase the leverage of challengers, since segments of the divided elite seek the support of challengers to solidify their own position (Jenkins 1985; Jenkins and Brents 1989; McAdam 1999; Piven and Cloward 1979b). Also in nondemocracies, the elite-centered literature on democratization has emphasized divisions within the military or between the military and upper-classes as important prerequisites for political change. A potential conse-quence of elite divisions in nondemocracies is regime defection, whereby significant elements of the previously stable ruling coalition align themselves with the challengers (McAdam et al. 2001, chapter 7).

Challenges may also be facilitated by third parties that support their cause. Michael Lipsky goes so far as to state that "the essence of political protest consists of activating third parties to participate in controversy in ways favorable to protest goals" (Lipsky 1968, 1153).[12] In the United States, for example, William Gamson found that the presence of allied third parties facilitated challenger success across the fifty-three challenging groups that he examined (Gamson 1990), and Craig Jenkins and Charles Perrow found that the presence of allied third parties in the 1960s facilitated the success of the United Farm Workers movement, while the lack of allied third parties in the 1940s inhibited its success (Jenkins 1985; Jenkins and Perrow 1977). In nondemocracies, the Catholic Church, religious workers, development workers, and human rights organizations and the international networks in which they are embedded have provided crucial support for the oppressed in their challenges to the state.[13] Yet the benefits of third-party support must be weighed against the possibilities that it will undermine the challenge by mak-ing it dependent upon outside support or inhibit its capacities to disrupt.

Criticism

The political process approach, as originally formulated, identified the in-herent power that the less powerful have by virtue of their position in the social structure and their potential for disruption through negative induce-ments (McAdam 1999; Schwartz 1976). The approach also accounted for dynamic interactions between challengers and the state (McAdam 1983, 1999). More recently, however, the emphasis of the political process ap-proach has shifted toward an emphasis on the political context external to movements. Whether or not the political process approach is characterized by a structural bias, as some suggest (Goodwin and Jasper 1999; Lichbach 1998), there has been a definite shift away from an analysis of the strategies and actions of social movements toward the external political context. Yet as Doug McAdam, John McCarthy, and Mayer Zald state emphatically,

"Movements may be largely born of environmental opportunities, but their fate is heavily shaped by their own actions" (McAdam et al. 1996, 15). Nevertheless, the primary focus of the analysis of social movements has tended to be on the former, that is, the contextual factors contributing to their emergence, rather than the latter, that is, how their fates are shaped by their attributes and actions.[14] Of course it is less difficult to demonstrate the emergence of social movements than it is to demonstrate how their actions shape their trajectories or their influence on social change (Amenta and Young 1999; Gamson 1990; McAdam et al. 1988, 727). Yet the munificent collection of studies on social movement emergence, participation, and maintenance means little if social movements do not influence political change or if their fates are entirely beyond their control (Burstein et al. 1995, 276).

Political process scholars have traditionally been most concerned with mobilization processes, to a lesser extent with movement outcomes, and to an even lesser extent with the mechanisms that link movement actions and characteristics with outcomes. Although I do not suggest a return to resource mobilization theory, I do suggest that movement attributes, such as their strategies and tactics, as well as their organization and framing, are theoretically relevant aspects that must be considered when examining the trajectories of social movements. While most would agree that there is a constantly evolving process by which movements respond to and shape the political context, the social movement literature has tended to emphasize the former to the neglect of the latter. Not only do social movements respond to political opportunities, but they also strategically overcome political constraints, thereby reshaping the political context.

A number of the weaknesses of political process scholarship can be addressed by insights from the literature on nonviolent action, which unfortunately has largely remained outside the purview of social movement scholars. There are a number of reasons for a lack of cross-fertilization between the two literatures. First, the nonviolent action literature draws on anarchist and Gandhian theories and philosophies, which are peripheral to mainstream sociology. In contrast, the social movement literature draws on Marxist theories and philosophies, which are central to mainstream sociology and which privilege macrostructural analysis and emphasize the role of violence in social change (Martin 1989). Second, much of the literature on nonviolent action is geared toward activists rather than academics. Thus, there is a disjunction between the instrumental-normative discourse of the nonviolent action literature and the social scientific discourse of the social movement literature. Third, the disciplinary division between peace studies scholars and social movement scholars contributes to the lack of cross-fertilization, although the two often attempt to explain many of the same phenomena. Finally, social scientists may be put off by the military analogies and some of the terms used by Gene Sharp, the most eminent theorist of nonviolent action. Take, for example, the terms *pluralist* and *consent*. Since these terms have been thoroughly critiqued by sociologists,[15] Sharp's use of them may deter sociologists from taking his work seriously. However, the meaning Sharp attributes to these terms differs from that commonly given to these terms by sociologists. Sharp's idea of the withdrawal of consent, for example, is akin to McAdam's notion of cognitive liberation, and Sharp uses the term *pluralist* not in the sense of competing interest groups, but rather in the sense that there are multiple loci of power from which states draw their resources and legitimacy.

While it is not without its own weaknesses, the nonviolent action literature has the virtue of addressing some of the biases in recent political process scholarship. The nonviolent action approach attempts to specify how power is used strategically by social movements to undermine the state and alter the political context. This approach recognizes that there are multiple factors determining the trajectories of movements, some partially controlled by movements and others outside their control. The role of movements is to organize and implement methods of contention that increase the likelihood of success, that is, to "widen the margin of victory" in a given political context (Ackerman and Kruegler 1994, 318). Thus, a cautious gleaning of insights from the nonviolent action approach may prove useful in supplementing the political process approach (and vice versa).[16]

The Nonviolent Action Approach

Perhaps the first modern social scientific analysis of nonviolent action as a method for political contention was by Clarence Marsh Case in 1923 (Case 1972).[17] Case maintained that studies of social conflict were biased due to their emphasis on violence and their neglect of nonviolent methods for producing social and political change. He identified a class of contentious acts involving nonviolent coercion, such as strikes and boycotts. Mohandas Gandhi drew upon Case's work and attempted to implement some of Case's insights on nonviolent methods in his campaign against British rule in India in the 1930s. The social scientific analysis of nonviolent action continued with first-hand analyses of Gandhi's nonviolent campaign. In 1935 Richard Gregg explicated the social psychological effects of violence and nonviolence (Gregg 1966), and in 1939 Krishnalal Shridharani identified the methods of nonviolent action used by Gandhi (Shridharani 1972).[18] Competing with Gandhi's approach of principled nonviolent action was a more pragmatic orientation that was given definitive expression in the publication in 1973 of *The Politics of Nonviolent Action,* the three-volume magnum opus by Gene Sharp. This was a major breakthrough in the social scientific study of nonviolence, as it clearly differentiated between principled and pragmatic nonviolence, identified examples of nonviolent action that had occurred throughout history, classified the techniques of nonviolent action into three broad methods, explained the mechanisms through which nonviolent action produces political change, and explicated a theory of power to explain how political change can occur through actions outside of the institutional sphere and without the use of violence.

In contrast to the principled approach to nonviolence, in which nonviolent methods are used as a matter of principle and the activists implementing them must adhere to a moral code, the pragmatic approach merely assumes that in some contexts nonviolent action may be more effective than violent action in promoting social and political change. The morality or beliefs of nonviolent proponents or activists are not issues. Aspects of the theoretical framework developed by Sharp have been incorporated into social scientific explanations of the dynamics and trajectories of a wide variety of social movements across diverse historical eras and political contexts (e.g., Ackerman and DuVall 2000; Ackerman and Kruegler 1994; Bleiker 1993; Bond 1988, 1994; Callahan 1998; Conser et al. 1986; Cooney and Michalowski 1987; Corr 1999; Crow et al. 1990; Dajani 1995; Eglitis 1993; Fukuda 2000; Holmes 1990; MacQueen 1992; Martin 1996, 2001; Martin and Varney 2003; Martin et al. 2001; McManus and Schlabach 1991; Parkman 1988, 1991; Rigby 1991; Roberts 1991; Routledge 1993, 1994; Smithey and Kurtz 2003; Wehr et al. 1994; Zielonka 1986; Zunes 1994, 1999b; and Zunes et al. 1999).[19] Some of Sharp's central ideas are discussed in the following section.

The Politics of Nonviolent Action

The theory of power developed by Sharp draws on, among other things, the political philosophy of Étienne de la Boétie and Hannah Arendt and the political sociology of Max Weber.[20] Drawing on their works, Sharp maintains that a government's power over its subjects is based on their obedience and cooperation. This "relational" view of power suggests that power is derived from sources within society, in contrast to a monolithic theory of power that assumes that power is imposed on people by the state from above due to the state's ability to enforce sanctions and apply repression.[21] "The most single quality of any government, without which it would not exist, must be obedience and submission of its subjects," writes Sharp. "Obedience is the heart of political power" (Sharp 1973, 16).

Thus, Sharp's theory is based on the assumption that the power of governments is ultimately based not on violence, but rather on obedience and cooperation. If a sufficient number of people disobey or do not cooperate for a sufficient amount of time, the government will be unable to rule, regardless of its coerciveness or brutality. In distinct contrast to Marxist-inspired theories and praxis, which suggest that the state apparatus must be captured through force, or theories and praxis of guerrilla warfare, which suggest that the state's capacities for violence must be worn down over time through a "people's war" of attrition, the nonviolent action approach maintains that methods of nonviolent action can produce "revolutionary" political change despite the state's superior coercive capacities. The target of nonviolent action is not the pinnacle of state power or where the state is usually the strongest, that is, its military or security apparatuses, but rather its social roots. Rather than challenging the state on its own terms, that is, with violence, social movements implementing nonviolent action challenge the state using methods that are designed to operate to their advantage. Since states depend on the constant replenishment of their power, it is not necessary to overpower the state to promote political change. It can also be done by denying the regime its sources of support or severing the regime from its sources of support. Thus, in calculating the chances for success in campaigns of nonviolent action, the fundamental variable is not the material or military strength of the state, but rather the withdrawal of support from the regime (Sharp 1973; Zunes 1999a).

Methods of Nonviolent Action

As discussed in chapter 1, state power may be challenged through struggles that depend primarily on nonviolent techniques, that is, techniques for wielding power that operate outside of institutional political channels and that do not involve violence or the threat of violence against human beings. Sharp classifies the methods of nonviolent action into three broad categories: methods of protest and persuasion, methods of noncooperation, and methods of nonviolent intervention (Sharp 1973; 1990, chapter 3; 1999). *Methods of protest and persuasion* are largely symbolic expressions, with communicative content intended to persuade the opponent or to produce an awareness of the existence of injustices and the extent of dissent. These methods do not consist of the use of reason, discussion, or persuasion exclusive of direct contentious action (McCarthy 1997, 320). Examples include protest demonstrations, marches, political funerals, rallies, symbolic public acts, and protest meetings. Protest and persuasion are important in that they may help aggrieved populations overcome acquiescence and the fear of repression, and provide them with social visibility while alerting reference publics and third parties to an unjust situation. Moreover, methods of protest and persuasion are often the crucibles in which frames are elaborated and disseminated, solidarity is forged, and members of the aggrieved group are mobilized to participate in other methods of nonviolent action. In democracies, some methods of protest and persuasion have become more or less institutionalized and therefore by themselves may not necessarily provide a direct and immediate challenge to the power of the state. However, in nondemocracies, where overt dissent is less tolerated and uncommon, protest and persuasion present a more direct threat to the state and have the potential for a greater impact on political relations.

Methods of noncooperation involve the deliberate withdrawal, restriction, or defiance of expected participation or cooperation. These methods, which may be social, economic, or political, are intended to undermine the power, resources, and legitimacy of the government. Social noncooperation involves refusal to carry out normal social relations through means such as social boycotts, social ostracism, student strikes, stayaways, and offering sanctuary to dissidents. Economic noncooperation consists of the suspension of existing economic relationships or refusal to initiate new ones through means such as labor strikes or slowdowns; economic boycotts; refusal to pay rent, debts, or interest; and the collective withdrawal of bank deposits. Political noncooperation involves refusal to continue usual forms of political participation. A common type of political noncooperation is civil disobedience, that is, the open and deliberate violation of laws or orders for a political purpose, such as the publication of banned newspapers or pamphlets and refusal to pay taxes, participate in the military, or obey orders of state agents.

To the extent that nondemocratic countries are less developed and their states control less resources than do democratic regimes, the probability is greater that sustained noncooperation in them will undermine state power. Moreover, if a regime is highly dependent on a single resource or a particular benefactor, methods of noncooperation that undermine that resource or sever the support of a key benefactor may have a considerable impact on the state's ability to rule.

Methods of nonviolent intervention are acts of interposition intended either to directly disrupt normal operations that support the status quo or to develop alternatives to state-dominated relations. Examples range from sit-ins, nonviolent obstructions, land occupations, paralyzing transportation, and sabotage[22] to developing alternative markets and creating parallel institutions during the course of contentious struggles. These methods can be subdivided into two categories: disruptive and creative (Burrowes 1996, 98).

Disruptive nonviolent intervention upsets or destroys normal or established social relations, while *creative nonviolent intervention* involves the forging of new autonomous social relations. Methods of creative intervention represent a more direct challenge in nondemocracies than in democracies, where autonomous social relations are less threatening to elites.

A virtue of these methods is that the means for challenging the regime are at hand. Symbolic actions, noncooperation, and intervention can theoretically be implemented by anyone at any time. Of course the mobilization and prosecution of nonviolent challenges can be vastly improved with access to transportation and communication technologies (Martin 1996; Martin and Varney 2003), but no special equipment beyond what is typically available to people is needed to undermine state power and legitimacy through nonviolent action. Moreover, although some particular acts of nonviolent action may require more physical strength and endurance than others, just about anyone in the population can participate in nonviolent action: men as well as women, the old as well as the young, the less physically fit as well as the physically fit. This contrasts sharply with violent action, which requires special weapons—weapons that are likely to be monopolized by the state—and military campaigns, in which participation has historically been limited to young, physically fit, ideologically indoctrinated or mercenary males. It also contrasts sharply with theories of social change that privilege a particular class or "vanguard" as the agents of social change, thus excluding networks of exploited groups from struggles against oppression (Galtung 1980, 396–98). Thus, nonviolent challenges have the potential to allow the maximum degree of active participation in the struggle by the highest proportion of the population. Whereas the arrest or killing of a dozen or so members of a guerrilla cell can devastate an armed campaign, the death or arrest of hundreds or even thousands of nonviolent activists may fail to weaken challenges incorporating mass nonviolent action due to their much greater size (Zunes 1994, 415; Zunes and Kurtz 1999). The greater scale of participation in such challenges also makes it more difficult for the state to differentiate between movement participants and nonparticipants, making targeted repression, which is more effective in quelling dissent, more difficult to implement and indiscriminate repression, which may undermine the regime and promote more widespread mobilization.

Mechanisms of Change

Sharp identifies four mechanisms through which nonviolent action can produce political change: conversion, accommodation, nonviolent coercion, and disintegration (Sharp 1973; 1990, chapter 3). Through *conversion* the government, as a result of nonviolent action by challengers, adopts the challenger's point of view and concedes to its goals. Conversion may occur through reason and argumentation or as a result of changes in the emotions, beliefs, attitudes, or morality of the oppressors. At the most basic level, conversion is based on the fact that the oppressor and the oppressed are related to each other as human beings, and this may be a basis for an alteration in their relations.

The likelihood of conversion increases as the social distance between the oppressors and the oppressed decreases. If the oppressed are viewed by the oppressors as members of a common moral order, the likelihood of a sympathetic response is greater. Conversely, if the oppressors view the challengers as outside of their moral order or as inferior, the oppressors are more likely to be indifferent to the demands of the oppressed. Thus, gender, race, ethnicity, religion, and language may be divisions that form the basis of dehumanizing ideologies and decrease the likelihood of conversion. In addition to social distance, physical distance or a lack of communication between the oppressors and the oppressed may also inhibit conversion (Martin and Varney 2003). As discussed in chapter 1, conversion is commonly (mis)understood as the only way or the main way in which nonviolent action produces political change. In reality, however, it is the least likely mechanism of change.

Through *accommodation* the government grants concessions to the challengers even though it is not converted to the challengers' point of view, is not forced to concede by the challengers' actions, and has the capacity to continue the struggle. A government may accommodate challengers when it perceives that the costs of ignoring or repressing the movement are greater than the costs of giving in to some or all of its demands, views the movement as more of a nuisance than a threat, or calculates that by giving in to some or all of the challengers' demands the development of a more broad-based movement will be pre-empted.[23] From the government's point of view, accommodation is the optimal mechanism of change, since the government retains the upper hand in power relations.

Accommodation is a more likely mechanism of change in democracies where the goals of challengers are often less of a direct threat to the regime. The most likely mechanism of change in nondemocracies is *nonviolent coercion*. While the term *coercion* is typically associated with violence, coercion can also be effected through nonphysical pressure whereby violence against humans is not used or threatened. Through nonviolent coercion, change is achieved against the government's will as a result of the challengers' successful undermining of the government's power, legitimacy, and ability to control the situation through methods of nonviolent action.

Nonviolent coercion promotes political change in one of three ways: (1) the challenge becomes too widespread to be controlled by state repression, (2) the state loses its willingness or capacity to repress, or (3) the movement's implementation of nonviolent action creates situations whereby it is too disruptive for the state to function without significant alterations in its policies or structure. Several factors facilitate nonviolent coercion, including the size of the movement; the degree to which the state is dependent upon resources targeted by nonviolent action; the skill of the challengers in choosing strategies, tactics, methods, and techniques and appropriate times and places for their implementation; the resilience of the movement in the face of repression; the cultivation of third-party support, and the presence of elite or military divisions.

Disintegration occurs when the government breaks down in the face of widespread nonviolent action. That is, the challenge undermines the sources of the state's power to such an extent that the state simply falls apart and there is no longer any effective political body to challenge or resist.

Nonviolent Action and Political Transformation

According to Sharp, if methods of nonviolent action are implemented in a disciplined, organized, and persistent manner, certain dynamics may be activated that contribute to the alteration of power relationships within society. One dynamic that may occur, for example, is that repression, rather than demobilizing a movement, actually contributes to its mobilization. The dynamic by which persistent nonviolent action in the face of violent repression produces a decrease in support for the state and an increase in support for the challengers is referred to by Sharp as "political jiujitsu" (Sharp 1973; 1990, chapter 3). Others have referred to this dynamic as the "critical dynamic" (McAdam 1999) or the "paradox of repression" (Smithey and Kurtz 1999). In effect, the repression applied by the state rebounds and undercuts the state's power. This process may operate through the aggrieved group, the political elite, security forces, and third parties or reference publics.

First, repression directed at dissidents may make them more committed to their struggle, and when they maintain collective action in the face of repression, additional members of the aggrieved group may be motivated to participate. Second, the violent repression of unarmed citizens is far more likely to generate questions about the legitimacy of authority within the political elite than is the violent repression of a violent challenge. If elite divisions exist, such repression may provide one elite segment with the opportunity to align with challengers against another elite segment. If elite divisions do not exist, it may be one factor that contributes to their emergence. Third, divisions within the military or security forces and mutinies or the refusal to obey orders by subordinates may result from the violent repression of unarmed citizens or orders to do so. Disaffection, disobedience, and mutiny may be more likely in response to nonviolent resistance where there is a possibility that sympathy for the challengers may develop than in response to violent resistance where the lives of security personnel are threatened if they do not respond with violence. Fourth, third parties and reference publics, such as the general public, transnational social movements, international organizations, and foreign governments may be more likely to take action against a regime or provide support for challengers in situations where violence is used to repress an unarmed challenge, since violence highlights the fact that the government's rule is based on force rather than on legitimacy. For the political jiujitsu dynamic to take place through third parties, they must be aware of the repression and must be concerned about its consequences. Significantly, violent confrontations between armed state forces and unarmed protestors are likely to generate intense media coverage that negatively impacts the state's position and encourages third-party involvement (Barkan 1984; McAdam 1996; Sharp 1973; Smithey and Kurtz 1999; and Wolsfeld 1997).

In an analysis of protest campaigns in five southern U.S. cities during the civil rights movement, it was found that challengers were more likely to succeed when whites responded with violence to nonviolent protest, especially when the violence was reported nationally. When whites responded with legal tactics rather than violent repression, protest efforts were less successful (Barkan 1984). Similarly, another study found that violent attacks on civil rights activists by Southern officials mobilized the support of reference publics (Garrow 1978). Others found this dynamic to operate in various nondemocracies as well (Sharp 1973; Martin et al. 2001; Zunes et al. 1999).

Thus, the use of violent repression against nonviolent challenges may invoke a dynamic that increases resistance to the regime by promoting mobilization, producing or exacerbating divisions within the political elite or the security forces, and cultivating influential domestic or international allies.[24] The more sustained a nonviolent movement is in the face of repression, the more likely it is that this dynamic will be activated. Exposing the violence of the state in contrast to the nonviolence of protestors casts the state in a negative light and may lead to shifts in opinion that alter power relations. In situations where the challenge to the state is violent, violent repression by the state is more likely to be viewed as justifiable.

An important attribute of challenges that facilitates this dynamic, according to Sharp, is nonviolent discipline, that is, strict adherence to only nonviolent methods of contention (Sharp 1973; 1990, chapter 3). From a pragmatic standpoint, nonviolent discipline has absolutely nothing to do with morality and everything to do with strategy. It involves educating participants about the power of nonviolent action, the potentially negative consequences of violence, and the state's use of agents provocateurs and attempts to provoke violent responses in order to justify violent repression. If the injury or killing of state agents occurs during the course of a struggle, the movement should clearly distance itself from these acts, since violent action may have a number of negative consequences. First, it may divert attention from the grievances and issues of the challengers and turn it toward the act of violence itself. Second, by implementing violent action the movement has begun to fight the government on the government's terms, using means in which it is most likely inferior. In effect, the initiative is taken away from the movement and given to the government. Third, violence implemented by challengers usually has a polarizing effect, forcing reference publics and third parties to take sides. When activists use violence, it often alienates potential supporters and third parties and solidifies the regime, regardless of the justness of the challengers' cause. Fourth, challengers implementing violent action provide justification for the state's use of repression in the name of "law and order" or "national security." If there are any limitations on the state's use of violence, it is usually removed when violence is incorporated by challengers. Thus, according to Sharp, nonviolent discipline is required for an advantageous shift in power relations to occur through methods of nonviolent action.

Criticism

Given its individualistic and voluntaristic assumptions, Sharp's theory has been severely criticized by more structurally oriented scholars. First, Sharp's theory of nonviolent action has been criticized because of its incompleteness with regard to specification of the sources of obedience and cooperation (Burrowes 1996, 89–90; Dajani 1995; Lipsitz and Kritzer 1975; Martin 1989; McGuinness 1993; Summy 1994, 12–13). As discussed earlier, Sharp emphasizes how obedience and cooperation are derived from consent. While individual choice exists in theory, in reality tradition, ideology, socialization, and social structures constrain people's knowledge of and capacity for individual choice, and it is very difficult for people to escape from their regular-ized patterns of behavior. People must become aware of structures of oppres-sion and the structural impediments to challenging oppression, and they must overcome deeply rooted ideological hegemony before they can begin to resist. Thus, processes of consciousness raising and frame alignment, which the nonviolent action approach does not adequately consider, must be implemented before acts of resistance are undertaken. Moreover, struc-tural transformations that affect the distribution of resources and provide opportunities for or constraints to dissent need to be considered. Framing and political opportunities, of course, are the strengths of the political pro-cess approach; thus, supplementing the nonviolent action approach with political process assumptions would give us a better understanding of the structures that constrain dissent, the processes that people go through before withdrawing consent, and how structural transformations may provide op-portunities for a challenge.

Second, the theory has been criticized for not being sufficiently ap-plicable to challenging systemic relations, as opposed to rulers or govern-ments. It has been argued that discursively embedded systems of exclusion and oppression, such as statism, militarism, patriarchy, capitalism, and bureaucracy (not to mention their mutual reinforcement), cannot simply be overthrown through popular dissent (Bleiker 2000; Burrowes 1996, 90–91; Martin 1989; McGuinness 1993). To challenge structural relations, alterna-tive structures must be developed to promote social and political change. While Sharp acknowledges creative nonviolent intervention as a technique of nonviolent action, he undertheorizes its centrality for promoting political change. A more comprehensive understanding of unarmed insurrections, and more generally of resistance to structures of oppression and the process of democratization, must consider the existence or creation of alternative structures capable of resisting co-optation, corruption, and destruction by existing institutions. Autonomous structures may gradually develop as a by-product of large-scale social change, or autonomous structures may be con-sciously established through implementing constructive programs, develop-ing autonomous organizations, appropriating existing organizations, and, more generally, expanding the sphere of oppositional civil society (Burrowes 1996, 95–96; Gramsci 1971; Havel et al. 1985; Mann 1986).

Third, the theory has been criticized because it assumes that the ruler's power is dependent upon the cooperation or obedience of the ruled. It is true, as Sharp suggests, that states are always dependent, but they are not necessarily dependent on the cooperation and obedience of the people they actually rule (Burrowes 1996, 87–88; Galtung 1989; Lipsitz and Kritzer 1975; Summy 1994). The power of a state may derive from sources outside of society, such as foreign states or international capital. Therefore, the degree and form of state dependence must be considered, and the crucial role of third parties in conflicts between challengers and the state must be theorized. Noncooperation by the oppressed may be a necessary but not sufficient prerequisite for a successful unarmed insurrection.

Thus, where the political process approach is strong, explaining the emergence of challenges and identifying the structures that constrain them or the opportunities that propel them, the nonviolent action approach is weak. Moreover, where the political process approach is underspecified in terms of accounting for the trajectories of movements once they have emerged and for how the actions of movements may contribute to the recasting of the political context, the nonviolent action approach provides useful insights. Thus, a cautious gleaning of insights from each approach may prove useful in developing the other.

Significantly, a growing body of scholarship on nonviolent action has emerged that, while drawing on Sharp's framework and recognizing the power of nonviolent action in nondemocratic contexts, also recognize the limitations of Sharp's framework (e.g., Burrowes 1996; Dajani 1995; Galtung 1980, 1989; Martin 1989, 1996; Martin and Varney 2003; Martin et al. 2001; Routledge 1993, 1994; Summy 1994; Wehr et al. 1994; Zunes 1994; and Zunes et al. 1999). But rather than simply dismissing Sharp's framework, this scholarship recognizes its limitations, but also its fundamental and irrefutable insight that states must constantly replenish their power, that states depend on the cooperation and obedience of at least some segments of the ruled, and that violence is not the ultimate source of power. Later in this chapter I draw from the political process approach as well as from scholarship on nonviolent action to develop a framework that may shed light on the trajectories of unarmed insurrections in nondemocracies. But first I must address two significant points of divergence between the political process and the nonviolent action approaches.

Political Process and Nonviolent Action Approaches: Points of Divergence

One fundamental difference between the two approaches is that from the nonviolent action perspective there is a tendency to view nonviolent action as a phenomenon sui generis, while the political process approach makes explicit the assumption that nonviolent action is part of a broader continuum of political contention, ranging from institutional politics to military warfare. Neither approach, it seems, is "right" or "wrong," but each has implications for the analysis of social movements.

Empirically, cases of resistance that implement only nonviolent action are rare, as struggles often implement various methods of political action, institutional and noninstitutional, nonviolent and violent. By viewing nonviolent action as a phenomenon sui generis, scholars may underestimate the role of violence or the implicit threat of violence in promoting political change. On the other hand, by conceptualizing nonviolent action as part of a broad continuum of contention, scholars may underestimate the power of nonviolent action independent of violence in producing political change. More generally, by not making conceptual distinctions between different methods of contention, the importance of strategy and tactics may be downplayed or overlooked, as different strategies along the continuum may invoke different dynamics of contention.

The political process approach assumes that political violence is an unproblematic or natural extension of ordinary social movement processes. Yet a number of questions are not addressed. For example, who decides that there is no choice but to take up arms? What knowledge, if any, do movement participants and leaders have about the power and strategy of nonviolent action? What criteria are used to gauge the effectiveness of methods of nonviolent action? Who benefits from shifting the struggle to more violent domains? The strategic shift from predominantly one form of struggle to another is often explained away, as the transgressive nature of contention and important questions are largely left unaddressed.[25]

A second significant way in which the two approaches diverge is with regard to the radical flank effect, an important feature of social movement activity that, unfortunately, has received scant scholarly attention. A positive radical flank effect occurs when the leverage of moderates is strengthened by the presence of a so-called radical wing that has more extreme goals and incorporates violent strategies. The presence of a radical wing makes moderate strategies and demands appear more reasonable, and radicals may create crises that are resolved to the moderates' advantage. A negative radical flank effect occurs when the activities of a radical wing undermine the leverage of moderates. The activities of radicals discredit the entire movement's activities and goals and threaten the ability of moderates to invoke third-party support (Haines 1984, 1988).

Although social movement scholarship suggests that radical flanks and violence may have positive or negative effects on a challenge, the nonviolent action approach suggests that the use of violence by a segment of the challengers is likely to have only negative consequences, based on the assumption that it will decrease support for the challenge, justify repression, and shift the conflict to the state's terms. Herbert Haines attributes the increase in funding of moderate U.S. civil rights organizations during the 1960s to the rise of a radical flank (Haines 1984, 1988).[26] Others, however, maintain that a negative radical flank effect occurred, since the emergence of a radical flank in the civil rights movement in the late 1960s produced organizational fragmentation and contributed to a white backlash and increased repression (Masotti et al. 1969; McAdam 1999; Muse 1968; Powledge 1967). Moreover, even a "positive" radical flank effect may be interpreted as having negative consequences. The increased funding of moderate groups, in effect, channeled the civil rights movement into less disruptive and institutionalized political channels. In the process, the movement lost its capacity to disrupt and therefore its power to promote political change (Jenkins and Eckert 1986; Piven and Cloward 1979a, 1979b).

A problem with the use of the radical flank concept is that goals and strategies are not always clearly distinguished. As discussed in chapter 1, it is entirely possible for challengers to be militant and confrontational and have "radical" goals, yet refrain from implementing violent action. This would seem especially relevant in nondemocracies, where challengers typically have "radical" goals in the sense that they are seeking fundamental changes in the political structure, yet they do not necessarily have to use or rely on violence to attain their goals.

Related to the radical flank effect is the relation between violent action and social movement outcomes. Some suggest that the use of violent action is likely to help challengers to attain their goals (e.g., Gamson 1990; Mueller 1978; Piven and Cloward 1979a, 1979b), while others suggest that the use of violence is likely to have the opposite effect, since it reduces third-party support and removes constraints on the authority's use of repression (e.g., Colby 1985; Schumaker 1975; Sharp 1973). However, a problem with the social movement literature on this topic is that violence is not clearly differentiated from disruption. The argument can be made that it is not violence per se that facilitates change, but the disruptiveness of violence. Some have suggested that violent protest is effective when it presents an economic threat through the disruption of business (Button 1989a, 1989b). Therefore, if violence works because it is disruptive, and since nonviolent action has the potential to be as disruptive as violence, it may be a functional equivalent to violence in producing political change in some contexts. Moreover, as suggested in chapter 1, there are reasons to believe that nonviolent action is increasingly being used as a functional equivalent to violence as repertoires of nonviolent action become more well known and as the ability of the oppressed to make their voice heard through methods other than violence increases. I return to the role of violence and radical flank effects in the concluding chapter.

Unarmed Insurrections and Political Transformation

In this section I sketch a relational framework for explaining the trajectories of unarmed insurrections in nondemocracies that pulls together elements from the political process and nonviolent action perspectives. While recognizing the importance of the political context, I also consider the fact that the less powerful have the inherent potential to withdraw their cooperation from the powerful and disrupt the normal functioning of the system. In accounting for the trajectories of unarmed insurrections, important considerations include the resilience of the challenger's campaigns of nonviolent action in the face of repression, whether or not the campaigns of nonviolent action invoke leverage vis-à-vis the state through the state's dependence relations, the role of third parties in supporting the challenge or pressuring the state for change, and the coherence of the political elite.

Two basic conditions must be met for a challenge to contribute to political transformations: (1) the challenge must be able to withstand repression, and (2) the challenge must undermine state power. These conditions are obvious enough. What is less obvious, though, are the attributes and actions of challenges that contribute to these conditions and the mechanisms that link movement attributes and actions to political change. Both primarily violent and primarily nonviolent challenges may successfully resist or wear down state repression, and state power may be undermined through primarily nonviolent or primarily violent challenges. Compared to the theories and literatures on how violent challenges promote change, however, the theories and literatures on how primarily nonviolent challenges can promote change in nondemocratic contexts are relatively underdeveloped. The following discussion specifies attributes and actions of struggles relying primarily on nonviolent action that may increase the likelihood that they will promote political change in nondemocracies.

Surviving Repression

Generally, when the interests of political authorities are threatened, repression is used as a means to control or eliminate the challenge. Unlike democracies, where dissent is expected and tolerated, nondemocratic regimes cannot simply ignore protest, as its mere existence represents a threat to the regime. If protest is ignored, the regime will appear helpless in the face of defiance, and resistance will spread. Thus, those engaging in overt challenges to nondemocratic regimes should expect a violent response by the government. Since violent repression is to be expected, safe spaces must be developed that lower the negative consequences of repression (Ackerman and Kruegler 1994; Evans and Boyte 1992; Gurr 1986; Lichbach 1995; Opp and Roehl 1990; and Scott 1990).

The organizational template most useful for challenging the state through nonviolent action in repressive contexts is network-oriented rather than hierarchical. According to Walter Powell, networks, in contrast to hierarchies, are characterized by lateral relations and reciprocal patterns of communication and exchange. Some of the virtues of networks, according to Powell, include being "lighter on their feet," which enhances the ability of participants to transmit and learn new knowledge and skills; possessing a comparative advantage in coping with an environment that places a premium on innovation; and, because individuals participate in the decision-making process, they may be more committed and enthusiastic in carrying out tasks than when they are simply given orders by superiors (Powell 1990). Although Powell was distinguishing between network and hierarchical forms of economic organization, his insights apply to social movement organization as well. Compared to hierarchically organized challenges, network-organized challenges are more flexible, are more adept at expanding horizontal channels of communication, are more likely to increase the participation and commitment of members and the accountability of leaders, are more likely to innovate tactically, and are more likely to weather repression.

Robert Burrowes suggests that decentralized organizations and network-oriented mobilizing structures have numerous advantages over centralized organizations in sustaining a challenge in a repressive context, such as the ability to satisfy the needs of individuals; to foster meaningful participation in the decisions and activities that personally affect the organization's members; to utilize individual differences to build collective strength; to minimize the susceptibility to institutionalization and co-optation; and to be less subject to targeted state repression. Moreover, leadership is diffuse in network-oriented mobilizing structures, so challenges may be sustained even if leaders are imprisoned or executed (Burrowes 1996, 184–99).[27]

Umbrella organizations and federations provide connections between diverse groups, facilitating the sustained and broad participation that is required for campaigns of noncooperation to be effective (Lichbach 1995; Marwell and Oliver 1993). Activists reside in the structures of everyday life, such as neighborhoods, churches, universities, and civic associations, and umbrella organizations are useful in activating these sites to mobilize on a national basis when necessary (Evans and Boyte 1992). Through "franchising," national umbrella organizations can coordinate the activities of a broad base without expending resources on maintaining the formal connective structures of a centralized hierarchical organization (McCarthy and Wolfson 1992). When umbrella organizations or federations are able to loosely coordinate the activities of diverse groups with common goals, it may be more difficult for the state to respond with focused and effective repression.

Like decentralized and network-oriented organization, the implementation of methods from all three classes of methods of nonviolent action increases the likelihood of sustaining a challenge in the face of repression. This is not tautological. Of course the ability to implement methods of nonviolent action is constrained by repression, but the mix of methods implemented may nevertheless influence the extent to which a challenge weathers repression. The more diverse the tactics and methods implemented, the more diffuse the state's repressive operations become, thus potentially lessening their effectiveness. Incorporating multiple methods also makes it easier to shift the emphasis from one class of methods to another if the state focuses its repressive capacities on a particular method. Moreover, each method has its own virtues and also reinforces the other methods. Protest and persuasion help overcome apathy, acquiescence, and fear; promote solidarity; contribute to the elaboration and dissemination of counterhegemonic frames; and signal to third parties and reference publics the existence of an unjust and intolerable situation. Noncooperation undermines the legitimacy, resources, and power of the state, and the collective withdrawal of cooperation from the state promotes cooperation and empowerment among the oppressed. Disruptive nonviolent intervention may be used in support of methods of protest and persuasion and methods of noncooperation, and creative nonviolent intervention undermines state authority and contributes to the ability of movements to sustain themselves by providing networks that are alternative to state-controlled institutions.

The ability to shift from methods of concentration to methods of dispersion in response to the political context is also important for weathering repression (Burrowes 1996, 224–25). Methods of concentration, in which a large number of people are concentrated in a public place (e.g., in a protest demonstration), provide a movement with the opportunity to build solidarity, highlight grievances, indicate the extent of dissatisfaction, and, if the state responds with repression, expose the fact that the state is based on violence rather than legitimacy. However, in the face of sustained repression, challengers must be able to shift to methods of dispersion, in which cooperation is withdrawn, such as a strike or boycott. These methods do not provide the state with a tangible target for repression and may overextend the state's repressive capacities due to the lack of a specific target. Methods of both concentration and dispersal are useful for promoting political change, but their effectiveness depends on the context.

Challengers and authorities tend to adapt to each other's actions over time (Francisco 1995, 1996; McAdam 1983, 1999; Tilly 1978; Trotsky 1980). If challengers adapt more quickly than the state, they increase their likelihood of weathering state repression. Thus, when the state learns to adapt to and counter certain methods, the challenging group must innovate to keep authorities off balance and to prevent the challenge from stagnating. Tactical innovation—activists' creativity in devising new noninstitutional tactics when the effectiveness of earlier tactics is offset by the responses of authorities (McAdam 1983)—is more likely to occur when challengers are organized as networks rather than hierarchies (Gamson 1990; Gerlach and Hine 1970) and when a range of methods of nonviolent action are used, since implementing a variety of methods increases the probability of novel recombinants of existing actions. Since tactical innovation occurs on the margins of existing repertoires (Tarrow 1998; Tilly 1995a), the more expansive the margins, as represented by the implementation or knowledge of multiple techniques from various methods, the greater the likelihood of innovation.

In sum, challenges characterized by dispersed yet coordinated networks and decentralized organizations that can mobilize resources through channels not directly controlled by the state, and that implement a diverse mix of methods and respond effectively to the state's actions, are more likely to remain resilient in the face of violent repression.

Undermining State Power

Changes in the political structure facilitate the emergence of social movements, but once the initial constraints on mobilization have been overcome, challenges face another set of constraints that must be dealt with before they can contribute to a change in political relations. The political opportunities that encourage the mobilization of challenges, in other words, are not likely to be the same ones that facilitate their success (McAdam et al. 1996, 15; Tarrow 1991, 81). If challenges are to contribute to regime transitions, they must transform political relations. That is, they must contribute to the recasting of the political context by undermining state power, resources, and legitimacy; creating or exacerbating elite divisions; and invoking third-party support. Although the relationship between authorities, challengers, and the political context is nonrecursive and unpredictable (e.g., Markoff 1997; McAdam 1996, 38), there are, nevertheless, movement attributes and actions that may enhance their ability to promote political transformations once they have arisen.

The mere existence of a challenge in the face repression demonstrates that the regime is not unassailable, decreasing the effectiveness of repression as a deterrent. A point may be reached whereby the more that repression is applied by the authorities, the stronger the challenge becomes through increased mobilization and third-party support. Moreover, if increased mobilization is translated into the implementation of multiple methods of nonviolent action, the likelihood that the challenge will contribute to the undermining of state power is greater than it would be if the challenge depended on one particular method or class of methods.[28] Multiple methods are especially useful if challengers can make and deliver upon threats to escalate tactics if the state does not meet their demands (Button 1989a, 1989b).

To maximize the leverage of the challenge, the state's dependence relations must be targeted. A necessary but not sufficient component of a successful unarmed insurrection, according to Ralph Summy, is targeting the state's dependence relationships, either directly or indirectly through third parties (Summy 1994). In any society, the state directly depends on segments of its own populace to rule. If any of these segments, such as military personnel, police officers, administrators, or workers in energy supply, transportation, communications, commerce, or other key sectors, refuse or threaten to refuse to carry out their duties, the state's power is significantly undermined. The withdrawal of cooperation on which others depend is a valuable resource for exerting power over others. According to Piven and Cloward, noncooperation and the disruption it causes are "regularly employed by individuals and groups linked together in many kinds of cooperative interaction, and particularly by producer groups. Farmers, for example, keep their products off the market in order to force up the price offered by buyers; doctors refuse to provide treatment unless their price is met; oil companies withhold supplies until price concessions are made" (Piven and Cloward 1979a, 24–25). Similarly, noncooperation with the state may be used to force it to make political concessions or to undermine its capacities for continued rule.

Thus, undermining state power through disruption or noncooperation, especially through channels that tap into the state's dependence relations, thereby increasing the leverage of the challengers, is a crucial mechanism that must be considered in examining the trajectories of unarmed insurrections. A central task of all challengers is to increase their leverage against the state by directly targeting the state's dependence relations and by mobilizing pressure indirectly through third parties.

The amount of leverage that challengers can wield varies depending upon the directness of their ties to the oppressors. In instances of indirect dependence relative to the state, where there are no direct ties between the oppressors and the oppressed, third parties become crucial to the conflict. The degree to which the government depends on the support of third parties determines the potential indirect leverage of the challengers (Burstein et al. 1995). Challengers with no direct dependence relations with the state can increase their leverage by generating the support of third parties that do have direct relationships to the state. This can occur through appeals, pressure, or the nonviolent coercion of third parties that have links to both the challengers and the state. Johan Galtung refers to the indirect leverage exerted against the state through the support of third parties as the "great chain of nonviolence" whereby the two sides of the struggle are bridged by a concatenation of intermediate groups or third parties (Galtung 1989, 13–33). In the U.S. civil rights movement, for example, middle-class whites and the federal government constituted third parties that intervened on the side of African Americans in the South in their struggle against the white power structure. As discussed in chapter 1, the global processes that intensified at the end of the twentieth century created networks linking oppressed and intermediary groups, thereby increasing the potential for challengers to invoke the support of third parties. Transnational social movement organizations such as Amnesty International, Peace Brigades International, and the Unrepresented Nations and People's Organization concatenate the oppressors and the oppressed through concerned citizens in other countries and international institutions. The result is an increase in the strength of the links between the oppressors and the oppressed, so nonviolent action by the oppressed may have a greater likelihood of succeeding where these networks are involved. The support of challengers by third parties may be crucial in providing them with greater leverage or in tipping the balance of power in their favor. The likelihood of network concatenation increases the denser that domestic and global civil society becomes. Of course the expanse of domestic and global civil society is highly uneven, so the prospects for third-party influence vary across countries.

In democracies, potential dilemmas for challenges receiving third-party support include the channeling of dissent into less disruptive channels, becoming dependent on institutional funding, and co-optation of the movement's leaders. This may be less of a problem with regard to transnational support, where the sources of third-party support are not usually part of the power structure being challenged. On the other hand, new dilemmas arise; since the support is not coming from the power structure being challenged, there may be fewer constraints on repression. Moreover, in order to attract international third-party support, challengers may shift their issues or undertake risky mobilizations, which in turn may provoke violent state repression that third parties are unable to stop (Bob 2002). Thus, increased support or encouragement from abroad must be carefully weighed against intranational political opportunities and constraints.

An unarmed insurrection characterized by network-oriented mobilizing structures, the implementation of a broad range of nonviolent actions, and the effective targeting of the state's dependence relations is by no means guaranteed success. The factors influencing the trajectories of unarmed insurrections and their interactions are far too complex and subject to the influence of factors beyond the control or recognition of activists and social scientists. Nevertheless, there are reasons to believe that unarmed insurrections characterized by the attributes and actions specified in this section may increase the likelihood that a challenge will remain resilient in a nondemocratic context. And by sustaining a challenge in the face of repression, the challengers increase the likelihood that they will learn from past experiences; that the state's legitimacy, resources, and capacities for repression will be undermined; that elite divisions may be produced or exacerbated; and that influential allies may be cultivated, producing a political context more favorable to the challenge.

Conclusion

Theoretically, no regime is immune from the pressure of a broad-based and sustained unarmed insurrection. In all regimes, the methods of control used by the oppressors can be turned against them. Yet in reality unarmed insurrections are rare phenomena (despite the global wave at the end of the twentieth century), and when they do occur, they may not contribute to political change. In the next three chapters I examine the trajectories of six diverse unarmed insurrections that occurred across a broad range of nondemocratic contexts in the late twentieth century, and I attempt to explain in a preliminary manner why unarmed insurrections contribute to political change in some instances but not others.[29] I begin with the anti-apartheid movement in South Africa and the people power movement in the Philippines.

3

People Power Unleashed: South Africa and the Philippines

The movement for racial equality in South Africa was a protracted struggle that lasted most of the twentieth century, with the final push touched off by an incident in Soweto in June 1976, when students demonstrating in protest of the imposition of Afrikaans as the language of instruction were met with lethal force. The murder of students by state forces sparked a nationwide rebellion lasting into 1977 that, while unsuccessful in toppling the apartheid system, catalyzed a groundswell of grassroots activism that sustained unarmed insurgencies in the townships in the 1980s. By the end of the 1980s, bans on political organizations were lifted; political prisoners were released, including Nelson Mandela, who had been imprisoned since 1962; and pathways for a negotiated transition to a unitary, nonracial democratic state were blazed. In April 1994 the African National Congress (ANC) won the first-ever universal national elections in South Africa, and Mandela was inaugurated as president.

In contrast to the decades-long struggle against racial oppression in South Africa, a mere thirty months elapsed between the assassination of Benigno S. Aquino Jr. and the fall of the Marcos dictatorship in the Philippines. On August 21, 1983, Benigno "Ninoy" Aquino, a long-time competitor of Ferdinand E. Marcos for the spoils of the Philippine presidency, returned to Manila following three years of exile in the United States. Upon his descent from the airplane steps onto the tarmac at Manila International Airport, Aquino's life was taken by a gunshot to his head. Although resistance to Marcos had been increasing in the early 1980s, the assassination of Aquino triggered campaigns of noncooperation and civil disobedience, culminating in the "People Power Revolution" of February 22–25, 1986, the abdication of Marcos, and a transition to democracy when Benigno Aquino's widow, Corazón, assumed the presidency.

Of course violence accompanied these unarmed insurrections. In South Africa, the armed wing of the ANC, the Umkhonto we Sizwe (MK, Spear of the Nation), which had been operating since the early 1960s, was increasing its campaigns of violent sabotage and attacks on military targets in the 1980s. In black townships, violence was used against alleged collaborators of the apartheid regime, youths armed with rocks—and occasionally guns—engaged in battle with security forces, and coercion was sometimes used to promote participation in boycott campaigns. In the Philippines, the New People's Army, which initiated a Maoist insurgency in 1969, had been increasing in effectiveness while the competence of the Philippine military had been declining. Nevertheless, in both South Africa and the Philippines, violent challenges by themselves were unable to topple the regimes, and it was methods of nonviolent action rather than violence that provided the most serious challenges to the regimes and culminated in democratic transitions.

How can we account for the success of these two predominantly unarmed insurrections? Were there comparable mechanisms at work in both that transformed political relations and promoted regime change? An examination of movement strategies and the responses by states and third parties will help to illuminate answers to these questions.

South Africa

In 1910 the Union of South Africa was formed under a constitution excluding blacks from politics.[1] In response, the African National Congress was founded in 1912. From the 1910s through the 1940s, the ANC challenged the regime mainly through institutional channels, such as petitioning and lobbying for political rights; however, these methods were unsuccessful in promoting political change. In 1948 the political context became more restrictive when the National Party came to power and implemented the apartheid system.

Resistance to Apartheid

A second period of black protest emerged in 1949, when the ANC adopted a program of mass action. The Defiance Campaign, a nationwide campaign of civil disobedience in which people disobeyed segregationist rules in public places, was launched in 1952. The movement successfully mobilized a substantial portion of the nonwhite population, but subsequently declined after thousands were arrested between June and November 1952 and the government passed repressive laws such as the Suppression of Communism Act prohibiting political meetings and demonstrations. During the 1950s an increasing number of dissidents became critical of the movement's so-called moderate tactics and cooperation with whites. In response, the Pan Africanist Congress (PAC) was formed in 1959. The PAC organized mass demonstrations in 1960 protesting pass laws restricting the freedom of movement of blacks. In Sharpeville, thirty-five miles south of Johannesburg, the police fired indiscriminately into a crowd of 10,000, killing at least 69 and wounding 178 demonstrators as they fled from the police.[2] A state of emergency was subsequently declared, and thousands were arrested, decimating the PAC and ANC leadership. Concluding that nonviolent techniques would not be effective against the apartheid regime, the ANC and their communist allies organized the Umkhonto we Sizwe and turned their attention to violent sabotage and armed struggle. The ANC was banned in 1960, and security police captured Umkhonto leaders, including Nelson Mandela and Walter Sisulu, in 1962 and 1963, sentencing them to life imprisonment. By the mid-1960s the government had suppressed all overt activities and uprooted most of the underground activity of the ANC and PAC.

In the late 1960s and early 1970s a third period of black resistance emerged, spearheaded by the Black Consciousness Movement (BCM). The South African Students Organization (SASO), formed in 1968 with Steve Biko as president, and the Black People's Convention (BPC), formed in 1972, were the movement's main organizational vehicles. According to Biko, it was necessary to liberate blacks from their own attitudes of subservience and inferiority in order for political change to occur (Biko 1978). Like the PAC, the BCM rejected any role for whites in the resistance movement; however, the movement did not have an explicit political ideology or strategy for challenging the state, as it was more concerned with developing black cultural pride, psychological autonomy, and counterhegemonic frames, and with organizing literacy campaigns and cultural activities (Price 1991, 49–50).

Resistance after Soweto

In contrast to the spontaneous and often violent Soweto rebellion, the challenges in the 1980s became increasingly more organized and sophisticated in their strategic implementation of methods of nonviolent action. The shift in the strategy and organization of the anti-apartheid challenge was a deliberate response to the opportunities and constraints of the political environment. While the opportunities for organizing were exploited through creative nonviolent intervention, the constraints of the political context were recast through the implementation of methods of protest and persuasion, disruptive nonviolent intervention, and especially noncooperation. The result was the undermining of state power, the exacerbation of elite divisions, the cultivation of third-party support, and ultimately, by the end of the 1980s, the demise of the apartheid system.

In the following section I discuss three major social movement organizations of the anti-apartheid movement in the 1980s: (1) the United Democratic Front (UDF) and affiliates, (2) the Congress of South African Trade Unions (COSATU), (3) and the ANC,[5] focusing on the extent to which they were characterized by the attributes and actions that should theoretically be associated with a challenge's ability to promote political change through nonviolent action in a nondemocratic context.

The United Democratic Front and Affiliates

The early 1980s were characterized by the expansion of local groups that were emerging to defend and promote the interests of black urban residents and to protest government policies on housing, rent, transportation, education, and other urban services. The UDF was launched on August 20, 1983, to oppose the government's new constitutional proposals aimed at legitimating apartheid rule and to coordinate and aggregate the many local struggles throughout the country. The 565 organizations affiliated with the UDF at its inception included trade unions, youth organizations, student groups, women's groups, religious groups, professional organizations, and civic associations. At its peak, the UDF claimed the allegiance of approximately 700 affiliates embracing every major concentration of population throughout the country (Lodge 1992; Price 1991; Seekings 2000).

The UDF was an umbrella organization that linked diverse local grassroots movements and provided the coordination and direction necessary to promote a national political challenge. The strength of the UDF was in its decentralized grassroots organizational structure and networks of autonomous groups, which provided a means for communication and mobilization and resilience in the face of state repression. The organizations affiliated with the UDF were self-consciously democratic, requiring leaders to be accountable and to have a mandate from their members. The UDF proponents maintained that loyalty to grassroots affiliates was stronger than allegiance to a centralized, monolithic organization, and a great deal of decision-making power resided at the local level (Lodge 1992; Morobe 1987; Price 1991; Seekings 2000).

The organizations affiliated with the UDF implemented methods of protest and persuasion, such as demonstrations, marches, rallies, and political funerals, to promote the redress of local grievances, oppose the proposed constitutional changes, gain the release of political detainees, and commemorate those killed by the state. The first major campaign of noncooperation coordinated by the UDF was the Anti-Election Campaign, a boycott of the state's constitutional reform initiative in August 1984. Although white voters approved the plan by a two-thirds majority, the boycott campaign succeeded in contesting the legitimacy of state reforms, as fewer than one in five eligible mixed-race voters, and only one in seven eligible Indian voters, voted (Lodge 1992; Seekings 2000).

After the national election boycott, the UDF and affiliates applied methods of noncooperation to local community struggles by boycotting rents, services, schools, and businesses. As a result of rent and service boycotts, state authority collapsed in many townships (Lodge 1992; Seekings 2000). The campaigns of noncooperation proved so threatening to the regime that a partial state of emergency was declared on July 21, 1985, the first state of emergency declared in South Africa since 1961. However, the repression merely fueled the uprisings, including an outbreak of violent action by militant youth against the military occupation of the townships. In addition to throwing bricks, stones, and Molotov cocktails at police and military forces, militant youth occasionally engaged in gun battles with security forces. Violence against black township residents alleged to be collaborators with the apartheid regime escalated as well. The homes of black town council members and black police officers were bombed. Vigilante mobs immolated alleged collaborators by putting burning rubber tires over their heads in actions referred to as "necklacing," claiming hundreds of lives during the mid-1980s.

Drawing on the lessons of the Soweto uprising in 1976–77, where unorganized and often violent collective action by students and young unemployed men had been brutally suppressed by the state, the UDF consciously developed a strategy of "people power." While recognizing the role of the Soweto uprising in inspiring mass political activity, the UDF maintained that further spontaneous, violent unrest would be easily crushed by state repression. The people power strategy was designed to build local decentralized structures that were difficult for the state to repress, to reign in the violent direct action of militant youth and channel it into more constructive forms of resistance, and to implement methods of creative nonviolent intervention in order to develop autonomous structures.

For dealing with black collaborators and informants, street and area committees encouraged the use of nonviolent methods such as boycotts of the businesses of black collaborators and social ostracism of black town council members and police. The committees attempted to make a clear distinction between the nonviolent action and accountability of people power and the undisciplined violent action of "ultramilitant" youth, and they promoted highly organized forms of contention that would not lead to unnecessary violence. Significantly, these attempts to promote nonviolent discipline were not based on moral condemnations of violent action. The UDF, in fact, approved of violence when it was used in self-defense and never condemned the armed actions of the ANC. Nevertheless, the UDF realized the strategic virtue of methods of nonviolent action and understood that state power was more likely to be undermined through nonviolent action than through violence. Thus, the UDF took a more tactful approach involving constructive engagement with those implementing violent action, an approach that involved educating perpetrators of violence about the practical advantages of nonviolent action and providing nonviolent options for resisting the state. For example, it encouraged "unmasking," whereby the names and photographs of security police and informers are published for the purpose of neutralizing their activities and promoting social ostracism, while discouraging necklacing (Smuts and Westcott 1991). According to one scholar, "Street and area committees have helped activists bring militant youths under control, by dividing youth squads into smaller more disciplined units attachable to a street or area committee and they have proved reasonably effective in countering repression. Tight local-level organisation has helped to lessen the damaging effect which detention, disappearance or death of leaders might otherwise have had" (Swilling 1988, 104).

The implementation of methods of creative nonviolent intervention by UDF affiliates was a deliberate effort to replace state authority with "people power" and in so doing to create a situation of dual power that would facilitate a shift in the balance of power and a political transition in South Africa. Local structures assumed administrative, judicial, welfare, and cultural functions. Civic associations acted as institutions for local rule that bypassed the state-controlled community councils, creating a situation of dual power at the local level (Lodge 1992; Marx 1992). The National Education Crisis Committee (NECC), launched in March 1986, organized "people's education." Teachers fired by the state for implementing a "people's curriculum" were supported by community-raised funds. A system of alternative health care also emerged as UDF-affiliated health professionals began treating patients outside of state-run clinics and training community workers in first aid to treat victims of state terrorism (Price 1991, 211–15).

Facilitated by decentralized grassroots structures, the implementation of methods of noncooperation continued despite the state of emergency. By 1986, rent boycotts had spread to fifty-four townships nationwide, involving approximately 500,000 households and costing the state at least R40 million per month (Swilling 1988). By 1987, rent deficits in townships across the country had reached R178 million (Seekings 2000, 207). The rent boycotts led to the collapse of numerous state-controlled community councils, since they depended on rents for revenue.

In 1986 a number of factors converged, leading to an even greater intensification of state repression against the anti-apartheid movement. First, the state concluded that its policies of political reform and attempts at co-optation had failed. Second, economic sanctions were being drawn up by the United States, ending constraints on repression that had resulted from the threat of increased international sanctions. Third, the "securocrat" sector of the elite, which favored a "total war" strategy against perceived enemies of the apartheid state, rose to prominence and was initially unconstrained by other elite segments. Repression became more systematic on June 12, 1986, when the government imposed a second state of emergency. The first state of emergency, from July 21, 1985, to March 7, 1986, had covered thirty-six magisterial districts in Pretoria-Witwatersrand-Vereeniging (PWV) and the Eastern Cape and had been aimed at preventing mass political meetings and methods of protest and persuasion. The second state of emergency, which was nationwide, was aimed at eliminating methods of noncooperation as well. It was declared illegal to encourage, take part in, or publicize boycotts or stayaways. Methods of creative nonviolent intervention, the "structures of people power," were targeted by repression as well, as participation in alternative institutions was declared treasonous (Price 1991).

While the second state of emergency severely weakened the UDF's national organizational structures, its decentralized network of local organizations remained resilient. The state of emergency resulted in a decline in mass protest demonstrations against the regime, but it was unable to eliminate the organizational infrastructure of the community-based networks. Street committees headed by people unknown outside their neighborhoods provided low-profile leadership that was highly resistant to detentions and restrictions and provided channels of communication which facilitated resistance. Rent strikes continued, and in Soweto officials were forced to enter negotiations with the UDF over ending the strikes, indicating the extent to which the UDF continued to undermine state power despite the state of emergency (Lodge 1992; Price 1991; Seekings 2000).

Moreover, the UDF continued to expand nonviolent resistance as consumer boycotts initiated in the Eastern Cape spread throughout the country. The boycotts were most successful when they were organized in support of local community initiatives, such as rent reductions, improved housing and urban services, desegregation of stores, and the withdrawal of military personnel. Consumer boycotts of white businesses forced them to end segregation in stores and helped drive a wedge between white middle-class shopkeepers and the state. Local chambers of commerce were compelled to lobby the government to end segregation in town council meetings, withdraw police from the townships, release political prisoners, and construct new schools for blacks (Swilling 1988). The UDF and its affiliates also organized campaigns that brought attention to the plight of political prisoners. One campaign called attention to juveniles being held in detention. Another campaign in 1989 organized coordinated and disciplined hunger strikes by detained UDF activists. More than six hundred prisoners took part, demanding immediate release from prison. As the strike continued, over one hundred prisoners had to be admitted to hospitals due to physical deterioration. This brought increased international attention to political repression in South Africa, and eventually most of the political prisoners were released (Price 1991, 268; Seekings 2000, 240–41).

The sustained campaigns of nonviolent action successfully undermined the state's repressive capacities and facilitated further mobilization. While the intensification of repression had the effect of limiting methods of protest and persuasion, methods of noncooperation and nonviolent intervention continued despite the repression. As Anthony Marx has reported, the sustained campaign of resistance in the face of repression had the effect of "eroding the state's capacity and will to govern through repression. . . . In the meantime, the capacity and will of black South Africans to reject their continued domination grew more quickly" (Marx 1992, 162). That is, the "political jiujitsu" dynamic was activated.

The Congress of South African Trade Unions

As South Africa's economy industrialized, it became increasingly dependent on a larger and more urbanized black proletariat, and it was this dependence that afforded blacks potential leverage over the state. However, this power could be wielded strategically only through effective organization of the workforce and disciplined collective action. This potential began to be tapped when an independent trade union movement in South Africa emerged out of the Durban strikes in 1973. In 1979, in response to the growing labor movement, the state formally recognized African trade unions within the official industrial relations system in an attempt to institutionalize labor conflict, control labor relations, inhibit the politicization of workers, and co-opt the working class. However, the labor reforms failed to have their intended effect, as the legalized unions failed to adopt trade union economism and took up nonworkplace struggles as well (Adler and Webster 1995; Baskin 1991; Maree 1985; Marx 1992; Price 1991; Seidman 1994).

The Federation of South African Trade Unions (FOSATU) was organized in 1979, bringing together 20,000 workers in twelve industrial unions committed to democratic shop floor organization, nonracialism, and working-class struggle. In the 1980s, and especially after the formation of the UDF in 1983, unions became increasingly involved in community issues as well as workplace issues. In response to the state of emergency in July 1985 and the intensified repression of union activists for their political activities, the need for a national federation that pursued political as well and economic issues became evident. The need was met with the founding of the Congress of South African Trade Unions (COSATU), an umbrella organization for trade unions, in December 1985. COSATU grew from 460,000 workers in 1985 to 1.15 million by the end of the decade (Baskin 1991; Finnemore and Van der Merwe 1992).

The South African trade union movement's fusing of the formal organizational features of unions with the mobilizing capacity and looser structure of social movements has been referred to as "social movement unionism" (Adler et al. 1992; Adler and Webster 1995; Hirschsohn 1998; Lambert and Webster 1988; Seidman 1994; and Webster 1988). Social movement unionism has three main characteristics. First, it involves linking workplace struggles over wages, working conditions, and worker autonomy with broader community and national political struggles over human rights, justice, and democracy. This entails working with local social movement organizations and national political organizations while remaining autonomous. Second, union organization is decentralized and democratic. Third, a "radical reform" strategy is implemented in which institutional collective bargaining strategies are combined with methods of nonviolent action.[6]

All of these characteristics applied to the trade union movement in South Africa. First, the movement's focus on workplace issues did not result in its eschewing of larger political issues, as most trade unions took the position that they should be involved in community and national struggles as well. COSATU engaged in mass democratic politics, complementing its workplace strength and links to grassroots community organizations with national alliances with other labor, political, and social movements. By the mid-1980s, COSATU had formed strategic alliances with the ANC and the UDF, but remained independent of them (Adler and Webster 1995; Baskin 1991; Marx 1992; Price 1991).

Second, COSATU was organized in a decentralized manner to remain resilient in the face of repression, and was organized democratically to promote the mobilization and commitment of the workers and inhibit the development of professional leaders who could be co-opted into the state's labor relations apparatus. Shop stewards were directly elected by workers, were held accountable, and were subject to recall. Moreover, the elected worker representatives were required to be full-time workers (Adler and Webster 1995; Baskin 1991; Marx 1992; Price 1991).

Third, while participating in the institutionalized collective bargaining process, trade unions did not shun noninstitutional methods of nonviolent action. In addition to labor strikes, trade unions organized and implemented other methods of noncooperation, such as stayaways, which developed as a method of contention after public gatherings and demonstrations were banned. In stayaways workers or students (and supportive members of the populace) would stay at home in support of a variety of economic or political demands (Adler et al. 1992). Stayaways in the Transvaal in November 1984 involved eight hundred thousand workers and four hundred thousand students, and stayaways in commemoration of the Soweto uprising in June 1988 produced the most successful general strike in the country's history. The three-day stayaway was 70 percent effective and cost the South African economy an estimated R500 million. A stayaway in September 1988 in commemoration of the killings at Sharpeville produced almost 100 percent absenteeism in most of the largest industries in the Eastern Cape (Price 1991, 196, 267). Between 1986 and 1990, more worker days were lost to noncooperation in South Africa than in the preceding seventy-five years (Innes 1992). Methods of creative nonviolent intervention were employed as well. For example, COSATU developed alternative programs of education for workers and established the National Unemployed Workers' Coordinating Committee (NUWCC) to provide statelike collective goods such as training and support for cooperatives from which future employees would be drawn (Marx 1992, 212).

In 1988, when the UDF was banned, COSATU assumed a leadership position in the anti-apartheid movement, launching the Mass Democratic Movement (MDM) and providing support for the remobilization of civic, women's, student, and youth organizations (Hirschsohn 1998). Increased repression during the state of emergency failed to disrupt organizing, which took place largely inside factories and mines. According to Glenn Adler and Eddie Webster, "The range of union campaigns, protests, wildcat industrial action, and disruption on the shop floor demonstrated the limited effectiveness of repression in ending mobilization. Furthermore, the mass action took its toll on employers, many of whom abandoned their support for the repressive legislation" (Adler and Webster 1995, 82). In sum, the labor movement remained resilient in the face of repression and contributed to elite divisions between capitalists and the state and ultimately to a shift in the balance of power in South Africa.

The African National Congress

The ANC, UDF, and COSATU all shared the same goals of ending apartheid and making a transition to a nonracial, unitary democratic state. Therefore, the ANC cannot be considered more "radical" than the UDF or COSATU in terms of its political goals. There was, of course, a divergence with regard to strategies, as the ANC promoted the violent overthrow of the apartheid state. Nevertheless, the armed wing of the ANC was never a military threat to the state. By the 1980s, after more than twenty years of commitment to armed struggle and substantial military aid and training from the Soviet Bloc, the military wing of the ANC was incapable of challenging the state through methods of violence. By the mid-1980s, even the Soviet Union viewed armed struggle as counterproductive and suggested to the ANC that it attempt to negotiate with the apartheid regime instead (Price 1991; Uhlig 1986; Zunes 1999b).

According to Jeremy Seekings, by 1987 "the ANC had failed to infiltrate large numbers of military cadres into South Africa, had only a limited tactical influence on internal protestors and, above all, had made no significant progress in building integrated political-military command structures inside the country (Seekings 2000, 207). "The ANC simply did not have the capacity to provide detailed direction and coordination for political initiatives inside the country, and it was these rather than the muted activities of the MK that were driving forward the prospect of political change. . . . Where the ANC was decisive was in buttressing the leadership role of the UDF inside the country" (292–93).

More important to the anti-apartheid movement than the threat of armed insurrection was the ANC's reestablished public presence after the Soweto uprising and its provision of a culture of resistance and popular anti-apartheid frames. The prestige of the ANC was reinvigorated as copies of the Freedom Charter, originally adopted by the ANC in 1954, were disseminated in the townships; there was a renewed interest in Nelson Mandela and other ANC leaders who had been imprisoned since the early 1960s; and the symbols, songs, and slogans of the ANC were adopted by the broader anti-apartheid movement. Nevertheless, the frames, symbols, and violent rhetoric of the ANC adopted by the larger anti-apartheid movement must not be confused with violent action. According to Jeremy Seekings, "The symbolism of resistance was that of the exiled ANC. . . . Songs exhorted the ANC. . . . chants praised the armed struggle, not non-violent strategies; and the flags draped over coffins at political rallies were in the colours of the ANC" (Seekings 2000, 23). "But for all this revolutionary bombast, key

ANC leaders saw the armed struggle more in terms of 'armed propaganda'—shifting the consciousness of black and white South Africans—than an actual campaign for the armed seizure of state power" (Seekings 2000, 8). Thus, contrary to a typical armed insurgency where the civilian populace is relegated to a supporting role for armed insurgents, the struggle in South Africa can more accurately be described as an unarmed insurrection in which civilians were the main actors and they were supported by the symbolic resistance of the ANC.

By the mid-1980s, in addition to buttressing the leadership role of the UDF, the ANC began to realize the power of the unarmed insurrections occurring in the townships. The underground structures of the ANC were used to divert resources to the political uprisings within the country—telling indication that the ANC had realized that the power of protest, noncooperation, and creative intervention was more likely to topple the apartheid regime than an armed insurrection.

In addition to framing and funneling resources to the unarmed insurrection, the ANC also played a crucial role with regard to the mobilization of international resources and the activation of third parties. Taking advantage of the international media's coverage of repression in the townships after the Soweto uprising and renewed international interest in South Africa, the ANC was able to expand its external mission rapidly in the late 1970s and early 1980s. The ANC's division for external affairs, based in Lusaka, Zambia, administered an international network of offices. The ANC had diplomatic offices in over twenty countries, representatives at the United Nations, and numerous other groups operating abroad. Through these networks the ANC promoted third-party pressure against South Africa. The diplomatic networks also secured financial and other forms of assistance and cultivated international legitimacy for the anti-apartheid movement while undermining the legitimacy of the South African state. ANC groups in the United States and Western Europe promoted anti-apartheid movements in these countries and played a leading role when disinvestment campaigns broke out on college campuses in the 1980s (Harmel 1997; Lodge 1988).

From Political Transformation to Political Transition

The "securocrat" segment of the elite, who opposed meaningful reform of the apartheid system, ascended to a dominant position within Pretoria's policy-making apparatus in 1986. It was responsible for imposing the state of emergency in June 1986 and intensifying repression against the anti-apartheid movement (Price 1991, 252). However, as discussed earlier, the intensification of repression was unable to quell the challenge, due in no small part to its organization and tactics. And by sustaining the challenge in the face of repression, the anti-apartheid movement recast the political context; it became increasingly costly to maintain repression, third parties were activated, and elite divisions were exacerbated. According to Robert Price, "The failure of repression and the realization of the related infeasibility of an autarkic economic strategy precipitated a division within the ruling elite. On one side were arrayed the securocrats—those associated with the government agencies responsible for domestic and foreign security. . . . On the other side of the division within the ruling group were officials associated with the economy and foreign relations [the internationalist reformers]" (Price 1991, 275–76).

The internationalist reformers joined capitalists in recognizing that continued international isolation from foreign capital, in addition to strikes and boycotts, meant permanent economic decline. They also realized that meaningful political change was essential to end internal disruption and to overcome international isolation, and they concluded that negotiating a transition to democracy with the anti-apartheid movement was the only way to solve South Africa's endemic crisis. The legitimate participation of the ANC and UDF leadership could occur only if the state of emergency was relaxed; the ANC and the UDF were unbanned; restrictions on organizing, communication, and political activity were lifted; and political prisoners, especially Nelson Mandela, were unconditionally released. The path to a negotiated transition to democracy was cleared with the ascendance of the internationalist reformer segment of the elite over the securocrats in 1989. In October 1989, four months after F. W. de Klerk replaced P. W. Botha as state president, the state's security apparatus was dismantled. In the opening session of the 1990 parliament, de Klerk announced the unbanning of the ANC and UDF, the relaxation of the state emergency, and the release of Nelson Mandela. The anti-apartheid movement succeeded in forcing the government to negotiate a democratic transition to a unitary, nonracial state.

The Philippines

The declaration of martial law by Ferdinand Marcos on September 22, 1972, marked the end of formal, albeit elitist, democratic politics in the Philippines and the beginning of a neopatrimonial dictatorship. Marcos claimed that martial law was necessary to subdue the communist insurgency, eliminate corruption, and implement land reform. More realistically, martial law was declared to prevent a presidential election, in which Marcos would most likely have been replaced by Benigno Aquino, and to facilitate Marcos's concentration of wealth. Under martial law Marcos undermined competing centers of power and centralized the formerly decentralized patrimonial polity, extending his financial reach throughout society. Through state monopolies he subcontracted to his relatives and friends important areas of the economy for plundering. Through aid from the United States, loans from international banks, and state monopolies Marcos and his cronies amassed great wealth. While Marcos remained in power through repression, he relied on legalistic arguments and held a series of referenda and plebiscites in an attempt to certify his rule. These techniques were characterized by intimidation and fraud, and they ultimately failed to provide the regime with the legitimacy it sought (Aquino 1987; Hutchcroft 1991; Overholt 1986; Timberman 1991; Wurfel 1988).

Resistance to Marcos

Opposition to Marcos prior to the assassination of Benigno Aquino in 1983 fell into four broad categories: reformist opposition, revolutionary opposition, opposition by the Catholic Church, and progressive opposition. Each represents separate strands of resistance that would converge or diverge after the assassination.

Reformist Opposition

Upon the imposition of martial law in 1972, the traditional political parties fell apart when most political opponents transferred their allegiance en masse to Marcos to benefit from his patronage system. Deprived of access to resources for operating their patrimonial structures, political parties lost their mass base and collapsed in the face of co-optation and repression. The surviving elements of the formerly party-based opposition constituted a reformist opposition committed to human rights, democratic processes, and the removal of Marcos. Beyond these common goals the reformist opposition was divided, especially on issues concerning the extent of economic change and relations with the United States. Marcos tolerated the reformist opponents as long as they did not unify or mobilize a mass following (Wurfel 1988, 204–6).

Major figures of the reformist opposition included politicians, such as Jose Diokno, Raul Manglapus, Gerardo Roxas, Jovito Salonga, and Lorenzo Tañada. However, the earliest and most outspoken critic of the regime was Benigno Aquino, a former senator and political opponent of Marcos. Aquino, who was arrested shortly after the declaration of martial law, remained in prison until May 1980, when he was permitted to leave for the United States to receive medical treatment. While in the United States he remained in contact with the opposition and lobbied the U.S. government to withdraw support from Marcos.

For the first six years of martial law, the reformist opposition was impotent, as most opposition leaders were in prison, in exile, or collaborating with the regime. However, by 1978 the reformist opposition was beginning to mobilize in response to the opportunities provided by the democratic façades that Marcos used in an attempt to maintain legitimacy. Lakas ng Bayan (Strength of the Nation, abbreviated to LABAN [the word for "fight"]), was formed by Benigno Aquino while in prison, with Senator Tañada as chairman, to contest the elections for the interim Batasang Pambansa (National Assembly) that were held on April 8, 1978. While the Liberals boycotted the 1978 interim Batasang Pambansa elections, LABAN participated but was, not unexpectedly, shut out by the Marcos-led Kilusang Bagong Lipunan (KBL, New Society Movement) as a result of government fraud and intimidation.

The United Nationalist Democratic Opposition (UNIDO), a broad coalition of reformist opponents, was formed in 1980 when the wing of the Nacionalista Party led by Jose and Salvador Laurel, which had been cooperating with Marcos, defected to the reformist opposition. UNIDO was led by Eva Estrada Kalaw, Salvador Laurel, Gerardo Roxas, and, from the United States, Aquino and Manglapus. A consensus was reached among the reformist opposition to boycott the plebiscite scheduled for April 7, 1981, and the presidential elections set for June 16, 1981. The plebiscite was approved, resulting in the ninth revision of the constitution to allow Marcos to legally retain his powers despite the lifting of martial law, and the presidential election resulted in an additional six year term for Marcos. Of course no one accepted these results as legitimate.[7] While there were signs of increasing collaboration among the reformist elements of the opposition, a wide gap remained between them and other challengers, since the reformist opposition was generally limited to a middle-class base and lacked mass support or the active support of the economic elite (Wurfel 1988).

Revolutionary Opposition

On Mao's birthday, December 26, 1968, Jose Maria Sison and a group of supporters dismayed with the Partido Komunistang Pilipinas (PKP), the communist party that had been operating in the Philippines since 1930, founded the Communist Party of the Philippines (CPP). A few months later it launched an armed wing, the New People's Army (NPA). The CPP, which was based on Marxist-Leninist-Maoist thought, and the New People's Army, which incorporated a Maoist strategy of guerrilla warfare, grew in importance after the imposition of martial law in 1972 drove hundreds of educated youth into the countryside to join the revolutionary guerrilla struggle. The NPA came under heavy military attack, but rather than destroying the NPA, the repression dispersed the resistance across the country. As disillusionment with Marcos's New Society program and repressive tactics increased throughout the 1970s, the NPA grew, becoming strongest in Samar, Negros, the Visayas, and areas of Mindanao and Luzon. By the 1980s the NPA encompassed all regions of the Philippines (Wurfel 1988, 223–27).

The NPA attempted to develop an urban base as well, forming the National Democratic Front (NDF) in April 1973 to aggregate a more broadbased movement. Unlike the reformists, the revolutionary opposition had an explicit and agreed-upon strategy for gaining power—armed insurrection. Nevertheless, while its policy of a united front was intended to mobilize support from among the urban poor and the middle classes, its strategy of violent action tended to inhibit the support they could mobilize. Moreover, its potential for aggregating Christian support was not realized due to the ideological rigidities of the CPP. While progressives in the church hoped to form a Christian-Marxist synthesis, the CPP's unwillingness to enter a dialogue on ideology with the church prevented it from developing a broader base (Wurfel 1988, 227–31).[8]

Opposition by the Catholic Church

When martial law forced oppositional political activity underground, the Catholic Church became an important channel for political dissent, since it was the only national institution that had retained its autonomy and credibility during Marcos's rule. While the Catholic Church's general policy toward the Marcos regime was one of "critical collaboration" at the beginning of martial law, elements of the Catholic Church openly opposed the Marcos dictatorship from the start and were involved with the reformist, revolutionary, or progressive opposition (Wurfel 1988).

Perhaps most significant was the role of Manila's Archbishop Cardinal Jaime Sin, the leader of the moderates in the church hierarchy. Archbishop Sin had been critical of martial law as early as 1974, when he had officiated at a prayer vigil in protest of a military raid on a seminary and the arrest of dozens of people. More than five thousand people attended the vigil, the largest protest against martial law to that time. Archbishop Sin continued to speak out against human rights violations and torture. While maintaining a stance of critical collaboration in the 1980s, Archbishop Sin became a more vocal critic of human rights violations. Moreover, he rejected the use of violence to oppose Marcos and attempted to attenuate the growing polarization resulting from the increased radicalization of elements of the Catholic Church and growth of the NPA. This would eventually facilitate the convergence of various strands of the opposition (Wurfel 1988, 220–22).

Progressive Opposition

Located between the reformist and the revolutionary strands of the opposition was a grassroots movement with a progressive orientation. Trusting neither the centralized communist-led military and civilian front organizations nor the elite-dominated political parties, activists from progressive organizations and the Catholic Church focused on grassroots organizing among marginalized segments of the population. The result was the development of a network of sectoral organizations concerned with issues relating to specific social aggregates, such as workers, peasants, women, students, and the urban poor (Zunes 1999a).

The more progressive and radical elements of the Catholic Church adopted liberation theology and organized Basic Christian Communities (BCCs) in rural areas. They were involved in raising political consciousness and demanding the redress of local grievances. The new linkages forged between activist clergy and peasants strengthened church-based mobilization. The noncommunist Left was further bolstered when a number of labor federations seceded from the government-controlled Trade Union Congress of the Philippines (TUCP) and founded the Kilusang Mayo Uno (KMU, First of May Movement) on May Day, 1980. The KMU emerged as a federation of independent trade unions that incorporated a strategy of social movement unionism (Lane 1990; Scipes 1992, 1996).

Prelude to Change: "Normalization" and Elite Divisions

In response to pressure from the United States, which was apprehensive of the growing communist insurgency, and international economic organizations, such as the International Monetary Fund (IMF), which was concerned with increasing political instability and corruption, a period of "normalization" was initiated in 1978 in what Marcos claimed was the beginning of the political liberalization of his "constitutional authoritarian" rule. Normalization was a process by which the regime attempted to legitimate itself, that is, attempted to maintain the certification of the United States and the economic elite. Marcos lifted martial law on January 17, 1981, but as in the case of the other democratic façades he erected, this had no real effect on political relations (Wurfel 1988, 234, 248).

Disillusionment with Marcos's rule and pressure for change from abroad produced elite divisions between those who benefited from Marcos's rule and those who did not. Four lines of elite cleavages emerged by the early 1980s: Marcos cronies versus the old economic elite, economic nationalists versus technocrats, military versus civilian bureaucrats, and, within the military,

Marcos cronies versus military professionals (Wurfel 1988, 237–40). The most important of these with regard to the anti-Marcos challenge were the divisions in the economic elite between the crony and noncrony capitalists and, in the military, between officers whose positions were based primarily on their loyalty to Marcos and officers with a more professional orientation.

The so-called cronies were the new economic elite promoted by Ferdinand Marcos and his wife, Imelda. They were relatives and close friends of the Marcoses who prospered through access to government credit and contracts and had an inside track for landing joint ventures with foreign investors. Large sums of money were funneled from the state treasury and government banks to crony corporations. Their rise increased the hostility of the old economic elite as well as indigenous entrepreneurs, contributing to mobilization against the regime. In 1981 the Makati Business Club was formed to articulate the business interests of the noncrony segments of the business class (Wurfel 1988).

Elite divisions within the military emerged in the late 1970s in response to Marcos's personalization of the military and corruption within the armed forces. By the 1980s the most significant rivalry within the armed forces was between Generals Fidel Ramos and Juan Ponce Enrile, on the one hand, and General Fabian Ver, on the other. Ramos was regarded as the epitome of professionalism and attracted respect from junior officers with high professional standards. His major competitor was Ver, a relative and former chauffeur of Marcos, whose rise to power was the result of personal loyalty. General Enrile would eventually spearhead the Reform the Armed Forces Movement (RAM), a reform movement within the armed forces.

By 1983, after five years of "normalization," little had been accomplished. The communist armed insurgency was growing, efforts at co-opting the reformist opposition had failed, segments of the reformist opposition were beginning to cooperate with the Left, elite divisions were becoming more pronounced, and the Catholic Church was becoming increasingly critical of Marcos. Adding to this the failing health of Marcos, Benigno Aquino sensed an opportunity too good to pass up, and returned to the Philippines from the United States to pressure Marcos to step down. However, upon his return to the Philippines on August 21, 1983, Aquino was assassinated by a military escort as he descended from the airplane at Manila International Airport.

Resistance after the Aquino Assassination: The People Power Movement

In the days following the assassination, hundreds of thousands of people filed by Aquino's open coffin, and an estimated two million people from all socioeconomic strata gathered to witness Aquino's funeral procession. Aquino had become a martyr for the anti-Marcos cause. In the aftermath of the initial shock and rage following the assassination of Aquino, the anti-Marcos opponents redoubled their efforts at mobilization, and various strands of the resistance began to converge. Although the revolutionary opposition and progressive grassroots groups had been resisting Marcos for years—and had been bearing the brunt of the regime's violent repression—the Aquino assassination served as the catalyst that produced a shift from passive acceptance to active opposition by the middle and business classes and by mainstream elements of the Catholic Church, groups that subsequently threw their support behind the reformist opposition movement.

The assassination of Aquino violated the unspoken rule in Philippine politics that exempted reformist opponents with elite backgrounds from deadly repression. On September 14, 1983, the Makati business community organized the first of what were to become weekly anti-Marcos demonstrations and rallies in the Makati business district of Manila. Approximately one hundred thousand office workers marched down the streets showered by yellow confetti tossed from the windows of surrounding skyscrapers. In February 1984, members of the middle class organized a 120 kilometer "Tarlac to Tarmac" run from Aquino's home province to Manila International Airport, mobilizing an estimated five hundred thousand people along the way (Thompson 1995, 115–20).[9]

The Christlike martyrdom of Aquino had an immediate and powerful religious significance for devoutly Catholic Filipinos (Thompson 1995, 116; Timberman 1991, 128). Mainstream elements of the Catholic Church came out in overt opposition to Marcos and provided institutional assistance to the pro-democracy challenge. By 1983 the moderates led by Manila Archbishop Sin came to the forefront of the Church in opposition to the Marcos regime and utilized its nationwide communications infrastructure to mobilize resistance.

While the reformist opposition uniformly boycotted the 1981 plebiscite and elections, some groups opted for participation in the May 14, 1984, Batasang Pambansa elections. UNIDO, now led by Salvador "Doy" Laurel and Benigno Aquino's widow, Corazón "Cory" Aquino, PDP-LABAN,[10] and the faction of the former Liberal Party headed by Eva Kalaw participated, while Jovito Salonga's wing of the Liberal Party continued to boycott the elections.[11] Although they did not expect free and fair elections, the reformist participants felt that the elections at least provided an opportunity to revitalize their mobilizing structures and organization. In response to the government-controlled Commission on Elections (COMELEC), the

National Movement for Free Elections (NAMFREL)[12] was organized as an autonomous election-monitoring body.

Although marred by fraud and intimidation, the May 1984 elections were fairer than expected, largely due to the actions of NAMFREL which placed some limits on electoral fraud in the urban areas in which it operated. Although the KBL enjoyed an overwhelming advantage, the opposition won sixty-one seats in the two hundred–seat Batasang Pambansa and most certainly would have won a majority of the seats if the elections had been free and fair. Moreover, the high turnout—almost 90 percent of the electorate participated in the election, the highest turnout since the declaration of martial law—encouraged most of the remainder of the noncommunist Left to participate in future elections, leaving the CPP isolated in its strict adherence to election boycotts and armed struggle (Thompson 1995, 131–32).

While the middle class, the business class, and traditional politicians were finally beginning to oppose Marcos overtly, the extant grassroots popular movement, including independent labor unions, peasants' organizations, student and teacher associations, women's groups, human rights groups, and groups of the urban poor, accelerated their activity after the Aquino assassination. Common tactics included *lakbayan* (people's freedom marches) and mass demonstrations, referred to as the "parliaments of the streets" (Timberman 1991, 131–32).

In the months immediately following the assassination, progressive left-leaning groups, such as Justice for Aquino, Justice for All (JAJA), organized numerous protests. Led by former senator José Diokno and Agapito "Butz" Aquino, the younger brother of the slain Aquino, JAJA organized more than one hundred protest demonstrations between October 1983 and February 1984. By May 1984, JAJA had been superseded by the Coalition for the Restoration of Democracy (CORD). CORD was organized to boycott the May 1984 elections for the Batasang Pambansa, but after many opposition groups participated in the election, it turned its attention to other methods of noncooperation, especially to *welgang bayan,* or people's strikes. A *welgang bayan* involves a general workers' strike, but it is more comprehensive, as all stores are closed, all public transportation is stopped, and community members construct barricades to stop the operation of private vehicles (Scipes 1992, 91). In early 1984 the first *welgang bayan* was held in Davao City. The tactic signified the weakness of the government in the face of mass noncooperation, and it spread to other cities. By the end of 1984, transportation strikes paralyzed areas of metropolitan Manila and Central Luzon, as well as southern cities, such as Davao, Butuan, Cagayan de Oro, Bacolod, and Cebu. In December 1984 a *welgang bayan* in Bataan shut down approximately

80 percent of transportation in the entire province. In some areas the strikes were up to 95 percent effective (Timberman 1991, 132; Zunes 1999a, 134–35).

In May 1985, *Bagong Alyansang Makabayan* (New Nationalist Alliance, known as "Bayan") grew out of CORD as an umbrella organization to unite numerous progressive organizations, including the Kilusang Magbubukid ng Pilipinas (KMP, National Farmers' Movement) and the KMU, the labor federation, to promote campaigns of noncooperation in opposition to the Marcos regime. On May 2 and 3, 1985, a massive *welgang bayan* was held throughout Mindanao. On June 18–20, 1985, a *welgang bayan* was implemented in protest of the nuclear power plant under construction on the Bataan Peninsula and more generally in protest of Marcos's corrupt capital-intensive development schemes. Approximately 10,000 people attended a rally at the plant, and there was a simultaneous strike by transport workers. Approximately 6,000 workers from the Bataan Export Processing Zone walked out en masse to join the *welgang bayan*. In February 1985, a one-day general strike was implemented in which 140,000 workers from 187 labor unions protested the killing of union leaders. The same month, approximately 7,500 peasants from the Alliance of Central Luzon Farmers marched into Manila and staged a nine-day sit-in in front of the Agricultural Ministry (Zunes 1999a, 134–37). By 1986, Bayan claimed a national membership of two million people, including 600,000 KMU members and 100,000 KMP members, and affiliations with approximately 500 grassroots organizations (Timberman 1991, 133; Zunes 1999a, 134).

Political Transformation and an Abrupt Political Transition

By 1985 mass campaigns of nonviolent action had shorn Marcos of almost all legitimacy and political power. In an attempt to shore up his rule, in early November Marcos called for snap elections to be held the following February. Confident in his ability to hold fraudulent elections and intimidate the apparently divided opposition, Marcos fully expected to remain in power.

On December 11, 1985, the reformist opposition united under the banner of UNIDO, with Corazón Aquino and Salvador Laurel as the presidential and vice presidential candidates. The Liberal Party and the Social Democratic Party also participated in the presidential elections, while the communists continued to boycott them. From the outset of the campaign, Cory Aquino urged followers to use nonviolent discipline, making it clear that violent attacks against opponents, not uncommon in the Philippines' rough-and-tumble electoral history, would not be tolerated (Zunes 1999a, 142).

Meanwhile, the progressive opposition, led by Bayan, decided to boycott the elections, reasoning that the reformist opposition was not committed to progressive social change. Bayan also hoped to build upon the anticipated failure in the 1986 presidential elections to generate support for future campaigns of noncooperation and for the local elections scheduled for May 1987. In retrospect, by boycotting the presidential elections, the progressive opposition ceded control of post-Marcos politics to the reformers (Timberman 1991, 141–42).

UNIDO received crucial support from the Catholic Church and NAMFREL. Since Marcos directly or indirectly controlled all of Metro Manila's television stations and most radio stations and newspapers, the church-owned Radio Veritas and *Veritas* newspaper were crucial in providing coverage of the UNIDO campaign. Archbishop Sin played an important role in forging the Aquino-Laurel ticket, and more generally in promoting the convergence of members of the reformist opposition. On January 19, 1986, he issued a pastoral letter calling on the population to vote for candidates who were honest and respected human rights. The same month, the Catholic Bishops' Conference of the Philippines (CBCP) urged Catholic voters to combat the conspiracy that threatened to thwart the people's will during the election through nonviolent resistance (Timberman 1991, 145–48).

Closely tied to the Catholic Church was NAMFREL, the independent election watchdog organization that paralleled the state-controlled COMELEC. NAMFREL mobilized and trained more than 500,000 volunteers to monitor the elections in about 90 percent of the country's precincts. On election day, the counts of election returns by NAMFREL were accepted as credible, while the COMELEC counts were viewed with suspicion. After the elections, the count discrepancy between NAMFREL and COMELEC widened. Marcos's position, already damaged by the watchdog activities of NAMFREL, was further undermined when thirty COMELEC workers responsible for the computerized tabulation of votes walked off their jobs on February 9, 1986, in protest of the election fraud being committed. COMELEC claimed that the Marcos-Tolentino ticket had won over 53 percent of the vote, while NAMFREL claimed that the Aquino-Laurel ticket had won about 52 percent (Timberman 1991, 145–48).

On February 15, the KBL-dominated Batasang Pambansa certified the COMELEC-reported election results and declared Marcos the winner with 53.8 percent of the vote. On February 16, in response to the obviously fraudulent declaration of an electoral victory for Marcos, Cory Aquino led a rally of approximately two million people, proclaiming victory for herself and "the people," condemning Marcos, and outlining the Tagumpay ng Bayan (Triumph of the People) campaign of nonviolent civil disobedience. The campaign called for a general strike beginning on February 26 (the day after Marcos's planned inauguration), the mass withdrawal of funds from seven crony-controlled banks, a boycott of the crony- and government-controlled media, a refusal to pay utility bills, a boycott of the crony-controlled San Miguel corporation and subsidiaries, a nightly noise barrage, and other appropriate forms of nonviolent action. The CBCP called for support of the nonviolent campaign of civil disobedience, and Bayan and the NDF endorsed the general strike to be held on February 26, calling on its two million members to participate (Elwood 1986, 4; Zunes 1999a, 144–46).

The planned campaign of civil disobedience most certainly would have toppled Marcos, but before it was implemented the four-day "EDSA (Epifanio de los Santos Avenue) Revolution" occurred.[13] Minister of Defense General Enrile and a group of officers in the RAM had planned an attack on the Malacañang Palace to force Marcos out of office. When their plan was discovered by General Ver, Enrile led two battalions of soldiers in a mutiny on February 22, barricading themselves in Camps Crame and Aguilnaldo, two major military camps just outside of Manila. Enrile was joined by Vice Chief of Staff General Ramos, and they announced their defection from the Marcos government and their support of Aquino. That evening, Archbishop Sin urged people to support the mutiny, and in response tens of thousands of pro-democracy sympathizers assembled at EDSA. Moreover, the independent media disobeyed Marcos's orders for censorship, and citizens openly disobeyed the curfew and orders to disperse from the area surrounding the military bases where the military rebels were barricaded.

Marcos ordered two battalions to go to the military camps to crush the mutiny, but as their tanks approached the military camps, unarmed civilians led by nuns and priests formed a human barricade between the tanks and the rebels in the camps. The unarmed protestors effectively immobilized the troops sent in by Marcos, and they subsequently retreated. The dramatic events sparked a nationwide defection of soldiers and officers. Jet fighter pilots ordered to attack the military bases refused to carry out the orders, since doing so would have led to widespread casualties of unarmed civilians. By February 25, hundreds of thousands of civilians were gathered outside the military bases. Significantly, nonviolent discipline was maintained throughout. Soldiers were met by gestures of friendship rather than abuse. Activists trained in nonviolent action, along with nuns and priests, took a leading role in calming the masses and limiting provocative actions against troops still loyal to Marcos (Elwood 1986; Zunes 1999a, 146–52). The military revolt did not succeed because of the popularity of Generals Enrile and Ramos or because of their military strength, but rather because of the organized and disciplined nonviolent support they were given by hundreds of thousands of civilians. Contrary to popular interpretations of the events, the success of the people power movement was not a function of the military revolt. More accurately, the exact opposite was true—the success of the military revolt was a function of the people power movement. What some refer to as a "civilian-backed military revolt" can more accurately be termed a "military-backed civilian revolt" (Zunes 1994, 1999a).

On the morning of February 25, a parallel government was formed when Cory Aquino took the oath of office as the seventh president of the Philippines. The parallel government included Salvador Laurel as vice president and foreign minister, Juan Ponce Enrile as defense minister, and Fidel Ramos as the chief of staff of the New Armed Forces of the Philippines. That evening, four United States military helicopters transported Marcos and his entourage from the Malacañang Palace to the United States' Clark Air Base, north of Manila. The following morning, Marcos and his entourage of about thirty, including his family and General Ver, were flown by the United States military to Guam and then Hawaii. On board the airplane were $1.1 million in newly minted pesos, jewelry, and other assets reported to be worth $30 million, and passbooks to foreign bank accounts (Timberman 1991, 150, 161). The allegiance of a majority of the Philippine population to the Aquino government and the whisking away of Marcos ended the period of multiple sovereignty and led to an abrupt transition to democracy.

Nonviolent Action and Political Transformation

The unarmed insurrections in South Africa and the Philippines were, to a degree, characterized by the attributes and actions specified in chapter 2 that should theoretically promote the success of an unarmed insurrection in a nondemocratic context: loosely coordinated networks of decentralized organizations, the implementation of a broad range of actions from across the methods of nonviolent action, and the withdrawal of support from the state and the mobilization of pressure against the state through its dependence relations. These attributes enhanced their ability to operate in repressive contexts, undermine state power, activate third parties, exacerbate elite divisions, and promote regime defection; that is, they facilitated the recasting of the political context to one more favorable to the challengers' goals.

Sustaining the Challenge

In both countries, diverse local strands of resistance emerged that were subsequently united by umbrella organizations. The townships of South Africa experienced an explosion of associational life in the early 1980s. Diverse local organizations emerged that emphasized a grassroots form of association, such as community, youth, women's, labor, student, and political groups. While serving somewhat different geographical, class, gender, and functional constituencies, they all shared the common goal of rejecting the limited reforms of the government and ending apartheid. These organizations subsequently formed the crux of the anti-apartheid movement after becoming loosely coordinated by the UDF. The 565 local organizations affiliated with the UDF at its inception grew to over 700 local organizations within a few years. After the second state of emergency banned the UDF, the COSATU-backed MDM emerged as an umbrella organization to continue the mobilization and coordination of the local struggles.

During the martial law period in the Philippines, left-leaning activists from the Catholic Church and progressive organizations engaged in the grassroots organizing of women, peasants, workers, students, and the urban poor. The mobilizing structures were characterized by affinity groups, that is, small autonomous groups of activists linked to similar groups that came together in campaigns of nonviolent action (Zunes 1999a, 131–33). This was part of a larger movement of building networks of decentralized sectoral organizations that were independent of the elite-dominated political parties and the hierarchical communist movement, as well as the state.

By 1985 there were hundreds of mass and sectoral-based organizations in the Philippines that formed and reformed shifting coalitions. A number of umbrella organizations emerged to unite the organizations, including the communist NDF and the progressive JAJA, CORD, and Bayan. While the NDF failed to mobilize the support of noncommunists due to its strategic and ideological intransigence, Bayan became the largest and best-organized umbrella organization in the Philippines, claiming a national membership of approximately two million, including 600,000 KMU members, 100,000 KMP members, and affiliations with over 500 provincially based organizations (Timberman 1991, 132–33). Bayan was growing stronger and mobilizing increasingly more people to participate in *welgang bayan*. However, Bayan was less than a year old when the snap elections were held in 1986, and its decision to boycott rather than participate in the elections guaranteed that UNIDO would lead the democratic opposition. While Bayan was in a position to align itself with UNIDO in a post-election campaign of civil disobedience that most certainly would have deposed Marcos, its leverage was once again undercut by the unfolding of the EDSA Revolution and the formation of a U.S.- and military-backed reformist government.

A second organizational parallel that stands out across the two cases was the adoption of social movement unionism by the labor movements. Although it was certainly more central to the anti-apartheid movement than to the anti-Marcos movement, in both cases social movement unionism contributed to the ability of the labor movements to withstand repression and undermine the regime. Social movement unionism, according to Glenn Adler and Eddie Webster, "has been characterized by patterns of organization suited to a movement fighting an authoritarian enemy: leadership devolved to local levels, a wide repertoire of mass protest tactics and strategies, and alliances with community and political groups" (Adler and Webster 1995, 89). In both South Africa and the Philippines, the labor movements were characterized by decentralized structures that provided resilience in the face of intense repression; democratic structures that inhibited bureaucratization, co-optation, and institutionalization; ties with, but independence from, local social movements and national political movements; and implementation of a wide array of methods of nonviolent action.

In both South Africa and the Philippines, the range of methods implemented by the movements enhanced their ability to sustain the challenges despite their repressive contexts (see Tables 2 and 3). Neither challenge relied on a single method of resistance, and both implemented a variety of actions from across the methods of nonviolent action: protest and persuasion, noncooperation, and disruptive and creative intervention. When the state focused its repressive capacities on one type of nonviolent action, the challengers shifted to other types. Each method reinforced the other and promoted the resilience of the resistance and its escalation over time.

In South Africa the methods of protest and persuasion used included marches, rallies, political funerals, and vigils in memory of those killed by state terror. The methods of noncooperation and disruptive intervention used included election, school, rent, and consumer boycotts; refusal to pay taxes; strikes and stayaways; nonviolent obstructions, occupations, sit-ins, and raids; hunger strikes by political prisoners; and disobedience of segregation laws. The methods of creative intervention used included building alternative structures of "people power" such as local governments and people's courts by street and area committees, schools by the National Education Crisis Committee (NECC), and cooperatives, community clinics, and legal resource centers by organizations such as the Organisation for Appropriate Social Services in South Africa (Oassa).

In the Philippines the methods of protest and persuasion used included marches, rallies, demonstrations, and protest jogs. The methods of noncooperation and disruptive intervention used included *welgang bayan* and work stoppages, sit-ins, the construction of human barricades, and the disobedience of emergency edicts. The methods of creative intervention used were implemented in numerous ways, such as through the development of

Table 2. Major Nonviolent Action Campaigns and Events in South Africa, 1983–1990

Action	Date	Location	Method of nonviolent action
Rally to launch the UDF	Aug. 1983	Cape Town	Protest and persuasion
Protest demonstrations and rallies in opposition of the whites-only referendum on political reform	Oct. 1983	Nationwide	Protest and persuasion
Million Signatures Campaign	Jan. 1984 to July 1984	Nationwide	Protest and persuasion
Rallies in support of election boycott	Aug. 1984	Nationwide	Protest and persuasion
Boycott of Tricameral Parliament elections	Aug. 1984	Nationwide	Noncooperation
Occupation of British consulate	Sept. 1984	Durban	Disruptive nonviolent intervention
Stayaway	Nov. 1984	Soweto	Noncooperation
Rally in support of occupiers of British consulate	Dec. 1984	Durban	Protest and persuasion
Political funeral	July 1985	Cradock	Protest and persuasion
Consumer boycotts	Beginning July 1985	Nationwide	Noncooperation
Implementing structures of people power	Beginning Aug. 1985	Townships	Creative nonviolent intervention
Stayaway	May 1986	Nationwide	Noncooperation
Stayaway	June 1986	Nationwide	Noncooperation
Rent boycotts	Intensified and spread June 1986	Townships	Noncooperation
Vigils	Dec. 1986	Nationwide	Protest and persuasion
Stayaway	May 1987	Nationwide	Noncooperation
Stayaway	June 1988	Nationwide	Noncooperation
Occupation of American consulate	June 1988	Johannesburg	Disruptive nonviolent intervention
Boycott of local elections	Oct. 1988	Townships	Noncooperation
Mass hunger strikes	Jan. 1989	Nationwide	Disruptive nonviolent intervention
Civil disobedience of segregation laws	Aug. 1989	Nationwide	Noncooperation
Stayaway	Sept. 1989	Nationwide	Noncooperation
Protest demonstrations	Sept. 1989	Nationwide	Protest and persuasion
UDF's "unbanning" of itself	Jan. 1990	Nationwide	Noncooperation

Note: Based on Seekings (2000) and Foreign Broadcast Information Service (1983–90).

Table 3. Major Nonviolent Action Campaigns and Events in the Philippines, 1983–86

Action	Date	Location	Method of nonviolent action
Political funeral	Aug. 1983	Manila	Protest and persuasion
Protest demonstrations, Makati business district	Beginning Sept. 1983	Manila	Protest and persuasion
Lakbayan	Beginning Oct. 1983	Manila	Protest and persuasion
Welgang bayan	Beginning Jan. 1984	Initially Davao City, then other cities	Noncooperation
Tarlac to Tarmac run	Feb. 1984	Tarlac to Manila	Protest and persuasion
Boycott of national assembly elections by leftists, progressives, and segments of the liberal-reformist opposition	May 1984	Nationwide	Noncooperation
Organization and operation of NAMFREL	Beginning May 1984	Nationwide	Creative nonviolent intervention
Sit-in by peasants	Feb. 1985	Manila	Disruptive nonviolent intervention
Boycott of presidential elections by leftists and progressives	Feb. 1986	Nationwide	Noncooperation
Walkout by COMELEC workers	Feb. 9, 1986	Manila	Noncooperation
Rally by UNIDO	Feb. 16, 1986	Manila	Protest and persuasion
Civil disobedience (openly violating censorship and curfews)	Feb. 22–25, 1986	Manila, Quezon City	Noncooperation
Surrounding military camps with human barricades	Feb. 22–25, 1986	Quezon City	Disruptive nonviolent intervention
Formation of a parallel government	Feb. 25, 1986	Manila	Creative nonviolent intervention

Note: Based on Lane (1990), Timberman (1991), Zunes (1999a), and Foreign Broadcast Information Service (1983–86).

alternative educational institutions and communications centers, the organization of rural cooperatives that attempted to build an indigenous economy outside the control of the state and transnational corporations, the organization of NAMFREL as an independent election commission operating parallel to the government-run COMELEC, and ultimately the organization of a parallel government led by Cory Aquino.

In both struggles, tactical innovation occurred whereby new methods were implemented in response to government restrictions and repression. These novel actions effectively overcame the constraints of the political context and prevented the movements from stagnating. In South Africa, stayaways were developed in response to the government's repression of protests. Rent strikes were held and alternative township governments were developed in response to the government's attempts to co-opt urban blacks. In the Philippines, the *welgang bayan* was developed in response to the repression of protest demonstrations. As with stayaways in South Africa, the government's use of force was virtually powerless against the *welgang bayan*. Challengers in both countries learned that when repression is focused on methods of concentration, such as protest demonstrations in public places, methods of dispersion, such as boycotts and general strikes, had to be implemented to sustain the struggle.

Undermining State Power

By sustaining their challenges in the face of repression, the anti-apartheid and anti-Marcos movements promoted political transformations by undermining the states' legitimacy and resources. This was done directly by undermining the states' power derived from sources within society, and indirectly by severing the states from sources of power derived from external sources.

In South Africa, the dependence of the apartheid system on black labor was directly exploited by the trade union movement. As indicated in Figure 3, strike activity in South Africa increased with the emergence of independent trade unions in 1973, then decreased after 1976 as a result of the intense repression in the aftermath of the Soweto rebellion. By the 1980s, strike activity began increasing again. Significantly, strike activity escalated after the states of emergency were imposed in 1985 and 1986, reflecting the ability of the social movement unionism strategy to withstand the repressive context.[14]

These trends are reflected even more dramatically in Figure 4, which indicates the number of worker days lost to methods of noncooperation. Temporary increases in noncooperation occurred around the time of the Durban strike wave in 1973 and the Soweto rebellion in 1976; however, these were both suppressed by the state. In the early 1980s, autonomous

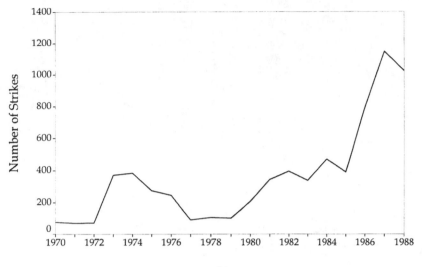

Figure 3. Strikes in South Africa, 1970–88. Data from the National Manpower Commission, government of South Africa, for various years. The figures are based on government-collected data that underestimate worker noncooperation, since the data are based on reports from employers, who are required to report only work stoppages resulting from disputes over terms of employment or where the strike is legal as defined by the Labour Relations Act. Thus, sympathy strikes, work slowdowns, political strikes, and other forms of worker noncooperation are not officially recorded.

organizations emerged and noncooperation escalated, beginning with the UDF's Anti-Election Campaign in 1984. Subsequently, various campaigns of noncooperation intensified, and the state was unable to quell the challenge despite the implementation of two states of emergency, due in no small part to the decentralized organization of the challenges and their implementation of a wide range of methods. The continued implementation of strikes and stayaways directly undermined the state's resources and its ability to control the political situation, contributed to the flow of foreign capital out of South Africa, and promoted divisions between capitalists and the state, as well as elite divisions within the apartheid government.

The dependence of the apartheid system on foreign capital and international legitimacy was exploited by the anti-apartheid movement as well. In addition to strike activity, the rejection of political reforms by non-whites directly undermined the state's legitimacy both at home and abroad.

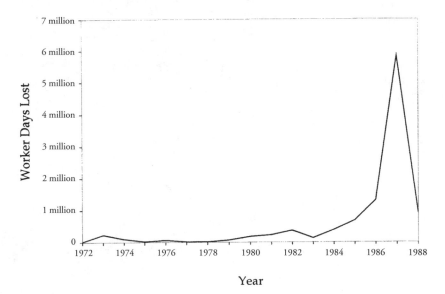

Figure 4. Worker days lost to noncooperation in South Africa, 1972–88. Data from the National Manpower Commission, government of South Africa, for various years.

International pressure on the apartheid regime was a function of the anti-apartheid movement's rejection of political reforms and its sustained collective action. If the movement had either accepted the regime's political reforms or been crushed by the regime's repression, international pressure on the regime would most likely have abated.

Figure 5 indicates the number of sanctions applied against South Africa. Figure 6 indicates the number of economic and arms embargoes of South Africa. Both figures indicate the same trends: an increase in sanctions and embargoes around the time of the Soweto rebellion in 1976 and immediately thereafter, followed by a decline in the late 1970s and early 1980s and a dramatic increase from 1984 onward. These data suggest that the spontaneous and often violent Soweto rebellion had the effect of bringing international attention to the plight of nonwhite South Africans, but when the rebellion was crushed by repression, the interest and pressure of international third parties waned, as indicated by the decline in sanctions and embargoes in the late 1970s and early 1980s. The anti-apartheid movement retooled with the political openings in the early 1980s, and became more organized and sophisticated in the implementation of nonviolent action. Its boycott of political reform in 1984 and its ability to continue to implement

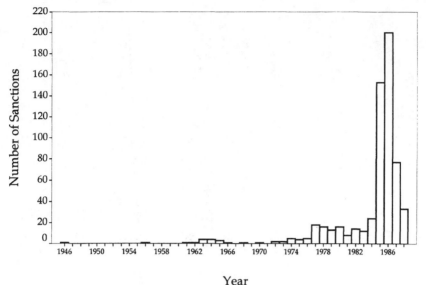

Figure 5. Sanctions against South Africa, 1946–88. Data from Schoeman (1988). These data include actual sanctions imposed, as well as calls for sanctions, boycotts, disinvestment, divestment, and isolation by foreign national and subnational governments, churches, banks, trade unions, educational institutions, social movements, and regional and international organizations. The data for 1988 are for only the first ten months of the year.

protests, strikes, and boycotts despite the states of emergency implemented in 1985 and 1986 contributed to reinvigorating international pressure on the regime, thereby undermining the apartheid regime's resources, legitimacy, and ability to control the political situation. In effect, the sustained pressure applied within the country facilitated the cultivation of pressure from outside the country.

In the Philippines, significant political pressure was put on the Marcos regime by strike activity. The number of strikes in the Philippines increased from 155 in 1983 to 282 in 1984 and 405 in 1985, and the number of working days lost from strikes increased from over a half million in 1983 to over 1.9 million in 1984 and over 2.4 million in 1985 (Scipes 1996, 32). In addition to directly undermining Marcos's ability to rule, the strikes indirectly undermined Marcos's ruling capacities by destabilizing the business climate and promoting capital flight from the Philippines. Capital flight intensified in the period leading up to the 1986 presidential election and especially after plans were announced for a nonviolent campaign on

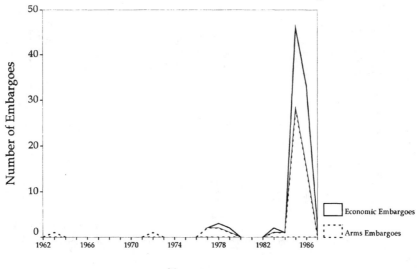

Figure 6. Economic and arms embargoes of South Africa, 1962–87. Data from Mozia (1991).

February 16, 1986, that included work stoppages, withdrawal of funds from crony-controlled banks, boycotts of Marcos- and crony-owned businesses, and refusal to pay utility fees (Zunes 1999a, 143–44).

The sustained challenge undermined Marcos's external support as well. The indiscriminate repression of the democratic opposition as well as the growing communist insurgency led members of the U.S. State Department and Congress to break with the Reagan administration and the Pentagon, which continued to support Marcos in the belief that such support was justified given his anti-communist rhetoric and the importance of maintaining control over two strategic military bases (Bonner 1987; Thompson 1995).

Segments of the U.S. government were also crucial in exacerbating elite disunity within the Philippine military by actively promoting the reformist sector of the military led by General Enrile. In an effort to stem the growth of the NPA and to build up the democratic opposition, the anti-Marcos faction in the U.S. government provided key support to both the reformist elements of the people power movement and the reform movement within the military. Once the military-backed civilian uprising against Marcos occurred, even Marcos's close friend and most ardent supporter, U.S. President Ronald Reagan, withdrew his support of Marcos.

The Paradox of Repression

By sustaining unarmed insurrections in the face of violent repression, the "political jiujitsu" dynamic may occur whereby the resolve of the challengers increases, the ability of the authorities to maintain control through repression decreases, and the support of third parties is invoked. In South Africa, the implementation of nonviolent action as a method of resistance by the anti-apartheid movement influenced white South Africans, from the general public through the political and economic elite. According to Stephen Zunes, "Armed revolution, in the eyes of the white minority, would have confirmed their worst stereotypes of the Africans as 'violent savages,' [and] would have reinforced the *laager* mentality. . . . On the other hand, nonviolent action not only challenged the popular image of the 'black terrorist,' but also that of the 'subservient house boy,' creating significant attitudinal changes among whites" (Zunes 1999b, 165). The same logic applies to international support as well. According to Robert Price, "The imposition of the July 1985 state of emergency was not only a disastrously unsuccessful effort to control the mass uprising, it also galvanized European and American elites into pushing for economic sanctions" (Price 1991, 250). Although an armed insurrection most certainly would have been crushed by the military, the implementation of a wide array of predominantly nonviolent strategies contributed to the struggle's resilience. Moreover, sustained nonviolent resistance cultivated support from home and from abroad, particularly from the West, that it most likely would not have received had it been undertaken primarily through armed methods of resistance.

The same dynamic occurred in the Philippines. According to David Wurfel, "A growing portion of the citizenry was appalled at the brutality and the haphazard selection of victims. Detention and torture may have deterred some organized expression of dissent, but many Filipinos found in it a course for disaffection from the regime" (Wurfel 1988, 127). Mobilization was greatly facilitated by the assassination of Benigno Aquino, which had the effect of transforming him into a martyr for the anti-Marcos movement (Ileto 1985). Martyrdom is a potent catalyst for the political jiujitsu dynamic; that is, the murder of unarmed activists highlights the brutality of the regime and encourages previously uncommitted persons to join the cause in a manner that the murder of a violent activist would not. Capitalists and mainstream elements of the Catholic Church, as well as the general public, were mobilized by the Aquino assassination in a manner that the murder of guerrillas or terrorists would never have accomplished. Once these elements were mobilized, violent repression and coercion failed to inhibit organized mass noncooperation.

The refusal of the military to use force against the "people power" movement contrasts sharply with the military's capacity and willingness—and the encouragement of the United States—to use force against the NPA's armed resistance movement. If the people power movement had been violent, the United States would have claimed justification for a military coup or, more dramatically, military intervention to prevent it from taking power (Zunes 1999a). Thus, nonviolent action as a method of resistance had the effect of unifying a large segment of the opposition, and it succeeded in depriving the United States of justification to intervene in the conflict militarily.

Conclusion

The struggles in South Africa and the Philippines provide evidence against the argument that nonviolent forms of resistance are ineffective against repressive regimes. Although factors external to the challenges influenced their trajectories and outcomes, the claim that outcomes of movements are determined solely by the results of external forces is questionable. An overemphasis on structural factors does not adequately consider how strategy and the dynamics of contention recast the political context so that it is more favorable to the challengers.

The anti-apartheid movement in South Africa and the anti-Marcos movement in the Philippines demonstrated that there is a mass-based insurrectionary path to regime transitions in nondemocratic contexts that is an alternative to guerrilla warfare. Unarmed insurrections may promote elite-negotiated transitions to democracy, as in South Africa, or they may topple dictatorships unwilling to negotiate, as in the Philippines. Nevertheless, not all unarmed insurrections within the third wave of democratization contributed to regime change. Two unsuccessful unarmed insurrections, in Burma and China, are examined in the next chapter.

4

People Power Suppressed: Burma and China

During the third wave of democratization, pro-democracy movements in one-party socialist countries emerged in Poland in the early 1980s and spread to other Eastern Bloc countries by the late 1980s. Asian Marxist-Leninist regimes were not unaffected by these events. Following the emergence of the Solidarity movement in Poland but prior to the opening up of the Berlin Wall in November 1989, unarmed insurrections challenged the rule of the military-dominated one-party socialist regime in Burma[1] and the one-party communist regime in China. Unlike the unarmed insurrections in Eastern Europe, however, these failed to contribute to political transitions.

The unarmed insurrection in Burma erupted in the spring of 1988 at the major universities in Rangoon. By summer the protests escalated into a broad-based nationwide pro-democracy movement that continued into September 1988, when the regime reorganized itself and brutally suppressed the movement. The unarmed insurrection in China was short-lived as well. Students in Beijing grasped the opportunity to engage in the collective mourning of Chinese Communist Party (CCP) Politburo member Hu Yaobang shortly after his death on April 15, 1989, and collective action was quickly transformed from mourning into protest against government corruption and pressure for political reform. The student movement spread to other cities and gained momentum, especially after the initiation of hunger strikes in May. However, by early June 1989, the movement collapsed in the face of martial law and military repression.

Violence accompanied these unarmed insurrections despite the attempts by movement leaders to promote nonviolent discipline. In Burma, some government officials were murdered by outraged citizens, state property was torched in acts of arson, and some segments of the opposition used whatever weapons they could muster, such as sharpened umbrella and bicycle spokes (*jinglee*) that they slung against the military. When the movement was suppressed by the military, many students headed to the peripheral areas of the country to join forces with armed insurgents. However, the military regime in Burma, which had kept the ethnic and communist insurgencies at bay since the early 1960s, was never directly threatened by the armed insurgents even after the influx of students into its ranks in 1988 and 1989. Moreover, the regime had the military capacity to easily counter violent resistance that occurred in Rangoon and other cities. The more serious threat to the regime occurred through unarmed methods of resistance.

In China, fights broke out when Beijing students and residents attempted to block soldiers from making their way to Tiananmen Square. During the forced removal of protestors from the square, angry crowds firebombed some tanks, killing military personnel inside, and some soldiers were beaten to death. Yet, as in Burma, the main threat to the regime's power did not occur through violent means, where the government's power was superior to that of the challengers, but rather through methods of nonviolent action.

Burma

In contrast to the situation in communist China, in Burma the military (Tatmadaw) has played a central role in governing the country. General Ne Win assumed dictatorial power in March 1962, staging a coup against the democratic regime of U Nu and organizing a twenty-four-member Revolutionary Council. The raison d'être of the military's assertion of control over the state included a perceived turning away from the state's founding socialist principles, U Nu's policy of establishing Buddhism as the state religion, U Nu's negotiations with leaders of non-Burman states for greater autonomy, and the possibility that the Karen and Shan states would exercise their constitutional right to secede from the union. Upon the declaration of martial law, Ne Win centralized politics and expanded the role of the military in the government, the bureaucratic administration, and the economy. The Burma Socialist Program Party (BSPP) was formed in 1962 as a means for mass mobilization and political indoctrination, and independent trade unions and political parties were banned. Within the BSPP, the Peasants' Asiayon, the Workers' Asiayon, and the Lansin Youth Organization were the primary bodies for political mobilization and control. All institutional rivals of the Revolutionary Council were eliminated by law or force, new institutions were created with direct ties to the state, and independent associations and newspapers were shut down (Taylor 1987).

The regime's economic policies concentrated control and management in the hands of the state, limiting the development of autonomous centers of wealth and power. After 1962, all banks, industries, and large commercial enterprises were nationalized. As a result of nationalization and demonetization without compensation, hundreds of thousands of Indian and Chinese business owners lost their property and savings and left the country. Military personnel were brought in to run business enterprises and the civil service. Burma subsequently attempted to disengage from the world economy and pursued an autarkic economic policy. The result of the military-run economy was gross inefficiency, rampant corruption, and economic decline, leading to widespread grievances throughout the population.

In 1972, Ne Win and nineteen other senior officers resigned from the military and assumed civilian positions. A new constitution was implemented with elections to a People's Assembly *(pyithu hluttaw)* and local councils. In practice, however Ne Win, the military, and the BSPP remained firmly in control of politics (Maung 1991, 1992; Silverstein 1977; Steinberg 1982, 1990; Taylor 1987).

The Pro-democracy Movement

Resistance to military rule in Burma was consistently met with violent repression. In July 1962, four months after Ne Win's military coup, the army killed up to one hundred students at Rangoon University who were protesting against the regime.[2] The military subsequently arrested students; used explosives to raze the student union building, which had been the center of student political activism since colonial days; and shut down the university for four months. Riots that broke out in Rangoon in 1967 due to food shortages, and student unrest at the universities during the Southeast Asian games held in Rangoon in 1969, were similarly met with violence. In 1974, workers and students in Rangoon protested against inflation and food shortages after the implementation of economic policies favoring the rural sector. The protests began with strikes in state-owned factories and spread to the universities. They ended with the use of force, in which at least twenty-two people were killed, and with the closing of universities. In December of that year, students and Buddhist monks protested against the state's handling of the funeral arrangements for former United Nations Secretary-General U Thant. In response, the government shut down the universities, arrested approximately three thousand people, and killed as many as one hundred people (Taylor 1987). Riots broke out in response to the government's treatment of Buddhist monks, and martial law was imposed. According to Robert Taylor, the military consistently responded to protests with "minimal manpower and maximum firepower to demonstrate, as rapidly as possible, its determination to keep the unrest from spreading and to serve as a deterrent" (Taylor 1987, 336).

Overt protest against the regime during the 1980s was minimal until grievances intensified in 1987. On September 5, 1987, Ne Win changed the denominations of the country's currency without warning or compensation, leading to the immediate loss of many people's life savings. In December 1987, after decades of military mismanagement of the economy, Burma was designated a "least developed country" by the United Nations. University students began expanding their underground political networks, and when a student from the Rangoon Institute of Technology was killed on March 13, 1988, and his assailant was not punished due to connections with the local BSPP, students took to the streets. Protest demonstrations and attacks on government property ensued. The Lon Htein, or riot police, were called in, and several university students were killed. Students at the Rangoon Institute of Technology protested against the killing of university students, and they were soon joined by students from Rangoon University in daily protests that took on an explicit anti-government and pro-democracy stance. Again the Lon Htein was called in to break up the demonstrations, killing scores of students and arresting more than one thousand students. On March 18, hundreds of students marched from the university campuses to downtown Rangoon, gathering supporters along the way. The number of anti-regime protestors grew into the thousands by the time the march reached downtown, where it was met with violence by the Lon Htein and by army troops as well. Scores of protestors and bystanders were killed, thousands were arrested, and the government shut down the universities, forcing the movement back underground (Lintner 1990; Moksha 1989).

When the universities reopened the first week of June 1988, students began organizing a mass movement, demanding the release of arrested students, the reinstatement of hundreds of students who had been expelled, and the right to organize an independent student union. By mid-June, large demonstrations within the confines of the university campuses were taking place. On June 21, thousands of students again took to the streets of Rangoon, joined by Buddhist monks and workers from nearby factories. The protests also mobilized people from the pool of disaffected and unemployed urban residents. By the time the protest march reached downtown Rangoon, its ranks had swelled into the tens of thousands. Once again, unarmed protestors were met by violence from the Lon Htein, and an estimated eighty to one hundred dissidents were killed. A new curfew was imposed, and the universities were closed again. Significantly, anti-regime protests erupted outside of Rangoon as well, with protests reported in Pegu, Prome, Mulmein, and Mandalay (Lintner 1990; Moksha 1989; Smith 1991; Taylor 1991).

In response to the spreading protests, the government announced that the BSPP would hold an extraordinary congress the next month. At the congress held on July 23, 1988, Ne Win announced that he would step down from his position of president and chairman of the BSPP. Unexpectedly, he also proposed that a referendum be held to gauge public support for a multiparty system. The proposed referendum, however, was rejected by the BSPP congress. The rejection of the proposal and the appointment of General Sein Lwin, the universally despised commander of the Lon Htein, to the posts of president of Burma and chairman of the BSPP on July 26, 1988, led to a new and intensified round of anti-regime protest (Lintner 1990; Moksha 1989).

The challenge subsequently focused on ousting General Sein Lwin and pressing for multiparty elections. A nationwide general strike was planned for the numerically auspicious date of August 8, 1988 (8-8-88). The demonstrations in Rangoon leading up to the general strike attracted tens of thousands of people, including students, monks, civil servants, workers, and the unemployed. On August 8, the general strike commenced and downtown Rangoon was filled with tens of thousands of peaceful pro-democracy protestors from all segments of society and ethnic groups. Huge demonstrations erupted in cities and towns throughout the country, including Sagaing, Mandalay, Taunggyi, Prome, Pyinmanar, Moulmein, Tavoy, and Bassein (Maung 1992, 59; Smith 1991, 4).

The festive atmosphere in Rangoon was broken on the night of August 8 when the military opened fire with automatic weapons. The brutal massacre left an estimated one thousand to three thousand unarmed citizens dead. Demonstrations in Sagaing and Bassein were brutally suppressed as well. Smaller demonstrations in Rangoon and throughout the country continued sporadically for a few more days in the face of repression. The violence was not entirely one-sided, as government buildings were attacked and it was reported that three policemen in a working-class section of Rangoon were beheaded by an angry crowd (Smith 1991, 5).

On August 12, the government announced that General Sein Lwin had resigned. Thus, despite the carnage, the unarmed insurrection forced General Sein Lwin from office. On August 19, the government announced his successor, Dr. Maung Maung, the highest-ranking civilian in the party and a "moderate" in the military regime. The next day, demonstrations resumed as tens of thousands of people rejected Dr. Maung Maung's nomination and demanded an end to one-party rule and the formation of a new interim government that would schedule multiparty elections. A second nationwide general strike was proclaimed on August 22. Strike centers were established in towns and cities across the country, daily anti-regime demonstrations took place, and many workers refused to return to their jobs until an interim government was formed (Lintner 1990; Moksha 1989).

The government made what at the time was perceived to be another concession by lifting martial law and withdrawing the military from the cities. Fear of being killed for participating in protests decreased, and on August 24 an estimated one million people participated in protest demonstrations in Rangoon alone, while other cities drew crowds of hundreds of thousands (Burma Watcher 1989). Much as had occurred in the townships in South Africa (chapter 3), citizens began organizing strike centers and people's committees to take care of local administration (Smith 1991, 6). Throughout the country, people resigned from their membership in the BSPP. Mass "burn-ins" took place in which crowds burned their BSPP membership cards in front of local BSPP offices (Fink 2001, 58–60). On August 26, a crowd estimated to number at least five hundred thousand gathered on the field beneath the Shwedagon Pagoda in Rangoon to hear Aung San Suu Kyi, the daughter of one of Burma's independence heroes, General Aung San, give her first public speech at a mass rally. She emerged as a leading voice of the pro-democracy opposition, calling for a multiparty democracy, national unity, nonviolent action, and nonviolent discipline (Aung San Suu Kyi 1991; Kreager 1991).

The general strike crippled the regime, and for a while it seemed as if the government would topple. However, by early September the festive Philippine-style people power movement in Burma turned lugubrious. Agents provocateurs and saboteurs from the military, along with criminals the government released from prison, engaged in arson, looting, violence, and other destabilizing activities, such as instigating food and race riots, apparently in an effort to provide justification for the military's restoration of "law and order." Enraged citizens responded with violence as well, murdering several Military Intelligence Service (MIS) agents alleged to be agents provocateurs or saboteurs. As the anti-regime demonstrations and general strikes continued, the country was thrown into chaos as the transportation infrastructure broke down and obtaining food became increasingly difficult for many people.

On September 18, a group of generals organized by Ne Win and led by Generals Saw Maung, Khin Nyunt, and Than Shwe staged a *"sui coup"*[3] and announced the formation of the State Law and Order Restoration Council (SLORC). Its stated purpose was to restore law and order and prepare the country for democratic elections. Martial law was declared, and the army returned to the cities to brutally repress all collective action. A curfew was imposed, restrictions on giving speeches and holding meetings were invoked, and strike centers throughout Burma were raided. Some people fought back with stones, swords, and *jinglees,* but these, of course, were no match for the machine guns and assault tanks of the Tatmadaw. By September 20, the military regained control, and in doing so killed several hundreds of civilians. Arrests and summary executions of alleged dissident organizers continued into October, and the universities remained closed. SLORC ordered all people to return to work and threatened those who did not with dismissal and arrest. Workers, in need of food and money, returned to work, and the general strikes collapsed (Lintner 1990; Moksha 1989). Collective action ground to a halt, and the regime reorganized and consolidated its power.

Using tactics similar to those of Marcos in the Philippines (chapter 3), SLORC scheduled elections to be held in 1990 in an effort to diffuse internal and external pressure, certify its rule, and receive foreign aid. However, draconian campaign restrictions were implemented, such as banning meetings of five or more people and forbidding criticism of SLORC or the military. In open defiance of these restrictions, the National League for Democracy (NLD), led by Aung San Suu Kyi, former general U Tin Oo, and former brigadier general Aung Gyi,[4] continued to hold rallies and print literature critical of the regime. Aung San Suu Kyi studied Gandhi while living in India and drew upon his theory and praxis of nonviolent action (Kreager 1991). From November 1988 through July 1989, Aung San Suu Kyi and NLD leaders traveled across Burma to mobilize support for the "Revolution of the Spirit," a campaign of nonviolent action in support of democracy. Wherever Aung San Suu Kyi spoke, thousands of citizens gathered, openly defying restrictions on assembly and risking imprisonment or death. On July 20, 1989, Aung San Suu Kyi was placed under house arrest, and most of the members of the NLD executive committee were subsequently imprisoned. By November 1989, there were an estimated six thousand political prisoners in Burma (Aung San Suu Kyi 1991, Kreager 1991).

Nevertheless, the scheduled elections for the Pyitha Hluttaw (National Assembly) were held on May 27, 1990. The regime fully expected to win the elections due to the severe restrictions on organizing and the arrest of opposition party leaders in the months leading up to the elections, and the actual voting was considered relatively free and fair. The descendent of the BSPP, the National Unity Party (NUP), received 21.2 percent of the votes (2.1 percent of the seats), while the most outspoken opposition to the military regime, the NLD, won 59.9 percent of the votes (80.8 percent of the seats) (Guyot

1991). Stunned by the election results, SLORC refused to honor them. By this time, however, unlike in the Philippines (chapter 3), the demobilized mass movement was no longer in a position to resist through campaigns of noncooperation, and regime defection was not forthcoming. Thus, after more than two years of resistance, the challenge, though successful in ousting Sein Lwin from power and forcing the government to hold multiparty elections, was ultimately unsuccessful in toppling the military regime.

China

Following a century plagued by foreign occupation, social turbulence, and civil war, the Chinese Communist Party (CCP), led by Mao Zedong, came to power on October 1, 1949, establishing the People's Republic of China. Mao unified China and carried out radical reforms in the economy and society in an effort to wipe out feudalism and create an industrialized socialist state. In an attempt to restructure Chinese culture, particularly to eliminate remnants of bourgeois ideology, Mao unleashed the Cultural Revolution in 1966. By the time of Mao's death in 1976, the Chinese economy was on the verge of collapse due to crises produced by extreme centralization and the chaos of the Cultural Revolution.

Beginning in 1978, China's new leaders, led by Deng Xiaoping, pushed for economic reform and modernization. Market relations were gradually introduced, and the standard of living of the Chinese improved. Limited political reforms were implemented as well, including policy rationalization, controlled political participation, separation of the CCP from the government, and separation of party leaders from the administrations of universities, research institutions, newspapers and publishing, and the management of state-run factories. State control over intellectual activities and public and private life was relaxed, and repression of those who challenged the state's legitimacy was softened (Meisner 1999; Zhao 2001).

By the mid-1980s, China's economic reforms were facing serious problems, as inequality was increasing, inflation soared, and corruption was rampant. Moreover, the post-1978 reforms had the effect of exposing China's urban population to the outside world. Their growing awareness of their lower standard of living compared to that of their East Asian neighbors and the West, their knowledge about the transnational wave of democratization, especially the recent political changes in Eastern Europe and the Soviet Union, and their bitter memories of the Cultural Revolution promoted criticism of the regime from segments of the urban population.

Students and intellectuals in particular were adversely affected by the economic reforms. They expected that a market economy would lead to economic prosperity in general, and in particular that they would benefit. However, university students were experiencing greater difficulty finding satisfactory jobs after graduation, and the standard of living and social status of students and intellectuals had declined, while those of uneducated entrepreneurs had increased. More and more students and intellectuals came to believe that economic reform without substantial political reform was contradictory and that democratization was the solution to China's problems. Small protests were not uncommon in China during the 1980s, but from 1986 onward student protests became more frequent, culminating in 1989 in the pro-democracy movement (Zhao 2001).

The year 1989 coincided with the anniversaries of three historical events of political significance—the two hundredth anniversary of the French Revolution, the seventieth anniversary of the May 4 Movement in China, and the fortieth anniversary of the founding of the People's Republic of China. Without much coordination, a number of dissident political activities surfaced in 1988 and continued into 1989 in anticipation of these anniversaries. Petition movements urging amnesty for political prisoners and the release of Wei Jingsheng, who had been imprisoned for participating in the 1978–79 Democracy Wall Movement, were initiated in early 1989, and political conferences and democracy salons were organized on major university campuses. *Dazibao* (large-character posters) appeared in public places, and small-scale protest demonstrations broke out, setting the stage for the 1989 Movement. The opportunity for widespread collective action arose when Hu Yaobang, the general secretary of the CCP from 1982 to 1987, died of a heart attack on April 15, 1989 (Dittmer 1990; Zhao 2001).

The Tiananmen Square Democracy Movement

Hu was dismissed as the general secretary of the CCP in January 1987 due to his lenient handling of student protests, although he remained a member of the Politburo. Hu's sudden death was significant to students and intellectuals, as he was considered the most supportive of political reform of anyone within the highest ranks of the CCP. At Beijing University scores of *dazibao* appeared on the evening of his death, mourning his passing or criticizing the government. In the following days, the content of the posters centered on promoting a free press, free association, political reform, and opposing official corruption (Zhao 2001, 147–48).[5]

Since mourning the death of a top-ranking state leader was a legitimate action, engaging in collective action at the time of Hu's death lowered the possibility of repression. On April 16, 1989, several hundred students from Beijing University went to Tiananmen Square, the symbolic center of

Chinese communist politics, to lay wreaths in honor of Hu. On April 17, several hundred students from the University of Political Science and Law in Beijing marched to Tiananmen Square to lay wreaths as well. That evening approximately two thousand Beijing University students marched to Tiananmen Square. In the following days, the students' focus shifted from mourning Hu to demanding official recognition of independent student organizations and dialogue with the government. In effect they were challenging the political monopoly of the CCP (Saich 1990; Zhao 2001, 148).

The government announced that demonstrators would be prohibited from entering Tiananmen Square on April 22, 1989, when the official ceremony for Hu was to be held in the Great Hall of the People on the west side of the square. However, on the evening of April 21, up to fifty thousand students marched from their Beijing campuses to the square, staying there overnight and staging a sit-in in defiance of the ban. During the funeral, three students knelt on the steps of the Great Hall of the People for about forty minutes to deliver a petition and to demand a meeting with Premier Li Peng. Li Peng did not appear, fueling the anger of students. Shortly thereafter, movement organizations emerged, demonstrations were mobilized, and a class boycott was initiated (Zhao 2001, 150–55).

Threatened by the protest demonstrations, the state sent a clear warning by publishing a harshly worded editorial in the *People's Daily* on April 26, 1989. In the editorial the state labeled the movement counterrevolutionary turmoil instigated by a small number of conspirators and threatened to dispatch military troops if the demonstrations continued. In response, as many as one hundred thousand students marched to Tiananmen Square on April 27 in defiance of the government's caricature of the movement and its warnings against further protest, marking the first large-scale defiance of the state since the Communist Party had taken power in 1949. Security forces made only token efforts to prevent students from entering Tiananmen Square, giving the protestors an illusory sense of invulnerability. An estimated one million Beijing residents took to the streets and cheered the students on (Dittmer 1990, 31; Zhao 2001).

The state initially tolerated the protest activities and praised Hu Yaobang in the media, which encouraged further mobilization. When the police were finally called in to oppose the student activity, students were repeatedly allowed to break through the understaffed police lines. Over the course of the movement the government shifted its responses back and forth between concessions and threats, which contributed to a misreading of the political context on the part of the students. Although the government had initially threatened the movement via the April 26 *People's Daily* editorial, following the massive protest demonstrations on April 27 the government adopted a more conciliatory approach and held dialogues with the students. In the eyes of the students, the government had reversed the evaluation of the movement it had given in the April 26 *People's Daily* editorial.

Protest demonstrations against the regime continued into May, and on May 4, 1989, students held a march to commemorate the seventieth anniversary of the May 4 Movement. By this time, many students were satisfied by the government's announcement that it would hold a dialogue with the students. Nevertheless, a group of students who questioned the government's sincerity about dialogues proposed a hunger strike, and about three hundred students commenced such a strike in Tiananmen Square on May 13. The hunger strike successfully mobilized more activists, and the number of hunger strikers quickly grew to over three thousand. On May 17 over one million Beijing residents of all occupations came out to express their support for the movement (Zhao 2001, 159–64, 171). Once commenced, the hunger strike took on a life of its own. Student leaders calling for an end to the hunger strikes and the occupation of Tiananmen Square were marginalized by those calling for its continuance.

On May 19, 1989, the day after the Sino-Soviet meeting in Beijing ended, the government imposed martial law. Over one hundred thousand soldiers entered Beijing; however, the troops were blocked from advancing on Tiananmen Square by an estimated two million Beijing residents and students on May 20. The students perceived the soldiers' retreat as another victory. Moreover, many came to believe that the state would not actually use force to suppress the movement, thereby lowering the risk of activism. However, after the movement defied the strongly worded editorial, repelled the initial show of force, and continued with the occupation of Tiananmen Square, from the government's point of view the only option other than giving in to the students' demands was to suppress the movement with violence. Since the political elite were not willing to give in to the students' demands, a military crackdown was ordered. The military began using violence to end the demonstrations, the hunger strike, and the sit-in occupation of Tiananmen Square on the evening of June 3. Around 9:00 p.m., soldiers advanced on Tiananmen Square, and by 6:00 a.m. on the morning of June 4, Tiananmen Square had been cleared through force. As many as one thousand people were killed during the confrontation, most of whom were unarmed citizens attempting to block the advancing troops. Afterward the government arrested thousands of political activists, forcing others to go underground or abroad (Dittmer 1990, 34; Zhao 2001, 184–207). The resistance collapsed in the face of intense repression.

The Suppression of Unarmed Insurrections

The unarmed insurrections in Burma and China were watershed events in those countries' post–World War II histories. In Burma the military regime, which had ruled the country since 1962, seemed to be on the verge of collapse, while in China the pro-democracy movement posed the most serious threat to the communist regime since its founding in 1949. Why did these unarmed insurrections, unlike those in South Africa and the Philippines (chapter 3) or in Nepal and Thailand (chapter 5), fail to promote a political transition? Their outcomes were predetermined neither by the political context nor by the actions of the challengers. Instead, these two elements combined in ways that shaped the movements' trajectories, by reducing the resilience of the challengers and limiting the leverage that they were able to generate against the state.

Lack of Resilience

Neither movement, of course, remained resilient in the face of repression. While the challengers in Burma implemented a diverse range of methods of nonviolent action, factors contributing to the movement's demise included the lack of a national umbrella organization to aggregate and coordinate the resistance and the inability of the challengers to organize a parallel government or create a situation of multiple sovereignty.

The Burmese pro-democracy movement emerged rather spontaneously in the spring of 1988, and when it reemerged that summer, student activists engaged in a frenzy of organizing. When the military withdrew from the cities in late August 1988, independent organizations among students, monks, professionals, workers, and civil servants sprang up throughout the country. In Rangoon, Mandalay, and various towns throughout the country, local strike committees were organized by university students or monks to handle security and food distribution, maintain law and order, and promote nonviolent discipline (Fink 2001, 58–60).

The challenge was spearheaded by students; however, their organization was in disarray. The All Burma Federation of Students' Unions (ABFSU), led by Mo Thee Zun and Min Ko Naing,[6] emerged as a major student organization, but hundreds of other student organizations were operating on various college campuses and acting independently, without overall coordination. As Mya Maung states, "The student protest movement was marred by disorganization, factionalism, and lack of a single charismatic student leader or organization to lead and fight against highly organized and efficient security forces" (Maung 1992, 86).

Furthermore, the students failed to coordinate the support that had been mobilized from other sectors of society. According to Christina Fink, "While demonstrations drew widespread participation, the lack of a unified leadership became a problem. Block, neighborhood and village organizations emerged to handle local affairs, but there was still no recognized national organization. Student groups took the lead in organizing demonstrations, but they were not capable of establishing a new administration" (Fink 2001, 61). A major push for a national umbrella organization occurred in September 1988 with the formation of the General Strike Committee (GSC). The GSC represented an attempt to bring together various sectors of the society, such as students, monks, workers, and professionals. Over one hundred GSC representatives met in Rangoon in early September; however, with transportation at a standstill and communication across Burma difficult, the GSC was unable to forge a coordinated nationwide network (Smith 1991, 8).

Moreover, there was no single recognized overall leadership of the prodemocracy movement in the crucial period before the military crackdown on September 18, 1988. On September 9, 1988, former prime minister U Nu released a statement announcing the formation of an interim government, with himself as prime minister. However, he was unable to mobilize widespread support, as most people had lost faith in him and were dismayed by his apparent political opportunism and by his appointment of relatives and old political cronies from the 1950s to his cabinet. Meetings were subsequently held on September 13 and 14 in an attempt to forge a widely supported interim government. The meetings were attended by U Nu, Aung San Suu Kyi, former general U Tin Oo, and Aung Gyi, as well as student leaders. U Nu, however, insisted that everyone support his government. The others were unwilling to do so, and the meetings ended without a widely supported alternative to the military regime (Fink 2001, 61).

Frustrated that the political elders were unable to forge a parallel government and recognizing that a leadership vacuum was detrimental to the challenge at this critical time, young activists from the GSC and the ABFSU called a meeting on the afternoon of September 18, 1988, to declare the formation of a parallel government composed of strike committees and workers' unions. However, the opportunity to create a parallel government at the local or national level and to promote a situation of dual sovereignty, which were crucial to the success of the people power movements in South Africa and the Philippines (chapter 3), had passed. That same afternoon SLORC brutally imposed its control over the country (Smith 1991, 15).

Another attempt to form a national umbrella organization to coordinate the resistance was made on November 5, 1988, in Karenni-controlled territory near the Thai border. Representatives of eighteen groups announced the formation of the All Burma Students Democratic Front (ABSDF). A few weeks later, representatives of twenty-two parties, including the ABSDF, met in Karenni-controlled territory to form the Democratic Alliance of Burma (DAB) (Smith 1991, 17). However, because DAB had little interaction with activists in central Burma, there was not much it could do to coordinate resistance to SLORC. Two years later, on December 18, 1990, after SLORC failed to honor the elections, a parallel government, the National Coalition Government of the Union of Burma (NCGUB), was formed in Manerplaw (in Karenni-controlled territory) by Dr. Sein Win. By this time, however, the mass movement had demobilized, and the role of the NCGUB was more to mobilize support from the international community than to act as a parallel government within Burma.

Given its lack of overall coordination, the movement in Burma implemented surprisingly diverse actions from across the range of methods of nonviolent action, including protest and persuasion, noncooperation, and disruptive and creative nonviolent action (see Table 4). However, when SLORC imposed its control over the country in September 1988, as many as ten thousand students traveled to the Thai, Chinese, Indian, and Bangladeshi borders to join the armed insurgents. According to Christina Fink, "The military regime was eager for the students to move out of the cities, recognizing that as successful as the students had been in organizing people in urban areas, they were no match for the battle-hardened Tatmadaw troops in the jungle" (Fink 2001, 62). In other words, the military regime understood its comparative advantage in the use of violence, while the students who left the cities failed to recognize their comparative advantage in methods of nonviolent action. The abandonment of the people power movement in order to engage in a people's war was certainly understandable given the fact that the universities had been closed and student organizers were being hunted down, arrested, tortured, and executed. The consequence, however, was the decreased resilience and leverage of the mass movement and a shifting of the battle against the government to strategies in which the government had a decided advantage.

Much as in Burma, factors contributing to the Chinese movement's lack of resilience included disorganization and the absence of a widely supported umbrella organization to aggregate and coordinate the resistance. The student movement was initiated by many individuals and small groups through independent actions and mutual influence, but it lacked any sort of general coordination and was fraught by conflicts among different student factions. The uprising produced a plethora of student organizations; however, none

Table 4. Major Nonviolent Action Campaigns and Events in Burma, 1988–90

Action	Date	Location	Method of nonviolent action
Marches and protest demonstrations	Mar. 1988	Rangoon	Protest and persuasion
Marches and protest demonstrations	June–Sept. 1988	Rangoon and larger towns and cities	Protest and persuasion
Alternative press	June–Sept. 1988	Rangoon, Mandalay	Creative nonviolent intervention
General strike	Aug. 8–12, 1988	Nationwide	Noncooperation
Protest demonstrations	Aug. 20 to Sept. 18, 1988	Rangoon and larger towns and cities	Protest and persuasion
General strike	Aug. 22 to Sept. 18, 1988	Nationwide	Noncooperation
"Burn-ins"	Aug. 22 to Sept. 18, 1988	Rangoon	Noncooperation
Rallies led by Aung San Suu Kyi	Aug. 26 to Sept. 18, 1988	Rangoon	Protest and persuasion
Hunger strike	Sept. 12–18, 1990	Rangoon	Disruptive nonviolent intervention
Local citizens' committees	Aug.–Sept. 1988	Rangoon and larger towns and cities	Creative nonviolent intervention
Patta ni kozana kan (refusal of monks to perform services)	Aug.–Oct. 1990	Mandalay	Noncooperation
Civil disobedience of restrictions on electoral campaigning	1989–90	Nationwide	Noncooperation
Parallel government	Aug. 1990	Mannerplaw	Creative nonviolent intervention

Note: Based on Fink (2001), Lintner (1990), Maung (1992), Moksha (1989), Smith (1991), and Foreign Broadcast Information Service (1988–1990).

of them had a pre-history or a grassroots membership, none of the leaders was elected by a reasonable number of movement participants through recognized procedures, the leaders of the various organizations did not work with each other, and the movement participants did not necessarily follow the directives of the organizations or the leaders. Leaders or organizations who wanted to act strategically in their interactions with the state were marginalized by those who wanted to take more extreme actions, resulting in an upward spiral of actions that lacked a sufficient base of support (Zhao 2001, 146–47).

On April 18, 1989, students at Beijing University set up the first autonomous students' organization. Shortly thereafter, the first Beijingwide student organization, the Beijing Students' Autonomous Federation, was formed. Several universities followed, founding their own independent student unions. However, as more autonomous organizations emerged, fragmentation ensued. On May 5, the College Students Dialogue Delegation was formed to formulate demands and organize negotiations with the government. The beginning of the hunger strike on May 13 saw the formation of the Student Hunger Strikers' Delegation. These three organizations were at the forefront of the movement, but rather than strategically coordinating their activities, they ended up in competition with each other (Saich 1990, 35–37).

The development of the movement brought to the fore not only many newly formed organizations, but also numerous politically ambitious students with different ideas. These students, regardless of whether they were inside or outside the leadership of the movement organizations, tended to act on their own. As the movement progressed, it became increasingly fragmented, uncoordinated, and dominated by spontaneous mass activities. The students with a more refined understanding of China's problems and of the goals of the movement were marginalized by those who had gained their credentials through the promotion of more extreme demands and actions. Over the course of the movement, conflicts between student factions intensified. On May 14, 1989, for example, students from Beijing University established a broadcasting station in Tiananmen Square. The next day, students from Qinghua University constructed a more powerful broadcasting station. The two stations broadcast at the same time, providing conflicting announcements and orders (Zhao 2001, 179).

The more organized segments of the movement, represented by the College Students Dialogue Delegation and the Beijing Students' Autonomous Federation, were unable to sufficiently coordinate or direct the movement, as they were in conflict with the hunger strike leaders over the movement's tactics and goals. By May 18, 1989, many student leaders and activists wanted to end the hunger strike so as not to give the state an excuse for implementing martial law, and the student factions fought bitterly over whether or not the hunger strike should end.

Moreover, there were two types of hunger strike leaders, who were themselves divided. The first type, including Wuer Kaixi and Wang Dan, had organized the hunger strike as a strategic political action, to increase mobilization and take advantage of the opportunity provided by the presence of the international media to cover Mikhail Gorbachev's visit to Beijing for the Sino-Soviet summit. The second type, including Chai Ling, viewed the hunger strike in more idealistic terms and decided to continue the hunger strike until the government capitulated to their demands. Student leaders who were flexible and willing to negotiate with the government and consolidate gains were viewed as traitors and marginalized. Calls by Wuer Kaixi and Wang Dan to end the hunger strike and the occupation of Tiananmen Square in order to organize and consolidate gains were dismissed. After the hunger strike began, it came under the control of idealists such as Chai Ling, Feng Congde, Zhang Bole, and Li Lu, who received support from the students newly arriving from outside Beijing (Zhao 2001, 179–81).

In late May another umbrella organization, the Joint Federation, was formed. The deadlock between students and the government was apparently on the verge of being broken when the Joint Federation, including Chai Ling and Feng Congde, voted to end the occupation of Tiananmen Square and consolidate their gains. Shortly thereafter, however, Chai Ling and Feng Congde changed their minds. Chai Ling announced that her General Headquarters had decided to withdraw from the Joint Federation. The students who had come from outside Beijing also rejected the idea proposed by Beijing student leaders, that they end the occupation of Tiananmen Square. These factors contributed to the students' head-on confrontation with the government and the tragic outcome (Zhao 2001, 190–95).

Thus, a major organizational deficit of the Chinese resistance was that although preexisting student networks were able to mobilize students rapidly, they did not provide the organizational infrastructure necessary for overall coordination of the movement. Nor did an organizational infrastructure develop during the movement's short but intense duration (Calhoun 1989; Sharp and Jenkins 1989; Smith 1992; Zhao 2001). Attempts were made to organize umbrella organizations that could effectively coordinate the diverse student groups, but none was able to command the allegiance of most of the students. Had there been a recognized umbrella organization for the movement as a whole, the challengers might have been able to formulate agreed-upon demands, act strategically in pursuit of their objectives, and consolidate gains. Without sufficient coordination, this was not possible.

The resilience of the movement was also inhibited by tactical problems. The massive public demonstrations followed by the occupation of Tiananmen Square and the hunger strike had tremendous symbolic value.[7] However, the occupation of a public space is always risky for protestors. More generally, methods of concentration, such as protest and persuasion (marches, rallies) and disruptive nonviolent intervention (hunger strikes, sit-in occupation), are less resilient in the face of repression than are methods of dispersion, such as forms of noncooperation and boycott. Without expanding the methods of nonviolent action implemented (see Table 5) from methods of concentration to methods of dispersion, the Chinese movement was unable to remain resilient when repression intensified.

Lack of Leverage

The leverage that the challenge in Burma could generate against the regime was limited by its emphasis on institutional methods to challenge the regime in the period leading up to the multiparty elections, the lack of elite divisions, the lack of autonomous institutions, the lack of support from abroad, and the lack of effective pressure against the regime by international actors.

While the challengers implemented a broad range of methods of nonviolent action before SLORC took control on September 18, 1988, a much more limited range was implemented following the military's resumption of power and its announcement that multiparty elections would subsequently be held. Aung San Suu Kyi, the general secretary of the NLD, was placed under house arrest on July 20, 1989, and thousands of NLD workers from across the country were arrested as well. Once Aung San Suu Kyi was put under house arrest, the only dissident activities were isolated and largely symbolic gestures. Thereafter, the methods of noncooperation implemented were limited to acts of civil disobedience of the campaign restrictions, such as holding rallies and publishing political pamphlets (Kreager 1991). More threatening forms of noncooperation, such as strikes and the boycott of

Table 5. Major Nonviolent Action Campaigns and Events in China, 1989

Action	Date	Location	Method of nonviolent action
Marches and protest demonstrations	Apr .17 to June 4, 1989	Beijing	Protest and persuasion
Formation of autonomous organizations	Beginning late April	Universities (first in Beijing, then nationwide)	Creative nonviolent intervention
Class boycotts	Apr. 22 to early May 1989	Beijing	Noncooperation
Protest demonstrations	May 1989	Major cities	Protest and persuasion
Hunger strike and occupation of Tiananmen Square	May 13 to June 4, 1989	Beijing	Disruptive nonviolent intervention

Note: Based on Zhao (2001) and Foreign Broadcast Information Service (1989).

state institutions, were not implemented. Rather than continuing with campaigns of noncooperation and nonviolent intervention, Aung San Suu Kyi and the NLD committed themselves to bringing about change through the elections, based on the assumption that the military authorities would recognize the results. In effect, by participating solely in the state-controlled channels of political participation, the challengers minimized their ability to pressure the state through the power of noncooperation and disruption. When the regime refused to honor the elections, the inability of the challengers to disrupt the regime through campaigns of noncooperation ensured that it would not be able to contribute to political change.

The lack of leverage, of course, was also a function of the context in which the movement arose. In Burma there were no divisions among the elite concerning the supremacy of the military; the military was not divided; there were no third parties with sufficient autonomy from the state that could have provided support for the movement, thereby increasing the movement's leverage; and there was a lack of tangible international support for the challenge and pressure against the regime.

A lack of elite divisions contributed to the unfavorable context. Prior to the beginning of the people power movement in 1988, the only serious challenges to Ne Win's rule had come from elites within the military and at the apex of the BSPP (which overlapped to a great degree). Ne Win responded to real or perceived threats to his power with political purges. In 1963, Brigadier General Aung Gyi, second in command to Ne Win, was purged from the party. His replacement, Brigadier General Tin Pe, was removed from the inner circle of power in 1969. General Tin U, who urged restraint in responding to protests in 1974 and 1975, was purged in 1976. It was rumored that a split within the armed forces had emerged between a pro–Tin U faction of field commanders who faced the brunt of the fighting against ethnic insurgents and the officers who had taken a leading part in the development of the state in Rangoon. In July 1976, seven junior military officers were arrested and tried for allegedly plotting to assassinate Ne Win. General Tin U, whom some viewed as a potential successor to Ne Win, was charged with having knowledge of the assassination plot and was imprisoned. Less than a year later, another plot to assassinate Ne Win was alleged. Two former officials of the BSPP were arrested and tried. Subsequently, there was a major purge within the state apparatus as well as within the armed forces to root out potential bases of support for Tin U and to consolidate Ne Win's grip on power. The chief of the Military Intelligence Service and a protégé of Ne Win, Tin U (unrelated to General Tin U) was purged and sentenced to life imprisonment in 1983 (Lintner 1990; Maung 1990; Silverstein 1977).

No coup or assassination plots were reported in the 1980s, and no elite divisions within the military command manifested before or during the unarmed insurrection in 1988. The only documented defections from the military during the 1988 protests were by lower-level personnel, primarily from the peripheral services (Guyot 1989). There was no withdrawal of support by any high-ranking military officers, and most of the rank-and-file troops faithfully carried out their orders to fire on unarmed demonstrators. Thus, the military command in Burma remained cohesive prior to and during the pro-democracy challenge.

Another constraint was the lack of autonomous institutions that could have provided support for the movement. There was significant support for the unarmed insurrection in Burma among segments of the Buddhist *sangha* (monkhood). During the 8-8-88 general strike, for example, columns of hundreds of Buddhist monks carried their alms bowls upside down, a symbol that the entire nation was on strike (Lintner 1990).[8] However, the relationship between the *sangha* and the state and the propensity of the regime to repress the *sangha* undermined the institutional support that the *sangha* could provide to the challenge. In the 1960s the *sangha* had successfully resisted the government's efforts to register monks as a method of attaining control over the Buddhist monkhood (Silverstein 1977). Subsequent attempts by the Ne Win regime to exert control over the *sangha* had been relatively ineffective until May 1980, when the relationship between the state and the *sangha* was fundamentally altered. As a result of the state-sponsored First Congregation of the Sangha of All Orders for the Purification, Perpetuation, and Propagation of the Sasana, rules for registering monks and for the removal of monks who engaged in political activities were implemented. This meeting, along with a second congregational meeting in 1985, led to much greater control over the Buddhist monkhood by its older conservative leadership and by the state (Matthews 1993; Taylor 1987; Than 1988). The conservative leadership of the *sangha* did not overtly criticize the military regime and consistently disapproved of monks participating in anti-regime demonstrations (Kurzman 1998). Thus, the organizational infrastructure of the *sangha* was not sufficiently independent of the state to contribute to sustaining the movement in the face of repression. Dissident monks organized the All Burma Young Monks' Union (ABYMU), which in 1990 called for the transfer of power to the democratically elected national assembly, but SLORC arrested hundreds of monks alleged to be members of the union and effectively ended its operation.

On August 8, 1990, students and monks in Mandalay organized a commemoration of the 8-8-88 uprising for its second anniversary. Thousands of people participated in the event, which was met with violence by the military, who killed two monks and injured many others. In response to these events, monks in Mandalay organized a religious boycott *(patta ni kozana kan)* against the regime. Beginning on August 27, 1990, the monks participating in the boycott rejected alms from soldiers and their families and refused to perform religious ceremonies for military personnel or their families. After the religious boycott had continued for nearly two months and had begun spreading to other cities, the regime clamped down. Senior abbots met with General Saw Maung and formally called for an end to the boycott (Maung 1992, 185). Beginning on October 20, 1990, the military disrobed and arrested disobedient monks who continued with the boycott and disbanded independent Buddhist organizations, such as the ABYMU, alleged to be participating in anti-regime activities. The military crushed the opposition within the *sangha* by attacking over one hundred monasteries, disrobing, beating, imprisoning, and torturing hundreds of monks in Mandalay, the center of *sangha* activism against the regime (Fink 2001, 70–71; Lintner 1994, 311–12; Matthews 1993; Maung 1992).

Thus, while a significant segment of the *sangha* supported or participated in the unarmed challenge to military rule, the *sangha* leadership's refusal to oppose the regime and its disapprobation of dissident monks, along with the state's willingness to repress dissident monks, suggests that the *sangha* was not able to function as an autonomous influential ally to the people power movement as did, for example, the Catholic Church in the Philippines (chapter 3) or Buddhist organizations in Thailand (chapter 5).

The leverage of the movement in Burma also suffered from a lack of support from influential allies from abroad. Burma has historically been more isolated than the rest of Southeast Asia, and suspicion of foreigners and capitalism had been prevalent in the ideologies of Burma's intellectuals since the early twentieth century. Following the 1962 coup, Burma severed most of its international ties, pursued a nonaligned isolationist policy, and remained insulated from direct political influence by foreign powers. Travel into Burma was restricted, and foreign missionaries, scholars, and foundations were forced to leave the country (Taylor 1987). Thus, Burma remained cut off from transnational social movements except for a brief period during the "Rangoon Spring" of 1988. Amnesty International, for example, briefly set up an office in Rangoon during the summer of 1988, but it was closed down in September, when the military reasserted control. Nongovernmental organizations promoting the pro-democracy movement in Burma subsequently emerged after the military takeover, but they were located outside of Burma, mostly in Thailand, Europe, or the United States, and their links to the movement within Burma were weak. Moreover, no transnational social movements were in a position to provide direct support for the movement.[9]

The transnational Burmese pro-democracy movement developed only after the challenge had been suppressed in Burma in September 1988 and the government refused to honor the elections of May 1990. Amnesty International, for example, did not launch a worldwide campaign for democracy and human rights in Burma until November 7, 1990. International awareness of the situation in Burma was changed dramatically by Aung San Suu Kyi's campaign for human rights and democracy after the unconsummated elections of May 1990, but the leverage against the military regime applied by those touched by her message was not sufficient to contribute to political change. Thus, the situation differed from that in South Africa (chapter 3), where international support for the movement increased while the movement was still growing; in Burma, international support for the movement developed only after it had been suppressed.

The ability of foreign states to invoke pressure against the Burmese regime was also weak. Following the 1962 coup, Burma pursued an autarkic policy of development and followed a strict policy of neutrality, even to the extent of withdrawing from the nonaligned movement in 1979 when it perceived that the movement was too closely aligned with the Soviet Union. The military regime repeatedly made proclamations about the ultimate sovereignty of states and the illegality of foreign intervention in domestic affairs (Taylor 1987). Given Burma's relative isolation and lack of dependence relations with foreign powers, no country had the leverage to effectively pressure its military regime or provide crucial support for the people power movement. The Western powers denounced the regime's brutality, but there was little they could do, or were willing to do, but impose trade sanctions and restrict government aid (Guyot and Badgley 1990). These actions, however, had a minimal effect given the relatively low levels of international trade between Burma and the West. Japan, although it temporarily suspended aid, refused to join the West in an economic boycott due to its substantial economic interests in Burma.

Meanwhile, the government of Thailand arrested and deported Burmese dissidents who fled across the border,[10] and Thai corporations provided the Burmese military government with hard cash by setting up multi-million-dollar logging operations to clear-cut teak forests in Burma for sale on the international market (United Nations 1991). SLORC also received revenue from foreign investment and joint ventures formed with private corporations, including fishing rights, oil exploration rights, gemstones, infrastructure development, and tourism. These sources of income permitted the military government to purchase military arms from Pakistan, Singapore, and China. In the aftermath of the unarmed insurrection, the Burmese military regime strengthened its ties to China considerably. In September 1990, China agreed to sell SLORC $1.2 billion in military hardware, which, of course, is used to suppress Burma's own population (Fink 2001; Maung 1992, 227). China has become an important supporter of the Burmese military regime in international forums as well, as it, too, is opposed to foreign pressure in support of human rights and is supportive of the ultimate sovereignty of states.

As in Burma, the leverage of the challenge in China was diminished by characteristics of the movement as well as by the broader political context in which it occurred. Some have suggested that the pro-democracy movement failed to promote political change in China due to its lack of negotiating capacity. In the opinion of some, a challenging group has negotiating capacity "to the degree that a representative of the organization is able to make commitments on behalf of the movement organization to which movement activists will adhere" (Pagnucco and Smith 1992, 177). Certainly the disorganization of the students limited their negotiating capacity, but even if the students had been more coherently organized, by themselves they lacked the leverage to promote political change. Generally, one party will not negotiate with another party unless the second party has some sort of leverage. The government agreed to dialogues with the students not to actually negotiate a political transition, but rather to provide apparent concessions to the students in order to facilitate the end of the occupation of Tiananmen Square without engaging in the potentially more risky action of violent repression. Although the dialogues failed to satisfy the students, the students did not have sufficient leverage to force concessions from the state, due in part to their disorganization, but also due to their reliance on a limited range of methods, insufficient ties to a broader social base, a lack of elite divisions, and a lack of international support or pressure against the regime (Sharp and Jenkins 1989).

The tactical centerpiece of the movement was the occupation of Tiananmen Square and the hunger strikes. Forms of nonviolent intervention such as these have power to the extent that they disrupt normal activities, mobilize people into campaigns of noncooperation, mobilize the withdrawal of third-party support from a regime, or convert the views of the opponent. While disruptive, the occupation of a public place is not resilient in the face of repression. Moreover, the occupation and hunger strikes failed to convert the political elite to the students' cause, failed to mobilize sufficient support of third parties with leverage against the regime, and failed to mobilize people to form campaigns of noncooperation that would have increased the leverage of the challenge.

In effect, the meteoric rise of the student movement and its transformation of the conflict into a zero-sum game exhausted the tactics that the students might have used to escalate pressure in the face of government intransigence. The imbalance between the movement's political leverage and the students' demands to end the political monopoly of the CCP, on the one hand, and the state's inability to end the occupation of Tiananmen Square through either conciliatory gestures or threats, on the other, ensured that the state would use violence to end the occupation. In effect, the hunger strikes and the occupation of Tiananmen Square "turned the movement into a moral crusade and a zero-sum game," according to Dingxin Zhao. "From then on, a head-on collision was almost inevitable" (Zhao 2001, 232).

In addition to being undermined by the student's failure to implement campaigns of noncooperation, the power of the students was also undermined by their isolation from other social forces. The student movement had the organized support of intellectuals and journalists, but not of workers or peasants. Although the system of ideological control of workers had weakened in the post-Mao era, the work unit *(danwei)* remained the basic unit through which the state controlled citizens. Most workers are dependent on jobs in large state-owned collective enterprises that distribute an array of benefits to employees, such as salaries, housing, and medical care. Turnover is very low, and the fear of losing employment constrains organization behind factory gates (Walder 1989). When workers participated in the protest demonstrations, they did so for the most part as individuals rather than as a bloc.

An exception to individual worker participation occurred when censorship of the major official newspapers collapsed during a brief period in mid-May (as discussed later), providing an opportunity for workers to join the movement without risking arrest or job loss. During this brief period, workers came out in support of the movement, organized by their work units. In fact, during this time government officials in charge of work units actually supported work unit mobilization, since to go against worker participation not only would have made them unpopular with their workers, but would have made them appear to be going against the government, since the official newspapers were reporting positively on the movement at this time (Zhao 2001). However, once martial law was declared on May 19, most worker units ceased demonstrating, as it was clearly illegal and would constitute an open challenge to authorities. Workers' support could have continued only if they had had autonomous organizations.

An exception to work unit mobilization was the formation of the Beijing

Workers' Autonomous Federation (BWAF) on May 18, 1989. However, based on its participants, leadership, resources, and major activities, it was apparent that the Workers' Federation was merely an appendage of the student movement and was unable to generate substantial worker support (Zhao 2001, 173–76). The federation was largely symbolic, as its influence did not extend into a single factory and it lacked the ability to organize strikes or slowdowns to demonstrate its power (Tianjian 1990, 1203). Thus, there is little evidence suggesting that workers were able to organize autonomously or coordinate threatening actions with political leverage, such as work stoppages or strikes in support of the student movement.

The coherence of elites also limited the leverage of the movement. There were policy divisions among the political elite over the pace of economic reform in China and how to respond to the students, but not over the formula for political rule, which would have been a prerequisite for regime defection. Some of the state leaders disagreed over the most effective strategy for responding to the challenge—crackdown or conciliation—but there were no elite divisions with regard to the supreme political role of the CCP. The political elite was committed to one-party rule, and most saw no benefits to be derived from ending the CCP's monopoly on political power. The pro-democracy movement's only high-level backing within the political elite seems to have been from Zhao Ziyang, who attempted to use the movement to salvage his own political fortunes (Dittmer 1990; Nathan 1989; Strand 1989; Tianjian 1990; Zhao 2001).

International resources and support for the pro-democracy movement made their way into Beijing from overseas Chinese and from Hong Kong (Zhao 2001, 195–98), but, given the problems with organization and coordination discussed earlier, these resources were not effectively translated into organization building. Moreover, the pressure generated by foreign states against the Chinese regime was not substantial. Sanctions imposed on China by the United States following the massacre in Tiananmen Square, for example, were intended to relieve domestic political pressure in the United States rather than to have any instrumental impact on the Chinese regime (Hufbauer et al. 1990, 93).

The Paradox of Repression

At the beginning of the pro-democracy movement in Burma in March 1988, the government met collective action with excessive and indiscriminate repression. However, some feel that the state's "disproportionate and indiscriminate use of force had kindled a deep and massive response within the populace" (Moksha 1989, 556). "Instead of becoming afraid, more and more people joined the movement" (Lintner 1990, 9). That is, at the beginning of the people power movement indiscriminate repression had the unintended effect of increasing mobilization. Yet when the military returned to the cities on September 18 upon SLORC's assumption of power, repression was again applied indiscriminately. According to one observer, the army was a "brutal, blunt weapon incapable of discrimination" (Moksha 1989, 554). "Parts of Rangoon were turned into a free-fire zone, with troops shooting people in tea shops, at bus stops, and even in their homes" (Moksha 1989, 549). Thus, the paradoxical effect of the violent and indiscriminate repression was to promote mobilization of the movement from March to August 1988, but then, by September 1988, the violent and indiscriminate repression had the effect of demobilizing and suppressing the movement. This paradox can be explained by situating the movement-state interactions within the broader configuration of opportunities and constraints and identifying how these influenced the movement's ability to implement various methods of resistance.

Contributing to the movement's inability to weather repression were state censorship and the lack of information flows. After the 1962 coup in Burma, the state assumed control of all publishing and communications and there was a general suppression of nonstate publications (Taylor 1987). However, during the "Rangoon Spring" period, from June to September 1988, a spate of newspapers critical of the regime surfaced. By August 1988, Rangoon alone had nearly forty independent newspapers and magazines devoted to political criticism and mobilization of the opposition (Lintner 1990). The emergence of alternative print media was crucial in transforming the student-centered protests into a mass movement. State-run newspapers were taken over by the workers, who published news of the demonstrations and pressed for movement demands (Guyot 1989). However, when SLORC assumed power in September 1988 it immediately retook control of the media, shutting down all newspapers except for the government-run *Working People's Daily* (Lintner 1990). With no alternative information available to the public, it became increasingly difficult to sustain the movement.

Mobilization in response to repression was also facilitated by the apparent divisions within the regime over holding a referendum on a multiparty democracy, that is, the formula for political rule. However, by mid-September the regime had reorganized and reunified, and no divisions existed among the commanders of the military that would have provided opportunities for the challenge.

Thus, the violent and indiscriminate repression facilitated mobilization when it was combined with perceived elite divisions and less constrained flows of information. However, when violent and indiscriminate repression occurred in combination with the closure of elite divisions and a lack of information flow, its effect was to demobilize the movement. This suggests that the effect of repression on dissent is not merely a function of its level or intensity, but also a function of the configuration of opportunities in which it occurs as well as the attributes of the challenge.

As in Burma, variations in the mobilization of the challenge in China were directly related to increased information flows and to perceived divisions among the elite. According to Dingxin Zhao, journalists tried to avert government control and report positively on the movement from its beginning. When the government's control over the media weakened, positive accounts of the movement dominated the news coverage. Dingxin Zhao examined the movement-related news stories published in the two most important official newspapers in China and found that the government's control over the media was directly related to the ebb and flow of the movement. Prior to April 28, 1989, the government was in firm control of the mass media, as exemplified by the harshly worded editorial concerning the student movement published in the *People's Daily* on April 26. In the aftermath of the editorial, journalists began participating in the protest demonstrations and pressuring editors to publish more positive accounts of the movement. During the period from April 28 to May 13, the state began losing control of the major official newspapers, and more and more objective and positive accounts of the student movement were published. State censorship of the major newspapers temporarily collapsed between May 14 and 19, during the emergence of the hunger strike. The almost entirely positive coverage of the movement in the official newspapers during this period decreased the risk of activism and had a significant mobilizing effect, as millions of Beijing residents came out in support of the movement. However, on the evening of May 19 the government declared martial law, and from May 20 onward the state began to reassert its control over the mass media and the movement declined. On May 25, martial law troops occupied the major media outlets in Beijing, and the major official newspapers published negative stories about the movement. By June 1, censorship was reimposed (Zhao 2001, chapter 10).

The international media, in Beijing to cover the Sino-Soviet summit, also facilitated the mobilization of the movement. The international media reported on the student movement, and the coverage was broadcast back into China, facilitating mobilization not only in Beijing, but also in provincial capitals and college towns across China (Dittmer 1990, 32). However, by June censorship of international mail was reimposed, fax machines were cut off or carefully guarded, Chinese-language Voice of America (VOA) and

British Broadcasting Corporation (BBC) radio broadcasts were electronically jammed, and, most important, the government reimposed censorship over the domestic mass media (Dittmer 1990, 37). Thus, when violent repression commenced in early June, the configurations of opportunities were not auspicious for the movement and contributed to its demise. The movement had not grasped the opportunity to organize and implement methods of dispersion during the period of freer information flows.

As in Burma, perceived divisions among the political elite in China spurred on mobilization, but the divisions in the political elite were either nonexistent or quickly closed. Zhao Ziyang, the general secretary of the CCP, gave an impromptu speech on the student movement on May 4, 1989, at the Asian Development Bank Conference, and the tone of the speech was essentially positive. To the students this appeared as if Zhao supported the movement, and, more generally, as if there were elite divisions, decreasing the risks of activism and facilitating mobilization. More likely, however, Zhao was merely using the movement in an attempt to improve his precarious position among the political elite (Dittmer 1990; Zhao 2001).

Another apparent success of the movement was its ability to stop the initial occupation of Tiananmen Square by the military. Martial law was declared on May 20, 1989, and seven to eight divisions of ten to fifteen thousand troops each attempted to enter the city. Beijing residents were outraged at the imposition of martial law and blocked the troops, who subsequently withdrew on May 22. As in Burma, the withdrawal of the troops was viewed as success for the movement, encouraging further mobilization and an escalation of demands. However, the alteration in the government's policies was primarily due not to elite divisions—as interpreted by the students—but rather to the ineffectiveness of previous responses. According to Dingxin Zhao, "Western analysts have highlighted the factional nature of Chinese government during the 1989 Movement. But the crucial fact is that no top state leaders really supported the students during the movement. Their differences were more over strategies to calm down the movement" (Zhao 2001, 282). Since there were no elite divisions with regard to the formula for political rule, since the state was not going to give in to the demands of the movement, and since concessions and threats were unable to control the challenge, the only option left, from the state's perspective, was military repression. Given the factors discussed earlier, repression had its intended effect.

Conclusion

In both Burma and China, extreme repression contributed to the demise of the resistance, but it was not the sole factor determining the outcomes of those unarmed insurrections, as is often assumed with regard to challenges in nondemocratic contexts that rely on methods of nonviolent action. Repression effectively suppressed the movements, but this was due to a combination of broader political configurations and the attributes of the movements themselves as much as to the intensity of the repression.

Moreover, it is commonly assumed that a relatively democratic context is necessary for nonviolent action to succeed. However, nonviolent action may be the prevailing means by which an oppositional civil society asserts itself and then defends itself from state repression, thus promoting democratization. The struggles in Burma and China in the late 1980s were unsuccessful in toppling their states, but they may have set in motion a process of developing an oppositional civil society that will contribute to political change in the future.

Despite the outcomes of the challenges in Burma and China, the global wave of unarmed insurrections continued. In the early 1990s, China's southwestern neighbor, Nepal, and Burma's neighbor to the southeast, Thailand, experienced unarmed insurrections. Contrary to those in Burma and China, the unarmed insurrections in Nepal and Thailand contributed to democratization. These cases will be examined in the following chapter.

5

Challenging Monarchies and Militaries:
People Power in Nepal and Thailand

In the early 1990s, two Asian kingdoms that had never been formally colonized by European powers, Nepal and Thailand, experienced unarmed insurrections. In Nepal, a broad-based movement challenged the monarchy and the entrenched *panchayat* system of government.[1] The target of the opposition in Thailand was not the monarchy, but rather the military, which was attempting to reassert its control over the polity following a period of gradual political liberalization in the 1980s. The unarmed insurrections in Nepal and Thailand in the early 1990s contrasted with previous political struggles in these countries. In Nepal, communist parties had sporadically engaged in armed struggles, and in Thailand the Communist Party of Thailand (CPT) had engaged in a guerrilla insurgency from the 1960s into the 1980s; however, neither challenge succeeded in promoting political change due to the superior military capacity of the state's armed forces and a lack of broad-based support throughout the populace.

The unarmed insurrection in Nepal in 1990 developed in response to deteriorating economic conditions and a repressive political regime that inhibited significant political change. The challengers demanded the dismantling of the *panchayat* political system, the restoration of parliamentary democracy, and the reduction of the king's powers to those of a constitutional monarch. The struggle climaxed in a massive demonstration in Kathmandu by approximately two hundred thousand people on April 6, 1990. In what became known as the Massacre of Kathmandu, security forces opened fire on unarmed protestors, killing at least fifty people and injuring hundreds of others. Nevertheless, the protests continued, and on April 8 the king lifted the ban on political parties, setting in motion a democratic transition that culminated in multiparty elections in 1991.

The pro-democracy challenge in Thailand emerged following a military coup in February 1991. By May 1992, hundreds of thousands of people in Bangkok as well as in provincial cities took to the streets in opposition to the military.[2] They demanded the resignation of General Suchinda Kraprayoon from the prime ministership and the adoption of a more liberal constitution. The protests were met with violent repression, and hundreds of unarmed demonstrators were killed or injured and scores more disappeared.[3] Despite the violent repression, the protests continued, and after three days of bloodshed King Bhumipol Adulyadej intervened and forced General Suchinda to step down on May 24, 1992. Subsequently a more liberal constitution was written and the pro-democracy parties formed a ruling coalition after the September 1992 elections.

Nepal

Democratic movements emerged in Nepal in the 1930s and became more widely mobilized following India's attainment of independence in 1947, when British imperialists, who had supported the hereditary Rana regime in Nepal, left the subcontinent. In 1950 the Nepali Congress Party (NC) was formed to promote a liberation struggle against the Rana regime. Indian pressure forced the Rana regime to negotiate with the NC, and India subsequently brokered an agreement between the regime, the NC, and the traditional monarchy, whose political role had been negligible since the middle of the nineteenth century, leading to the formation of an interim government in February 1951 (Parajulee 2000, chapter 2).

The interim period was characterized by incessant conflict between the democratic forces and the ascendant monarchy. A series of constitutional amendments were implemented, and by 1954 the revised constitution laid the foundation for a return to an absolute monarchy. King Mahendra assumed the throne in 1955 and continued to strengthen monarchical rule. Nevertheless, democratic forces led by the NC continued to pressure the regime and in 1959 succeeded in forcing the monarchy to hold elections in which the NC received a clear mandate to govern. However, disunity within the NC and opposition by traditional elements increased, and in December 1960 King Mahendra ended the brief period of democracy in Nepal by dissolving the parliament, dismissing the government, and banning political parties. The multiparty parliamentary system was replaced in 1962 with a partyless *panchayat* system of governance. King Birendra succeeded his father in 1972 and maintained the political status quo (Parajulee 2000, chapter 2).

The *panchayat* system, which had the trappings of democracy, with a parliament, a cabinet, and a prime minister, essentially operated to provide sycophantic support for the monarchy, and in practice, all authority was concentrated in the monarch. The palace secretariat was directly appointed by the king and operated as an unofficial government parallel to the *panchayat,* though the king's appointees were more influential than their official counterparts in the elected *panchayat* body. Nevertheless, the "dual system" helped to maintain the myth of democracy for almost two decades. However, as economic conditions deteriorated and political change through institutionalized political channels proved ineffective, calls for noninstitutional political challenges gained wider support (Brown 1996, chapter 4).

Various banned political parties struggled against the monarchy through a combination of institutional political action, nonviolent action, and armed violence, but the divisions among the challengers limited the pressure they could effectively muster against the regime. By the late 1970s, student unions affiliated with the banned political parties began to mobilize in opposition to the regime. The democratic wing of students affiliated with the NC, the Nepal Student Union (NSU), and the progressive wing of students affiliated with the Nepal Communist Party (NCP), the All Nepal National Free Student Union (ANNFSU), mobilized opposition to the regime. In response to the mounting pressure, the king announced that a referendum would be held (Parajulee 2000, chapter 2).

In the 1980 referendum, voters were given the option of choosing between a multiparty system and a reformed *panchayat* system. The regime had a distinct advantage heading into the referendum, as it used the media, development funds, rewards of patronage, and the threat of withdrawal of these rewards to influence the vote. Meanwhile, the opposition forces were unduly complacent in their assumption that they would win the referendum, and they engaged more in competition among themselves for postreferendum political positions than in a coordinated competition against the regime. As a result, the challengers were unable to muster the necessary votes, and 54.7 percent of the people chose a reformed *panchayat* system over a multiparty democracy (Brown 1996, chapter 4; Parajulee 2000, chapter 2).

The opposition grudgingly accepted the results for the time being, but another challenge surfaced in 1985 when the NC launched a nonviolent civil disobedience movement *(satyagraha)* in opposition to the *panchayat* system and monarchical rule. Many of the leaders of the NC had been educated and become politically active in India, and their ideology and political activity had been shaped by Gandhian principles of nonviolence. Over the course of the *satyagraha,* several thousand political activists and supporters were imprisoned.

The NC called off the campaign, however, to disassociate itself from a number of suspicious bombings that had occurred after the campaign commenced.[4]

Nevertheless, the campaign was significant in that the NC began to realize the virtues of cooperating with the communist parties, and the communist parties began to realize the virtues of mass nonviolent action. Afterward, the NC and the communist parties began forging links with each other to promote a more broad-based and sustained challenge to the monarchy. On December 18, 1989, a loose coordinating committee of opposition forces was established by the NC, and on January 14, 1990, seven communist parties announced the formation of the United Leftist Front (ULF). The remaining communist parties joined together in the United National People's Movement (UNPM) to coordinate their activities with the NC and the ULF. The pro-democracy movement was subsequently undertaken through separate but coordinated and complementary campaigns by the NC, ULF, and UNPM (Brown 1996, chapter 5; Parajulee 2000, chapter 2).

The Pro-democracy Movement

On January 18, 1990, one of the first acts of civil disobedience occurred when the NC, in defiance of laws banning mass political meetings, convened a three-day convention in Kathmandu to plan the pro-democracy movement.[5] During the convention a decision was made to launch a campaign of nonviolent action, called the Movement for the Restoration of Democracy (MRD), beginning on February 18. The NC urged all parties, groups, and associations throughout Nepal to participate in the movement.

On February 4, 1990, when Tribhuvan University opened for a new term, pro-democracy rallies by student organizations and the University Teachers' Association commenced. On February 11, 1990, copies of the *Samalochana Daily* newspaper were surreptitiously distributed in Kathmandu before they could be confiscated by the government. The paper announced the plans for a campaign of nonviolent action that had been agreed upon by the NC and the ULF, which included calls for a protest demonstration on February 18 (Democracy Day), a general strike on February 19, another protest demonstration on February 25, and a second general strike on March 2.

Democracy Day had been held each year on February 18 to commemorate King Tribhuvan's historic proclamation in the early 1950s calling for the implementation of democracy in Nepal. The monarchy had used the day each year to stage pro-government rallies. In 1990 the MRD commenced the same day with counterdemonstrations. Approximately ten thousand people gathered near the center of Kathmandu carrying flags of the banned opposition political parties, shouting slogans, distributing leaflets to bystanders, and disrupting the official Democracy Day celebration. The counterdemonstrations were met with police violence, and clashes between police and demonstrators occurred throughout the city. Several hundred people were arrested, and scores of deaths and injuries were reported. In addition to the protests in Kathmandu, there were also protests in Birtamond, Jhapa, Biratnagar, Hetauda, Birgunj, Bharatpur, Narayangarh, Nawalparasi, Pokhara, Baglung, Palpa, and Mahendranagar.

A general strike *(bandh)* followed the next day in Kathmandu. Educational institutions, factories, and shops were closed, and vehicles stayed off the roads. Once again, the protests were met by police violence, and clashes broke out between unarmed demonstrators and government forces. Several vehicles that did not observe the *bandh* were stopped and set ablaze. Clashes between protestors and the police were reported in Kirtipur, Janakpur, Patan, and Bhaktapur as well.

On February 25, 1990, called "black day," a second major protest demonstration occurred in Kathmandu, with protestors carrying black flags and wearing black armbands. In an attempt to regain control of the political situation, the government again responded with violence, ushering in a period of terror unprecedented in recent Nepalese history. Riot police attacked the demonstrators, and approximately one thousand people were arrested, some of whom were subsequently tortured in police custody. The government also hired *mandales,* or thugs, to attack protestors. Nevertheless, Ganesh Man Singh, a leader of the NC, urged supporters of the movement to maintain nonviolent discipline, arguing that violence would only strengthen the government's position.

Despite the repression, the movement gained momentum in March. Workers, students, medical personnel, lawyers, government workers, housewives, airline employees, writers, and artists all engaged in nonviolent action against the regime. On March 5, 1990, members of the Bar Association of Nepal implemented a strike in protest of political arrests and detentions. On March 13, government workers at the Agricultural Development Bank organized a one-hour sit-in strike in support of the pro-democracy movement. By the end of March, the opposition movement was implementing "blackouts," whereby all lights were turned off between 7:00 and 7:30 p.m., signaling solidarity and widespread support for the movement.

Two cities in the Kathmandu Valley, Patan and Kirtipur, were designated by pro-democracy supporters as "liberated areas" after barricades and trenches prevented police and military vehicles from arriving after they had been dispatched to quell the insurrection. In Patan, citizens surrounded, or *gheraoed,* the main police station, effectively holding the police in custody, and on April 1, twenty thousand people gathered for a mass pro-democracy demonstration in the center of Patan.

On April 2, 1990, another general strike was implemented. Repression failed to compel compliance with orders to end the strike, and King Birendra was forced to reverse his hard-line stance against the movement and announce that reforms in the *panchayat* system were forthcoming. By this time the movement had invoked sufficient leverage against the regime that it could dismiss the regime's attempts at conciliation. Massive demonstrations occurred all over the country on April 6. In Kathmandu, up to two hundred thousand people gathered at the parade ground in the center of the city for a political rally. After the rally crowds began marching along the main thoroughfare toward the royal palace, where they were met by riot police. The unarmed crowd broke through police lines and began approaching the gates of the palace. The security forces opened fire on the demonstrators, leaving many dead and injured. In the aftermath, a twenty-four-hour curfew was implemented in the capital, but was defied by the movement.

Unable to co-opt the resistance through conciliation or quell it through violence, the king lifted the ban on political parties, as was announced shortly before midnight on April 6. The king issued a proclamation, broadcast over Radio Nepal, announcing the formation of a new cabinet and the establishment of a constitutional amendment commission. After the speech, hundreds of thousands of Nepali citizens poured into the streets in celebration. The next day crowds reassembled in the streets, where NC and ULF leaders, just released from prison, addressed the people.

From Political Transformation to Political Transition

On April 8, King Birendra began negotiating with opposition leaders for a democratic transition. The leaders of the NC and the ULF presented a set of demands to the king, including the establishment of an interim cabinet, the dissolution of the *panchayat* system, and the release of all political prisoners. The *panchayat* regime gave way to an interim government, which subsequently drafted a constitution. On November 9, 1990, a new constitution was promulgated that called for a constitutional monarchy under a parliamentary system. Parliamentary elections were held in 1991 and local elections in 1992. The unarmed insurrection succeeded in toppling the monarchy and set in motion the process of a democratic transition.

Thailand

Democracy was introduced in Thailand in June 1932 when a group of junior military officers and civilian bureaucrats seized power, overthrew the absolute monarchy, and established a constitutional regime. After an initial competition for state power between monarchical, democratic, and bureaucratic forces, the bureaucracy, and especially the military, emerged as the dominant social forces. From the 1950s onward, the polity and the economy were increasingly directed by the military. The military built up its economic base of power by operating its own business firms, controlling state enterprises, and placing generals on the boards of directors of private firms owned by Sino-Thais. In October 1958, Field Marshal Sarit Thanarat staged a coup, abolished the parliament and the constitution, and banned all political opposition. During Sarit's rule, from 1958 to 1963, the Thai state was transformed in three ways: a policy of vigorous anti-communism was pursued, an economic policy of state-directed technocratic capitalist development was implemented, and, in an effort to increase the state's legitimacy, the monarchy, which had been merely symbolic since 1932, was rehabilitated as a political institution. After Sarit died in 1963, his authoritarian policies were continued by General Thanom Kittikachorn (Chai-Anan 1995; Girling 1981).

The first serious challenge to military rule in Thailand occurred in the early 1970s. A student-led rebellion resulted in the toppling of the military dictatorship in October 1973 after hundreds of thousands of students, workers, and peasants protested against the military regime. However, the period of civilian democratic rule, which lasted from 1973 to 1976, was characterized by intense political conflict and extreme polarization between the Left and the Right (Girling 1981; Morell and Chai-Anan 1981).

In response to an increasingly chaotic and violent domestic political situation and to perceived external threats from communist movements in Vietnam, Cambodia, and Laos, the military seized power on October 6, 1976. A right-wing military dictatorship headed by Thanin Kraivichien engaged in extreme repression against liberal elements, thereby fueling the communist insurgency in the countryside. In an effort to decrease political polarization, the Thanin government was overthrown on October 20, 1977, by the same group that had staged the coup that had brought him into power one year earlier. General Kriangsak Chomanan was installed as the prime minister, and the new coup group attempted to mitigate polarization by relaxing repression and implementing a more liberal constitution. Amnesty was granted to dissidents arrested after the October 6 coup as well as to those who fled to the countryside to join the communist guerrilla insurgency (Girling 1981).

Kriangsak resigned in 1980 and was succeeded by General Prem Tinsulanond, who continued Kriangsak's policies of reconciliation through the 1980s until his retirement in 1988. The period from 1977 to 1988 was one of parliamentary and constitutional rule, and although it was dominated by military and former military leaders, the power of the parliament and of political parties gradually expanded. During this period, bureaucratic and nonbureaucratic groups forged a working partnership in what has been termed a "semidemocracy," "demi-democracy," or "half democracy" (see, respectively, Chai-Anan 1995, Likhit 1992, and Prudhisan 1992). The semidemocratic model of rule consisted of a political compromise between bureaucratic and nonbureaucratic forces, with bureaucratic elites appointed to the senate and members of the house of representatives popularly elected. Significant constraints were placed on political rights and civil liberties to prevent the organization of autonomous social forces that could challenge the power of the bureaucratic-military elite.

Chatichai Choonhavan, as the head of the largest party in the parliament, assumed power after the July 1988 parliamentary elections, and for the first time since 1976, Thailand had a prime minister who was an elected member of parliament rather than a military appointee. Chatichai implemented steps to transfer policy-making powers from the conservative military and civilian bureaucracy to elected politicians. However, resistance to the liberalization policies grew within the military-bureaucratic elite, and on February 23, 1991, a group of officers called the National Peace-Keeping Council (NPKC), led by General Sunthorn Kongsompong, seized power in a coup, arrested Chatichai, overthrew the democratically elected government, and annulled the parliament and the constitution. The NPKC framed the coup as necessary in order to replace corrupt politicians with impartial bureaucrats. However, the coup, led by the 1958 (Class 5) graduates of the military academy, was more realistically an attempt by the conservative military-bureaucratic elite to reverse political liberalization, limit the growing power of independent social forces, and return decision-making powers from civilians to the military (Chai-Anan 1995; Hewison 1996).

After the February 1991 coup, the NPKC attempted to diffuse pressure and legitimate its rule by promising a new constitution and the holding of free and fair elections. However, the military's desire to maintain control over politics was demonstrated by the establishment of a military-backed political party, and it soon became apparent that the constitution would be rewritten to perpetuate the power of the civilian-military bureaucracy (Surin 1993). The military also targeted labor unions, placing restrictions on private labor unions and banning unions and strikes in state-run enterprises (Brown 1997; Hewison 1996).

The Pro-democracy Movement

Initially there was not much opposition from the middle class or capital-ists following the February 1991 coup, as they accepted, or at least were indifferent to, the military's claims that the coup was necessary to weed out corruption in the civilian government and to clean up politics. The initial op-position to the regime was organized outside of the institutionalized political sphere by nongovernmental and social movement organizations. The core of opposition emerged from student organizations, labor unions, and non-governmental organizations concerned with human rights, development, and the environment. On April 19, 1991, nineteen organizations representing labor, academics, women, the urban poor, and nongovernmental organiza-tions coalesced with the Students' Federation of Thailand (SFT) to form the Campaign for Popular Democracy (CPD) in order to oppose military rule and promote a more democratic constitution. The CPD organized public forums to criticize the drafting of the 1991 constitution; served as a network between social movement organizations, non-governmental organizations, and opposition political parties; facilitated the coordination of local struggles into a national struggle; and organized mass rallies and protest demonstra-tions (Callahan 1998, 114).

The first major protests against the military occurred in November 1991, while a draft constitution written by a committee of NPKC ap-pointees was being considered in the National Assembly, a body of military appointees. If implemented, the proposed constitution would have reversed the process of liberalization that had occurred throughout the 1980s, al-lowing for an unelected prime minister and increasing the powers of the military-appointed senate. A mass rally on November 19, 1991, drew over seventy thousand protestors; it was the largest demonstration in Thailand since 1976 (Callahan 1998, 117). The protest demonstrations ended, how-ever, after King Bhumipol intervened and called for the passage of the military's proposed constitution. The king urged the opposition to wait until after the elections scheduled for March 1992 to amend aspects of the constitution that they considered unacceptable. To further diffuse the op-position that was building, General Suchinda, one of the generals behind the February 1991 coup, publicly announced that he would not seek the position of prime minister after the upcoming elections. The opposition was placated for the time being, and the demonstrations ceased.

In the March 1992 elections, a group of five mainly military-backed parties formed a ruling coalition and appointed Suchinda to the prime min-istership. By accepting the appointment on April 7, 1992, Suchinda broke his public promise. This, along with the continuation of the military rule of the NPKC and, more generally, the recognition of the military's attempts to reverse political and economic liberalization, touched off a more widespread pro-democracy movement.

In an effort to catalyze the remobilization of the opposition to military rule, Chalard Vorachart, a retired naval officer and former member of parliament, announced on April 8, 1992, that he would fast to death unless Suchinda resigned from office. Thereafter, the plaza in front of the parliament house where Chalard's fast was being held was filled with pro-democracy protestors. Public sentiment against the government intensified, and on April 20 a major protest demonstration called the People's Power to Preserve Democracy drew a crowd of approximately 100,000 people (Surin 1993). On May 4, a second hunger strike was initiated by Chamlong Srimuang, a former major general and the head of the pro-democracy Palang Dharma Party, who vowed that he too would fast to death unless Suchinda resigned from office. As in China (chapter 4), the hunger strikes struck a responsive chord, and mobilization intensified. On May 4, a crowd of over 100,000 people gathered and called for Suchinda's resignation, and on May 6, a crowd of over 150,000 people assembled in front of the parliament to participate in pro-democracy demonstrations. By May 8, the protests were drawing crowds of up to 200,000 people, and by May 17 the demonstrations swelled to 500,000. Pro-democracy demonstrations against the military were implemented in major provincial cities outside of Bangkok as well (Pasuk and Baker 1997; Somsak 1993; Suthy 1995).

Faced with a growing rebellion, the military felt compelled to respond. On May 17, 1992, in an attempt to regain control of the political situation, military troops under the command of General Issarapongse fired on unarmed protestors in Bangkok. Hundreds were injured or killed, thousands more were arrested, and scores of protestors "disappeared." The protests were met with indiscriminate shootings and brutalities committed against unarmed protestors and even against medical professionals who treated the injured (Callahan 1998; Chai-Anan 1995; Hewison 1997; Somsak 1993). Despite the violence, mass protest demonstrations and rallies continued throughout Bangkok. After each round of violence dispersed the crowds, the dissidents regrouped and again took to the streets in protest.

On May 20, 1992, after three days of bloodshed and increasing political polarization, King Bhumipol intervened, and the military withdrew from the streets. General Suchinda resigned as prime minister on May 24, yet protests continued against the military. People withdrew their money from the Thai Military Bank in protest against the military, and businesses with ties to the military were targeted for boycotts. Even Bangkok business associations came out in opposition to continued military rule (Callahan 1998, 124).

With General Suchinda out of office, opponents turned their attention to the elections scheduled for September 1992. The elections were subsequently held in a more democratic and transparent political environment than in the past. An independent citizen-run organization, PollWatch, monitored the elections, and military manipulation of the elections was considered minimal, limited to the usual practice of vote buying. Four pro-democracy parties won a majority, formed a new government, and subsequently drew up and implemented a revised constitution reflecting the demands of the pro-democracy forces. The pro-democracy movement succeeded in ousting the unelected prime minister from office and implementing a more democratic constitution, and more generally illustrated how grassroots social forces could effectively wield power against the military without the force of arms.

Nonviolent Action and Political Transformation

The unarmed insurrections in Nepal and Thailand were, to a degree, characterized by the attributes and actions specified in chapter 2 that should theoretically promote the success of an unarmed insurrection in a nondemocratic context: coordinated networks of decentralized organizations, the implementation of a broad range of actions from across the methods of nonviolent action, and the withdrawal of support for and mobilization of pressure against the state through its dependence relations. These attributes enhanced the ability of these insurrections to operate in repressive contexts, undermine state power, activate third parties, exacerbate elite divisions, and promote regime defection; that is, they facilitated the recasting of the political context to one more favorable to the challengers' goals.

Sustaining the Challenge

In the late 1980s, the NC in Nepal realized the strategic virtues of collaborating with the communist opposition, and a number of communist parties realized the virtues of abandoning a "people's war" in favor of promoting "people power." Without their usual fractiousness, the opposition forces were able to temporarily set aside their differences to support the NC's call for a people power movement, as they realized that a more broad-based popular movement had to be developed in order to generate a sufficient amount of pressure to promote political change. The people power movement in Nepal was implemented by a federation of the NC, ULF, and the UNPM. They remained independent of each other, yet engaged in coordinated campaigns of mass nonviolent action (Parajulee 2000, 79–80). Since the challenge was undertaken by a number of different independent organizations acting in a coordinated manner, the government could not focus its repressive capacities on a particular organization.

The resilience of the unarmed insurrection in Nepal was also enhanced by the implementation of a range of actions from across the three methods of nonviolent action (see Table 6). When methods of concentration such as protest and persuasion were met with repression, the movement turned to methods of dispersion, such as forms of noncooperation, that were more resilient in the face of repression. As in South Africa and the Philippines (chapter 3), those leading the movement realized that state violence could inhibit public demonstrations, but that it was less effective in compelling compliance with state orders and ending campaigns of noncooperation. The regime outlawed strikes by workers in essential occupations, but as the strikes continued they merely revealed the government's limited ability to compel compliance through repression. The *bandhs* illustrated the popular opposition to the regime in an incontrovertible manner.

Tactical innovation contributed to the movement's resilience as well. An innovative method referred to as "corner demonstrations" or "lightning demonstrations" emerged during the course of the insurrection, whereby small groups of activists assembled at strategic locations, distributed movement literature, and shouted anti-government slogans. When police or military authorities appeared, the protestors would suddenly disperse and reassemble at another predetermined location. Many of these demonstrations would be carried out simultaneously, thus stretching the authorities' capabilities to control the situation. As one scholar notes, "Groups of activists would assemble, demonstrate, disperse and then regroup in another location. Lightning demonstrations gave the impression that the Jana Andolan [people power movement] activists were ubiquitous. Not only did this keep the security forces confused and on the defensive but it also created the impression that the Movement had unlimited support. This was vital to the success of the Jana Andolan. In order for it to have any chance of posing a credible alternative to the panchayat forces, it had to be seen by wary and risk-averse potential supporters as a viable movement, likely to succeed in its objectives" (Brown 1996, 120–21).

Another novel method implemented in Kathmandu was the citywide blackout that was implemented during the evening curfew. This innovative response symbolized the widespread opposition to the regime and permitted the participation of people who were opposed to the regime, but were unwilling to engage in riskier forms of collective action. The blackouts provided

Table 6. Major Nonviolent Action Campaigns and Events in Nepal, 1990

Action	Date	Location	Method of nonviolent action
Defiance of bans on mass political meetings	Beginning Jan. 18, 1990	Kathmandu	Noncooperation
Rallies and protest demonstrations	Beginning Feb. 18, 1990	Nationwide	Protest and persuasion
Disruption of official Democracy Day parade	Feb. 18, 1990	Kathmandu	Disruptive nonviolent intervention
Bandh (general strike)	Feb. 19, 1990	Nationwide	Noncooperation
Strikes by various workers and professionals	Beginning Feb. 20, 1990	Kathmandu and other cities	Noncooperation
Class boycott by university students and professors	Beginning Feb. 25, 1990	Kathmandu	Noncooperation
"Lightning" demonstrations	Beginning Feb. 1990	Kathmandu	Protest and persuasion
Construction of physical and human barricades *(gheraoed)*	Beginning Mar. 1990	Patan	Disruptive nonviolent intervention
Bandh (general strike)	Mar. 2, 1990	Nationwide	Noncooperation
Burning of *panchayat* effigies	Mar. 9, 1990	Kathmandu and other cities	Protest and persuasion
Tax boycott and refusal to pay for utilities	Beginning Mar. 11, 1990	Kathmandu and other cities	Noncooperation
Bandh (general strike)	Mar. 14, 1990	Nationwide	Noncooperation
Sit-in strike by members of the Agricultural Development Bank	Mar. 13, 1990	Kathmandu	Noncooperation; nonviolent disruptive intervention
"Pen down" strike by employees of the Provident Fund Corporation	Mar. 22, 1990	Kathmandu	Noncooperation
Blackouts	Beginning Mar. 24, 1990	Kathmandu and other cities	Disruptive nonviolent intervention
Burning of the Panchayat Constitution	Beginning Mar. 24, 1990	Kathmandu	Protest and persuasion
Strikes by government employees	Beginning Mar. 24, 1990	Kathmandu and other cities	Noncooperation
Bandh (general strike)	Apr. 2, 1990	Kathmandu and other cities	Noncooperation
Protest demonstrations	Apr. 5–7, 1990	Nationwide	Protest and persuasion
Bandh (general strike)	Apr. 6, 1990	Nationwide	Noncooperation

Note: Based on Brown (1996), Parajulee (2000), Raeper and Hoftun (1992), and Foreign Broadcast Information Service (1990).

Table 7. Major Nonviolent Action Campaigns and Events in Thailand, 1991–92

Action	Date	Location	Method of nonviolent action
Rally and protest demonstration	Nov. 19, 1991	Bangkok	Protest and persuasion
Hunger strike by Chalad Vorachat	Beginning Apr. 8, 1992	Bangkok	Disruptive nonviolent intervention
Protest demonstrations	Apr. 8, 1992, to May 20, 1992	Bangkok and major provincial towns and cities	Protest and persuasion
Hunger strike by Chamlong Srimuang	Beginning May 6, 1992	Bangkok	Disruptive nonviolent intervention
Protest demonstrations	Beginning late May 1992	Major provincial towns and cities	Protest and persuasion
Organization and operation of PollWatch	Sept. 1992	Nationwide	Creative nonviolent intervention

Note: Based on Callahan (1998), Chai-Anan (1995), Pasuk and Baker (1997), Somsak (1993), Surin (1993), Suthy (1995), and Foreign Broadcast Information Service (1991–92).

a symbolic form of communication, serving as a means for people to indicate the extent to which the challenge was popularly supported, and they had a tactical function as well, as the darkness facilitated the movement of dissidents so as to avoid detection by security forces.

The resilience of the challenge in Thailand was also facilitated by features of its organization and methods (see Table 7). Nongovernmental organizations had operated in Thailand since the 1960s, but it was not until the gradual liberalization and the decline of the communist insurgency in the 1980s that their networks significantly expanded. During the 1980s, political space opened up for nongovernmental organizations, alternative visions of social justice and development were formulated, and nonviolent action was implemented to pursue these visions. The thrust of the pro-democracy movement in Thailand occurred though the grassroots networks of nongovernmental organizations (Callahan 1998; Chai-Anan 1997, 44; Hewison 1996; Prudhisan and Maneerat 1997; Pasuk and Baker 1997, 34; Suthy 1995).

The pro-democracy movement opposed state centralization and uncontrolled urbanization and economic growth, and it promoted sustainable development, environmentalism, democracy, and human rights. By 1985 nongovernmental organizations had established a number of networks, including the Development Support Committee (DSC) to coordinate small nongovernmental organizations and to act as an information clearinghouse, the NGO Coordinating Committee of Human Rights Organizations to co-ordinate human rights efforts, and the NGO Coordinating Committee on Rural Development (NGO-CORD) to facilitate sustainable development, empowerment, and political action by marginalized populations (Prudhisan and Maneerat 1997, 201). The environmental movement was also a cru-cial component of the groups that coalesced to challenge the centralized decision-making of the bureaucratic elite (Callahan 1998; Prudhisan and Maneerat 1997, 206; Surin 1993, 330–31). According to one scholar, "Environmentalists represent a potent challenge to the concept of power embodied in the Thai state. More challenging are the coalitions they build between activist monks, villagers, NGOs, students, academics, and urban activists. . . . It was these groups that formed the backbone of the move-ment opposing General Suchinda's premiership and the 1991 constitution" (Hewison 1993, 173).

The networks of nongovernmental organizations and social move-ment organizations were supported by networks of Buddhist monks as well. Buddhist political activism had historically been discouraged by both the state and the *sangha* (Buddhist monkhood). However, by the 1990s the state's control over the *sangha* had decreased and the *sangha* had experienced a decline in its authority over clerics. A range of Buddhist movements emerged outside of the official *sangha* to contest official religious interpreta-tions, criticize the state's desire to control the *sangha,* and engage in political activity or provide support to political activists (Jackson 1997; Taylor 1993). Activist Buddhists supported the marginalized segments of the populace in their struggle against state authority and also provided support for the pro-democracy movement.

The initial pro-democracy protests in 1991 were organized by the Cam-paign for Popular Democracy (CDP), an umbrella organization that coor-dinated a coalition of nongovernmental organizations, students, academics, labor groups, and opposition political parties. The organization provided information to people regarding the negative aspects of the military regime and its drafting of a new constitution, and it also offered suggestions on how to actively oppose the government.

Thus, the challenge was based in a diverse decentralized network of scores of organizations that came together in opposition to the military, making focused repression more difficult. Compared to the Thai student movement in 1976, which had been suppressed with violence, the 1992 pro-democracy movement was much more decentralized and resilient. The democratic movement in 1976 had collapsed when the military arrested and massacred students at Thammasat University. Thus, when the leader of the pro-democracy movement, Major General Chamlong Srimuang, and thousands of activists were arrested on May 18, 1992, the military assumed that the demonstrations would end. Yet the protests continued, as there was no single leader to be arrested or organization to be repressed that would put an end to the movement, as had been the case in 1976. According to William Callahan, "In 1992 the demonstration was not dependent on students, but had many centres, including professionals, health-care workers, business people, slum dwellers, workers, and farmers in Bangkok and the provinces" (Callahan 1998, 86).

The methods implemented by the challengers enhanced the resilience of the challenge as well. As in Nepal, "liberated" areas were created by the opposition. When a curfew was declared on May 19, 1992, more than fifty thousand protestors regrouped at Ramkhamhaeng University, where they constructed barricades and formed a nonviolent "commune," that is, a liberated area outside the control of the military (Callahan 1998, 86–87, 123). However, the main actions implemented in Thailand were methods of protest and persuasion, such as demonstrations, marches, and rallies. Their mobilization was facilitated by the hunger strikes, which were effective in bringing out huge crowds of people in Bangkok as well as in provincial cities. Significantly, as in Nepal, and in contrast to the situation in China, the protestors outflanked military forces and reassembled in multiple places rather than occupying a single undefensible public place. When the military responded with violent repression, people remained committed and risked their lives by regrouping and engaging in protests in different places. William Callahan states, "The May protest was multi-centered where various groups—aided by technology such as the telephone, the fax, and the cellular phone which facilitated communications all around the country—continued the protest after their so-called leader was arrested. Whenever the army dispersed a crowd in one spot, another would appear elsewhere" (Callahan 1998, 86). Thus, the decentralized and multicentered nature of the challenge enhanced its resilience. Had the protests stopped in the face of repression, the military would have remained firmly in control, but by persisting the challengers triggered the "political jiujitsu" dynamic.

Undermining State Power

By sustaining their challenges in the face of repression, the pro-democracy movements in Nepal and Thailand promoted political transformations by undermining the states' legitimacy and resources. They did this directly by undermining the power the states derived from sources within society, and indirectly by severing the states from the power they derived from external sources.

In Nepal, the regime was directly undermined by the withdrawal of co-operation by crucial sectors within Nepal upon which the government was dependent. By late March 1990, government employees began to openly support the pro-democracy movement, depriving the regime of a valuable base of support (Parajulee 2000, 88). Had the challenge not remained resilient in the face of repression, these sectors most likely would not have risked engaging in noncooperation. By remaining resilient, it was able to trigger the political jiujitsu dynamic. In addition to mobilizing internal pressure, the challenge mobilized significant external pressure against the regime as well.

The conflict between the Indian and Nepali governments was also a significant factor that weakened the government and strengthened the leverage of the opposition movement in Nepal. In 1988 tensions arose between the two governments after Nepal purchased military hardware from China and imposed a permit scheme on Indians working in Nepal. These actions were perceived by India as contravening the 1950 Treaty of Peace and Friendship between the two countries, and in response, India refused to renew the Trade and Transit treaty. This had a significant impact, since Nepal's trade is dependent upon Indian cooperation. Nepal is a landlocked country, and most of its imports come from or pass through India to the south, as the Himalayas form a natural barrier to transportation to the north into China (Tibet). When the Trade and Transit Treaty between India and Nepal expired on March 23, 1989, India closed thirteen of the fifteen points of transit along the Indo-Nepali border, creating acute shortages of several essential commodities and increased prices. As the crisis continued into the fall, grievances against the government in Nepal intensified (Brown 1996, 8; Parajulee 2000, chapter 5; Raeper and Hoftun 1992, 20).

The National Front government of India expressed its commitment to democratic values and the democratic aspirations of the Nepali people, but it did not directly support the opposition during the struggle. On the other hand, Indian political parties such as the Janata Dal, the Communist Party-Marxist (CPM), and the Communist Party of India (CPI) threw their support behind the pro-democracy movement in Nepal. The Janata Dal had close ties with the NC, and the CPM and the CPI had close ties with the ULF (Parajulee 2000, 202–3). Several prominent Indian political leaders participated in the NC conference in Kathmandu in January 1990 and openly expressed their support for the democratic challenge in Nepal

(Parajulee 2000, 160). Thus, the Indian government's stance toward Nepal with regard to the trade and transit dispute and the support of Indian political parties helped to loosen the terrain upon which the monarchy's political control was based.

In addition, Nepal's dependence on foreign aid provided external actors with considerable leverage over the regime, and the pro-democracy movement actively sought to exploit the monarchy's dependence relations. In 1989–90, foreign aid provided 49.4 percent of Nepal's total budget expenditure and 73.5 percent of its development expenditure (Parajulee 2000, 150). The pro-democracy movements sought to undermine the regime by mobilizing pressure through donor countries and international agencies. The NC and the ULF sent representatives to foreign countries to lobby governments and to pressure external actors to use their leverage to inhibit the regime's use of repression and to promote political change (Parajulee 2000, 223–24).

Aware of the donor community's sensitivity to human rights issues, the pro-democracy movement highlighted the regime's violation of human rights. They publicized human rights violations and urged donors to suspend their assistance to the monarchy. Transnational social movement organizations facilitated the efforts of the pro-democracy movement in this regard by amplifying the voice of the movement in the international community. Amnesty International and Asia Watch, for example, investigated and documented violations of human rights in Nepal, publicized the government's repressiveness, and lobbied donor countries to withdraw support from or pressure the regime (Parajulee 2000, 229). This made it increasingly difficult for the regime to justify violent repression in the name of "law and order." As a result, some donors withdrew aid and pressured the regime to negotiate with the opposition. The United States, Germany, and Switzerland publicly condemned the repression of the government, threatened to withdraw aid, and privately pressured the government to negotiate with the pro-democracy movement (Brown 1996, 139; Parajulee 2000, chapter 6). Aid networks thus acted as a fulcrum that the movement used to undermine the regime. In effect, the donor networks that were in place to support the monarchy and promote development in Nepal were transformed into networks of pressure against the regime by the activities of the pro-democracy movement. When the king realized that he could no longer violently repress the movement without jeopardizing the international support upon which the regime depended, he was forced to negotiate with the pro-democracy movement.

In Thailand, shifts in the internal distribution of power were related to external factors as well. The changing nature of Thailand's relation to the international system improved the leverage of challengers and decreased the power of the state. As the Cold War emerged in the aftermath of World War II, the United States and its Western allies pursued a policy of anti-communism and anti-neutralism. Cold War geopolitical concerns of the West were especially great in Asia, where communists took power in China and North Korea. In the view of the United States, Southeast Asia was of strategic importance in stopping the advancement of communism and Thailand was a front-line state in the struggle. In the late 1950s the United States supported Sarit's authoritarian transformation of Thai politics, and in the 1960s U.S. support for the military regime in Thailand intensified as Thailand became a base of operations for U.S. air strikes against communist insurgencies in Indochina. Support from the United States meshed with the agendas of the authoritarian state in Thailand, whose repression of political opposition was considered justified on the basis of anti-communist and pro-capitalist imperatives (Hewison and Rodan 1996; Saiyud 1986).

However, by the 1980s U.S. support for the Thai military regime loosened as the communist insurgency in Thailand was subdued and the threat of invasion from Thailand's communist neighbors became more remote. By the end of the 1980s, the Cold War was winding down and it was no longer in the interests of the United States to provide uncritical support to the Thai military regime. The role of the United States changed from that of a benevolent patron of the military regime to that of an economic competitor demanding trade liberalization, and the United States became increasingly critical of Thailand's role in the production and transportation of opium. As a result of changes in the international system, the two modi operandi of the military-bureaucratic elite's reign of power, anti-communism and state-centric capitalist development, became obsolete by the 1990s (Chai-Anan 1997). The effect was to undermine the power of the military-bureaucratic elite, making it more susceptible to challenges from below.

The growth of an autonomous capitalist class in Thailand also under-cut the leverage of the military-dominated state. In the post–World War II era, capitalists worked with the military as politically passive partners; however, from the 1980s onward, capitalists became more independent of the state and took a more active role in politics. During the period of rapid economic growth in the 1980s, Thai capitalism became much more internationally oriented as capitalists guided the economic transition to export-oriented industrialization. The globalization of business enterprises provided the entrepreneurial class with a greater degree of flexibility in investment strategies, reducing its dependence on state-directed investment schemes. The independent capitalists began to control an increasing amount of resources and organizational power and formed assertive interest groups, and independent capitalists became influential in political parties, either as candidates or as financial supporters. By the 1990s, the capitalist class was autonomous enough to provide an effective countervailing force to the military-bureaucratic elite (Anek 1991; Chai-Anan 1997; Hewison 1996; Pasuk and Baker 1997).

Globally oriented capitalists were pressured to internalize the norms of international agencies such as the World Bank, the International Monetary Fund, and United Nations development agencies—agencies that promoted a neoliberal agenda (Hewison 1996). Neoliberalism obviously conflicted with the interests of the traditional military-bureaucratic elite. Capitalists were not necessarily pro-democratic, but they were apprehensive about the military-bureaucratic elites' attempts to regain control over economic decision-making. Thus, the capitalist and middle classes supported democratization to the extent that it prevented a return to the bureaucratic paternalism of the past.

Capitalists pressured the military to end repression due to their concerns about its adverse effects on business. In April and May of 1992, capitalist opposition to the military government was mobilized when the actions of the NPKC were viewed as hurting the international business climate. Business analysts agreed that "the impact of the anti-military demonstrations and subsequent crackdown will severely damage Thailand's image among foreign investors, bankers, and travelers" (Friedland 1992). On May 23, the head of the Thai Chamber of Commerce urged the government to appoint a civilian prime minister so that tourism and foreign investment would not be driven away by violence and instability. Subsequently, the Thai Chamber of Commerce was joined by the Industrial Organization of Thailand and the Thai Bankers Association in declaring that if the NPKC did not call for a new government, they would shut down their factories and businesses in opposition. In an effort to promote a hospitable business climate, these groups supported political reform, such as a democratically elected prime minister and reduced military influence (Callahan 1998, 123; Thomson 1994; Pasuk and Baker 1997). The pro-democracy challenge created the opportunity for the capitalists, along with the middle class, to withdraw their support from the repressive state.

While these developments undermined the leverage of the military-bureaucratic elite, the pro-democracy movement was crucial in driving a wedge between the state, on the one hand, and capitalist and middle class forces, on the other. It was the nongovernmental social movement network that had originally opposed the military, and had it not been for its challenge, middle-class and capitalist opposition would most likely have been limited to institutional political channels, where the military had a decided advantage.

The Paradox of Repression

When unarmed insurrections are sustained in the face of violent repression, the "political jiujitsu" dynamic may occur whereby the resolve of the challengers increases, the ability of the authorities to maintain control through repression decreases, and the support of third parties is generated. In Nepal, this dynamic did indeed occur and enhanced the challenge. The monarchy threatened and intimidated the public by deploying thousands of police and military personnel and by engaging in mass arrests, violent repression, and torture. However, anti-government sentiment was only intensified by the violent repression of unarmed demonstrators. People continued to take to the streets in defiance of the government's show of force. In March 1990, state security forces in Patan engaged in indiscriminate shootings that had the impact of radicalizing an already anti-government population. On March 20, 1990, approximately five hundred Nepali intellectuals and professionals assembled at Tribhuvan University near Kathmandu to hear speeches about the pro-democracy movement. The government responded in a way that only encouraged alienation from the regime, by arresting many in the audience and interrogating them. These acts of repression served as a catalyst, making an influential sector of Nepali society hostile toward the system.

The resilience of the challenge in the face of repression triggered regime defection as well. Divisions within the political elite surfaced on April 2, 1990, when Foreign Minister Shailendra Kumar Upadhyay resigned in protest of the government's mishandling of the Indo-Nepali trade crisis and its violent repression of unarmed protestors. Upadhyay's resignation signaled to the public the existence of elite divisions and contributed to the fall of the Marich Man cabinet a few days later. Defections spread among the political elite as more and more members of the National Panchayat condemned the use of violence against the unarmed protestors (Parajulee 2000, 83). Mass political action and elite defection formed a combination that was potent in the toppling of the regime—to the extent that the regime was overturned despite the fact that the military remained loyal throughout the crisis.

Significantly, the flow of information enhanced the resilience of the challenge and helped to promote the withdrawal of support from the regime. Although the government imposed censorship on the national media, censorship failed to control the flow of information through personal electronic media. Moreover, the Indian media, which had a widespread international circulation and reported positively on the movement, were sent into Nepal over the open border with India, providing Nepali citizens with information about the movement that was not otherwise available.

The political jiujitsu dynamic was also triggered in Thailand, where three days of indiscriminate repression of unarmed civilian protestors had the unintended effect of undermining support for the military and increasing support for the movement. If the protests had been subdued by the repression, the military would have remained firmly in control. Yet the protests continued, largely due to the movement's decentralized organizational structure and tactical innovation. Middle-class support for the regime was alienated by the military's violence, and King Bhumipol was forced to intervene in the situation to end the violent repression.

The resilience of the resistance was also enhanced and the withdrawal of support from the regime facilitated by the flow of information through channels not controlled by the government. The Suchinda government imposed censorship in an effort to cut the flow of information. The censorship was most effective with regard to television and radio, which were mostly owned by the state or the military. Newspapers, on the other hand, were more difficult to censor, and videos and faxes were not censored (Callahan 1998, 17–26). The decentralized organizational infrastructure of the CPD, as well as the SFT and PollWatch, permitted information to continue to flow despite state censorship. Moreover, the government was unable to censor graphic reports on the repression of the unarmed protestors that were beamed to the world by the British Broadcasting Corporation (BBC), the Cable News Network (CNN), and the Nippon Hoso Kyokai (NHK) (Callahan 1998, 1).

Conclusion

In contrast to the situation in Burma and China, where the challenges lacked crucial support from abroad, in Nepal and Thailand the challenges were facilitated by external pressures, albeit in different ways. The geopolitics of Nepal as a landlocked country surrounded by India on three sides and the Himalayan mountains to the north, along with the dependence of the kingdom on foreign support, made Nepal vulnerable to outside influence. Meanwhile, in Thailand the leverage of the military-bureaucratic elite was undermined by shifting geopolitical relations related to the decline of the Cold War and the ascendence of neoliberalism, along with the emergence of an autonomous capitalist sector. Yet these structural shifts constitute only part of the story, as ultimately it was the actions of the people power movements, specifically their ability to remain resilient in the face of repression and their ability to exploit dependence relations, that promoted democratization and toppled the monarchy in Nepal and the military in Thailand.

6

Trajectories of Unarmed Insurrections

One view of unarmed insurrections is that they are merely epiphenomena of large-scale social change and class relations and that the specific attributes of the challenges are inconsequential with regard to the pace or direction of political change. Another view suggests that the mobilization and outcomes of unarmed insurrections are entirely a function of individual intentions and rational choice calculations. Fortunately, there is plenty of theoretical space in between the extremes of structural determinism and methodological individualism where explanations of the trajectories of unarmed insurrections may be pieced together that consider structural constraints as well as human agency. Political process theory is useful in this regard, as it accounts for aspects of the political context that facilitate or constrain mobilization and, through the concept of framing, helps us to understand the spirit of movement agency. But much of the political process literature suffers from an underspecification of the crucial role that strategies and tactics play in sustaining a challenge or recasting the political context. This theoretical lacuna can be addressed by developing a more relational approach to political contention in which political process theory is supplemented with selective insights from the literature on nonviolent action.

Central to a more relational approach are the concepts of resilience and leverage. *Resilience* refers to the capacity of contentious actors to continue to mobilize collective action despite the actions of opponents aimed at constraining or inhibiting their activities. This concept emphasizes the iterative interactions between challengers and opponents over time. *Leverage* refers to the ability of contentious actors to mobilize the withdrawal of support from opponents or invoke pressure against them through the networks upon which opponents depend for their power. The inherent potential of leverage is realized by directly severing the dependence relations between the ruler and the ruled or by mobilizing the withdrawal of third-party support from the ruler. This concept emphasizes the interdependence of the polity and society in the national sphere and the interdependence of states and also nonstate actors in the transnational sphere. In this chapter I draw on these concepts while summarizing by means of a synthetic explanatory sketch that may be useful in accounting for the power and trajectories of unarmed insurrections in nondemocracies and providing examples from the six cases examined in the preceding chapters.[1]

Trajectories of Unarmed Insurrections in Nondemocracies

The trajectories of unarmed insurrections are shaped by the extent to which interactions between challengers, the state, and third parties produce shifts in the balance of power. The probability that an unarmed insurrection will tip the balance of power in favor of the challengers is a function of its resilience and leverage. By remaining resilient in the face of repression and effecting the withdrawal of support from or pressure against the state through its dependence relations, the state's capacity to rule may be diminished, third-party support for the movement may be mobilized, and the coherence of the political or military elite may fracture, that is, the political context may be recast to one more favorable to the challenge.

Generally, when the interests of political authorities are threatened, repression is used to channel, control, or eliminate the challenge. Characteristics of unarmed struggles that enhance their resilience in the face of repression include decentralized yet coordinated organizational networks, the ability to implement multiple actions from across the three methods of nonviolent action, the ability to implement methods of dispersion as well as methods of concentration, and tactical innovation.

A decentralized structure may enhance the resilience of unarmed struggles in nondemocracies for a number of reasons. First, decentralized challenges are more likely to withstand repression since the repressive capacities of the state cannot be targeted against a particular organization. Second, the devolution of leadership inhibits the disruption of movement activities when movement leaders are imprisoned or murdered. Third, there is a tendency for decentralized movements to be more democratic, thus increasing the commitment of activists and the accountability of leaders and decreasing the likelihood of co-optation. Fourth, there is a tendency for decentralized movements to develop an oppositional consciousness that enhances the ability of diverse groups to work together toward a common goal despite a lack of ideological consensus. Fifth, due to their flexibility and capacity for horizontal information flow, decentralized challenges are more likely to innovate tactically than are more bureaucratically structured and ideologically rigid challenges.

A decentralized challenge, however, requires a sufficient degree of coordination and aggregation. Umbrella organizations or federative structures are useful in this regard, as they may facilitate the brokering of diverse groups, promote the flow of information and the aggregation of resources, coordinate local networks and struggles into national political challenges, and magnify the resources and power of a challenge. Umbrella organizations or federative structures also facilitate the forging of broad alliances of diverse groups that are necessary for effective campaigns of protest and noncooperation.

The resilience and leverage of an unarmed struggle may also be increased through an ability to implement actions from all three methods of nonviolent action. Of course the level of repression constrains the ability of challengers to implement collective action, but not, as discussed previously, in a deterministic manner. Similarly, the mix of methods of nonviolent action implemented is not a linear function of the degree of repression. The implementation of a diverse range of actions across the various methods of nonviolent action diffuses the state's repression, thereby lessening its effectiveness. Incorporating multiple methods of nonviolent action also makes it easier for the challengers to shift the emphasis from one set of methods to another when the state focuses its repressive capacities on a particular set of actions. Especially important is the ability to shift to methods of dispersion when heightened repression makes the implementation of methods of concentration more risky.

The resilience of a challenge may also be increased through tactical innovation. When the state adapts to and counters certain methods, the challengers must innovate to keep the authorities off balance and prevent the challenge from stagnating. As mentioned earlier, tactical innovation is more likely to occur when challengers are organized as decentralized networks rather than hierarchies. Implementing a mix of methods of nonviolent action increases the probability of tactical innovation resulting from novel recombinants of actions. Since tactical innovation occurs on the margins of existing repertoires, the more expansive the margins, as represented by the use or knowledge of multiple actions from various methods, the greater the likelihood of permutation and innovation.

The more resilient a challenge, the greater the likelihood that it will be able to mobilize the withdrawal of support or generate pressure against the state through the networks upon which the state depends for its resources and legitimacy. The withdrawal of cooperation from key sectors of society upon which the state depends is crucial for undermining state power. More often than not, a challenge must also contribute to the mobilization of pressure against the state through third parties tied to the state through dependence relations, either from within the society or from abroad.

South Africa

In South Africa, the United Democratic Front (UDF) acted as an umbrella organization coordinating diverse local struggles into an effective national anti-apartheid struggle. Its goal was to engage in a coordinated political struggle against the apartheid regime rather than to develop a single "correct" ideological stance; thus an oppositional consciousness was cultivated, which facilitated the mobilization of a broad base. Leadership was devolved to local levels, which facilitated the resilience of the challenge when more prominent leaders were arrested or killed. The UDF incorporated a wide range of actions across the three methods of nonviolent action and responded innovatively to government repression (see Table 2 in chapter 3). Methods of dispersion, such as stayaways and boycotts, were innovative responses to the increased repression that targeted methods of concentration, such as public rallies and protest demonstrations. Despite the extreme intensification of repression during the states of emergency, the challenge remained resilient due to its decentralized structure, its ability to shift from one set of methods to another, and its tactical innovation.

The implementation of social movement unionism, which combined noninstitutional with institutional political action, enhanced the resilience of the Congress of South African Trade Unions (COSATU), inhibited the labor movement from being co-opted into the state's industrial relations apparatus, and permitted it to pursue political as well as economic objectives. The federated relations between the UDF and COSATU, whereby each organization remained independent of the other while pursuing coordinated action against the state, enhanced the resilience of the struggle as well. For example, when the state directed its repression at the activities of the UDF during the second state of emergency, COSATU took the lead in the challenge to apartheid by organizing and implementing the Mass Democratic Movement.

The rejection of political reforms by nonwhites and their protests against the state directly undermined the state's attempts to legitimate its racist rule and control the political situation. The resilience of the challenge in response to the brutal states of emergency subsequently stripped the regime of legitimacy, contributed to the condemnation of the apartheid regime by third parties, and triggered increased international sanctions. The labor movement directly undermined the regime through strikes and slowdowns due to the state's dependence on black labor, and it also contributed to the flight of foreign capital. Moreover, the boycott of white businesses, in addition to methods of noncooperation implemented by the labor movement, made it clear to capitalists that the apartheid system had to be reformed, driving a wedge between capitalists and the state and promoting divisions among the political elite.

The Philippines

In the Philippines, two broad-based organizations emerged to coordinate unarmed struggles against Marcos—the Bagong Alyansang Makabayan (New Nationalist Alliance, or Bayan) and the United Democratic Opposition (UNIDO). Bayan acted as an umbrella organization, coordinating the activities of a diverse array of progressive organizations promoting the interests of women, peasants, and workers. Bayan encompassed the Kilusang May Uno (KMU, First of May Movement) as well, which, similar to COSATU in South Africa, engaged in the strategy of social movement unionism. UNIDO, which represented the interests of the traditional political elite opposition and their middle-class followers, acted as both a political party and a social movement organization, engaging in nonviolent action outside of institutional channels as well as electoral activity. Both strands of the anti-Marcos challenge implemented a range of methods and responded innovatively to government repression (see Table 3 in chapter 3). Similar to the stay-away in South Africa, the *welgang bayan* (general strike) in the Philippines was a method of dispersion that diffused and limited the effectiveness of state repression, thereby contributing to the movement's resilience.

The *welgang bayan*, the implementation of civil disobedience, and the rejection of the official election results undermined the state's ability to control the political situation. These actions, along with the growing armed communist insurgency in the countryside, promoted capital flight, contributed to regime defection, and led to the diplomatic intervention of the United States, which severed its ties to Marcos and threw its weight behind UNIDO.

Nepal

The people power movement in Nepal was coordinated and implemented through a federation of the Nepali Congress Party (NC), the United Left Front (ULF), and the United National People's Movement (UNPM). These diverse groups forged a working agreement to coordinate their struggle against the regime while remaining independent of each other. They developed an oppositional consciousness that allowed them to set aside their ideological differences and facilitated their collaboration. The challengers implemented a range of actions across the three methods of nonviolent action and innovatively responded to government repression through techniques such as blackouts and lightning demonstrations, thereby increasing the challenge's resilience (see Table 6 in chapter 5).

The resilience of the challenge in the face of repression led to regime defection as members of the *panchayat* became dismayed with the violence being used against unarmed demonstrators. *Bandhs* (strikes) directly undermined a regime that had already been destabilized by India's refusal to renew the Trade and Transit treaty. These actions, combined with the pressure mobilized by the pro-democracy movement against the state through the international donor networks upon which the regime depended to undermine the state's resources, legitimacy, and ability to rule, were effective in overthrowing the regime.

Thailand

The challenge to the military in Thailand was spearheaded by the Campaign for Popular Democracy (CPD), an umbrella organization that coordinated the oppositional activities of a diverse network of student, women's, workers', human rights, development, environmental, and engaged Buddhist organizations. The resilience of the challenge was enhanced by its decentralized structure and tactical innovation. For example, local groups continually reassembled to engage in public protest despite the arrest of hundreds of movement leaders and organizers and the killing or injuring of scores of activists. While the Thai challenge relied primarily on protest demonstrations—a more limited range of actions than was implemented during the course of the unarmed insurrections in South Africa, the Philippines, or Nepal (see Table 7 in chapter 5)—this challenge remained resilient during three days of violent repression, thereby catalyzing the support of third parties, which tipped the balance of power in its favor. King Bhumipol Adulyadej intervened in the conflict, ordering the military to cease the repression to prevent the conflict from escalating and to restore order to the kingdom. The capitalists and members of the middle classes sided with the pro-democracy challenge because they opposed the reversal of economic liberalization and, more immediately, because the violent repression of unarmed demonstrators exposed the illegitimacy of the regime and threatened foreign investment.

Thus, the four successful unarmed insurrections remained resilient in the face of violent repression, mobilized the withdrawal of support from the state, and generated sufficient leverage against the state to tip the balance of power in their favor. Sustained disruption and the undermining of state power created or exacerbated elite divisions and catalyzed the support of third parties upon which the state depended for resources and legitimacy. By contrast, the unarmed insurrections in Burma and China failed to promote political change due to their lack of resilience and their inability to generate sufficient leverage.

Burma and China

In Burma, during the short but intense period of organizing and protest prior to the military crackdown on September 18, 1988, protest demonstrations and general strikes implemented by the pro-democracy movement directly undermined the regime to the point that it was on the verge of collapse. However, no umbrella organization emerged that was capable of coordinating the diverse strands of resistance or organizing a parallel government. The National League for Democracy (NLD), a broad-based opposition organization, emerged only after the state had suppressed the unarmed insurrection and channeled opposition activity into tightly controlled electoral campaigning leading up to the May 1990 elections. In contrast to the people power movement in the Philippines, which continued to implement methods of noncooperation in addition to participation in electoral activity, the challenge in Burma, whose supporters had implemented a wide range of nonviolent actions before the military crackdown, was primarily limited to electoral campaigning after the crackdown (see Table 4 in chapter 4). Unlike the situation in the Philippines, where the movement could challenge the regime's refusal to honor the election results, the demobilization of the Burmese mass movement foreclosed this option.

The leverage generated by the challenge in Burma was also constrained by Burma's international isolation. Citizens were not integrated into transnational networks to the extent that they were, for example, in the Philippines, Nepal, and Thailand, thereby inhibiting the generation of third-party support for the challenge or pressure against the state.[2] Due to the regime's isolation, no foreign government was in a position to effectively pressure the Burmese government during the course of the unarmed insurrection.

As in Burma, the pro-democracy movement in China lacked an umbrella organization that could effectively coordinate the activities of students and other aggrieved sectors. The challengers in China also failed to implement a range of actions, depending almost entirely on methods of concentration, such as protest demonstrations and a mass hunger strike and occupation of

Tiananmen Square. Its failure to shift to methods of dispersion diminished its ability to remain resilient once repression intensified.

Moreover, the Chinese pro-democracy movement failed to generate sufficient leverage against the state, either directly or indirectly. Campaigns of noncooperation, which were fundamental to undermining state power in South Africa, the Philippines, and Nepal, were absent, and the Chinese state was autonomous enough to effectively deflect the international pressure that was mobilized. As in Burma, citizens in China were not integrated into transnational networks that could have promoted pressure against the regime.[3] Although the international media that were in China at the time of the student movement to cover Gorbachev's historic visit publicized the movement to the world and resources for the pro-democracy flowed into China from Hong Kong and from Chinese overseas, the resources were not converted into effective pressure against the state due to the movement's organizational deficits.

Should the Burmese and Chinese cases be taken as examples of the inevitable futility of unarmed insurrections against Leninist regimes that are willing to counter a challenge with military force? Although there are problems inherent to mobilizing and sustaining challenges in communist regimes where the government attempts to monopolize political space, unarmed insurrections in similar contexts have contributed to political transitions, so failure is not inevitable. Why might this be so? A brief examination of the Polish unarmed insurrection in the 1980s and a comparison of that challenge with those in Burma and China seems useful in shedding some light on the issue.[4]

Protest against the state by disgruntled Polish workers erupted in 1956, 1970, and 1976, with each episode following a similar logic. Workers struck, left their workplaces, and marched to the offices of party officials to demonstrate. They were met by security forces who responded with violence, and in turn some workers rioted, leading to an intensification of repression and the quelling of the protests without any significant reform. Following the events in 1976, the Komitet Obrony Robotników (KOR, Workers Defense Committee) emerged to provide assistance to the workers and their families who had participated in the protests. More significantly, KOR began forging a strategy of developing an oppositional civil society. This strategy entailed the transformation of society in a democratic direction, regardless of whether there was state reform. The goal was not to seize state power, but rather to forge an autonomous civil society so that the opposition could subsequently engage the state from a stronger position. The strategy was implemented through methods of creative nonviolent intervention, and wherever possible, state domination was resisted by boycotting official institutions as well. By encouraging the withdrawal of support from the state and creating alternatives, the movement mobilized people into activity that was independent of the state and promoted solidarity. Creating parallel structures, especially an underground press, was crucial for building an oppositional civil society and sustaining the movement.

In August 1980, a strike wave broke out in cities along the Baltic coast and spread to other parts of the country. The strike wave of 1980 was significant for a number of reasons. First, the workers made political demands as well as economic ones, as they sought the legalization of trade unions independent of the state and the relaxation of state censorship. Second, the workers were in a much better position to sustain their protests in the repressive context due to the oppositional society that had been forged over the previous four years. Third, drawing on the lessons of 1956, 1970, and 1976, when workers had been met with repression when they took to the streets, the workers innovated by prosecuting the strikes from their occupied workplaces instead. The walls and fences surrounding the factories and workplaces provided protection against repression and infiltration by government agents, and the workplace was turned into a democratic forum that enhanced the worker's sense of unity and solidarity. Strike leaders were directly elected by the workers, and the leaders who emerged became part of the Międzyzakładowy Komitet Strajkowy (MKS, Interfactory Strike Committee), which coordinated workers across the country under the banner of Solidarity.

As a result of strike activity in the Baltic cities of Gdańsk, Gdynia, Szczecin, and Jastrzębie, as well as in the province of Silesia, the government was nonviolently coerced to sign a series of accords legalizing autonomous trade unions and liberalizing censorship laws. The massive strike wave ended only when the government extended the agreements to the entire country. Thus, through the implementation of creative nonviolent intervention and methods of noncooperation such as strikes and boycotts, the movement was able to break the state's monopoly over civil society and politics and force the government to accept independent trade unions and a reduction of state censorship.

The Solidarity movement was characterized by a decentralized organizational structure that was sufficiently organized to coordinate workers. Moreover, independent associations organized by students and peasants emerged, such as the Independent Student Association and Rural Solidarity, and aligned themselves with Solidarity. Significantly, the movement had limited goals at first, namely the recognition of independent trade unions and the liberalization of censorship laws. Once these were accepted by the state, the leverage of the challenge increased and it was in a better position to press for further reforms.

In the months following the accords, conflict ensued between the Communist Party and the Solidarity movement over the interpretation and implementation of the agreed-upon concessions. The government began to undermine and pull back from the accords, which in turn led to a series of strikes and threats of strikes by Solidarity. The Polish government was threatened by the emergence of autonomous organizations and by freedom of speech, and it responded with an intensification of repression against the unarmed dissidents in order to hold onto power. Much as would happen in Burma in September 1988, the Polish government manufactured a power vacuum in late 1981 and created a sense of chaos and impending doom, leaving the country in such disarray that the military was then called in to "rescue" the country and impose "law and order." Martial law was implemented in December 1981.

The Solidarity movement was severely weakened by martial law, but not eliminated. Despite the arrest of the top leaders, the Solidarity movement remained resilient during the imposition of martial law and was able to survive through a decentralized and loosely organized underground. The strategy developed in the 1970s of forging an oppositional civil society permitted the movement to weather martial law. While overt strikes were crushed, as the government now responded to occupied workplaces with force, the challenge continued through methods of creative nonviolent intervention. The underground press thrived and maintained the oppositional civil society, and a point was reached at which the civil society had matured too much to allow a return to the past. By September 1986, the government finally recognized this and was compelled to declare a general amnesty, launch a series of meaningful reforms, and recognize the political opposition as a fundamental part of a stable political system. Reforms continued through 1988, and in 1989 Solidarity candidates won a spectacular victory in the first open elections in Poland since World War II.

Thus, while there were parallels in the contexts of the challenges, the strategy of the Solidarity movement in Poland differed from that of the struggles in Burma and China in a number of significant ways. First, the struggle in Poland occurred over a number of years, from the mid-1970s through the 1980s, gradually forging an oppositional civil society through boycotts and methods of creative nonviolent intervention. The spaces created were crucial for launching effective campaigns of noncooperation and for sustaining the movement when repression intensified after martial law was imposed. In contrast, the pro-democracy movements in Burma and China represented nascent movements toward the emergence of civil society. The challenges lacked preexisting organizational infrastructures, and during a few months of sustained collective action they were unable to build them sufficiently to endure in the face of intensified repression. Neither challenge developed an organization like Solidarity that was capable of aggregating diverse strands of the opposition and effectively coordinating collective action.

Second, while the challenge in Poland relied on methods of noncooperation, such as strikes, and on methods of dispersion, such as boycotting state institutions and creating alternatives to the state, the challenges in Burma and China relied to a large degree on methods of concentration; on methods of protest and persuasion, such as marches and protest demonstrations; and on methods of disruptive nonviolent intervention, such as the occupation of public places. The methods of concentration were not resilient in the face of violent repression, and the lack of sustained campaigns of noncooperation limited the leverage that the challengers could generate.

Third, the position of the workers in the Polish economy provided them with the leverage they needed to force concessions from the state through campaigns of noncooperation. Since the state was dependent upon the workers, the sustained collective withholding of their labor forced the state to recognize their demands to organize independently. In contrast, the movements in Burma and China were spearheaded by students, a social group with less potential leverage than workers. No organization emerged in Burma or China that was capable of effectively forging ties between students, workers, and peasants.

Fourth, the Solidarity movement had clear and limited goals, namely the state's recognition of autonomous trade unions and the liberalization of censorship laws. By contrast, the movement in China was characterized by unclear goals and a premature escalation of demands without the consolidation of any gains. Likewise, in Burma no gains were effectively consolidated before repression intensified.

Fifth, the resilience of the Solidarity movement in Poland bought the movement time, as divisions within the political elite subsequently emerged and the international political context shifted to one more favorable to the movement in the middle to late 1980s. By contrast, neither the Burmese nor the Chinese movement remained resilient long enough for the political context to shift to one that was more favorable.

Where a government attempts to monopolize civil society and the state and to penetrate potentially autonomous spheres, as in Burma or China, unarmed insurrections are unlikely to succeed unless they are resilient and disruptive enough to trigger regime defection. When elite or military defection is not forthcoming, challengers should focus on boycotting state institutions and forging an oppositional sphere independent of the state through methods of creative nonviolent intervention. Doing so will enhance the environment so that future overt collective action may be more resilient and powerful. The oppositional civil society forged in Poland prior to its successful challenge to state power suggests a model in this regard.

Unarmed Insurrections and Social Movement Theory

Analysis of the six unarmed insurrections in this study suggests a number of areas where social movement theory is underspecified. These are discussed below.

Structural and Perceived Opportunities

The political opportunity framework assumes that there is a close connection between structural and perceived opportunities. Contrary to these assumptions, however, there may be instances where structural and perceived opportunities are mismatched. Charles Kurzman argues that in the case of the Iranian Revolution in 1979, there was a mismatch between the two, as challengers perceived opportunities despite the absence of objective structural opportunities (Kurzman 1996).[5] Although the shah's regime remained strong and its capacities for repression were not diminished, the challengers' calculations about political opportunities and constraints were based on the growth of the opposition rather than on the objective strength of the state. People feared repression and the consequences of engaging in collective action, but they perceived that constraints on participation were decreasing as the challenge grew more widespread. Thus, Kurzman concludes that perceived opportunities may affect the mobilization and outcomes of social movements independent of structural opportunities.

Although the mismatch between perceived and structural opportunities promoted political change in Iran, the mismatch in China contributed to the challenge's demise. In China, there was a perception among the student challengers that divisions existed among the political elite. However, what appeared to the students to be structural elite divisions were merely differences among elites over how the state should respond to the movement. There were no divisions among the political elite over the supremacy of the Communist Party or the basic formula for political rule. According to Dingxin Zhao, "Rumors about governmental divisions gave people hope and encouraged them to continue fighting. . . . Had people known that the information around them was unfounded rumor and that the top state elites had consolidated even before martial law had begun, they would have thought that any efforts at resistance were risky and futile" (Zhao 2001, 320–21). Thus, perceived elite divisions lowered the perceived risk of mobilization and promoted the escalation of demands, but the calculations that led to this strategy were based on misperceptions about the coherence of the political elite rather than on objective conditions. Given the consequences of activists' perceptions about political opportunities and constraints on the trajectories of social movements that can result from the potential mismatch between perceived and objective opportunities, surprisingly little attention has been paid to this issue by scholars of social movements.

National and International Opportunities

The overwhelming focus of social movement scholarship has been on national political opportunities. Nevertheless, political opportunities operate at various levels, from the local to the global (McAdam 1996; Miller 2000). In this section I illustrate the importance of the international political context.

The international context may influence political contention directly by shaping the balance of power within countries or indirectly through its impact on national political structures (Jenkins and Schock 1992). The degree and nature of external influence are shaped by the level and types of a country's interdependencies with transnational actors. Here I note three levels and types of relations: (1) the extent to which a country is integrated with or isolated from the international system, (2) the extent to which a country is dependent upon another country, and (3) the nature of economic relations with other countries. First, the more integrated a state is into the international system of states and the more integrated its populace is into transnational networks, the more likely it will be that foreign states and transnational social movements will be in a position to provide support for a challenge or effectively pressure the state for change. Countries that are more isolated may be better positioned to resist international pressures for democratization. Second, states that are more dependent on external support are more susceptible to foreign influence in their domestic politics. In contrast, the less dependent a state, the less impact foreign pressure will have on its domestic politics. Third, the nature of economic ties to the international system has consequences for political contention within countries. Countries whose economies are characterized by export-oriented industrialization, for example, are more susceptible to pressures for economic and political liberalization than are countries whose economies are oriented toward providing natural resources to other countries.

A brief comparison of Burma and Thailand, two contiguous countries where unarmed insurrections had opposite outcomes, illustrates the contrasting effects of the three dimensions. First, Burma was much less integrated into the international system both economically and politically than Thailand, so Burma was less susceptible to international pressures for political liberalization.[6] Since 1962, Burma had pursued autarkic economic policies that had not only had negative consequences for its economic development, but had also shielded the state from pressures to conform to international norms and inhibited the society from developing ties to transnational social movement organizations.[7]

Second, the historical dependence of the Thai military-bureaucratic elite on the United States contrasts with Burma's lack of dependence on a foreign country. As the Thai regime saw at the end of the Cold War, political dependence can be a double-edged sword. The uncritical support provided by the United States to the Thai military-bureaucratic elite during the Cold War declined precipitously at the end of the Cold War. In contrast, Burma maintained a strictly neutral position during the Cold War, and it was not dependent on any foreign power whose shifting foreign policies would have had a significant impact on the internal dynamics of Burmese politics.

Third, Thailand's export-oriented industrialization contrasted with Burma's autarkic policies before 1988 and its increased role as a supplier of natural resources to other countries after 1988. Thailand's export-oriented economic growth during the 1980s had facilitated the development of internationally oriented capitalists and members of the middle classes who had developed a degree of independence from the state and supported economic and political liberalization. Prior to the 1990s, Burma's relative isolation inhibited the ability of foreign actors to directly influence political contention within Burma. Countries that did have some leverage at the time of the unarmed insurrection in 1988, such as Japan, which held substantial investments in Burma, did not exert effective pressure against the military regime. In the 1990s, the military regime in Burma began to open its economy by permitting foreign countries to exploit its natural resources in exchange for hard currency. Corporations from Thailand, Singapore, Malaysia, and South Korea, for example, were granted concessions to exploit Burma's timberlands, fisheries, and oil deposits. These relations with the Burmese military regime have proved profitable for the countries and corporations involved, and their economic interests would be threatened by a democratic Burma, since in a more democratic context, environmentalists would oppose the exploitation of timberlands and fishing areas, and indigenous people's groups would oppose the relocation or genocide of indigenous peoples in areas where there were explorations for oil or oil pipelines were being built. Thus, it is not to the immediate economic advantage of Burma's trading partners to promote democratization in Burma. In sum, the nature of a country's international relations, the ways in which those relations have direct implications for collective action, and how those relations shape national political opportunities need to be more clearly articulated by social movement scholars.

The Repression-Dissent Paradox

Many have noted the apparently paradoxical relationship between repression and dissent; that is, sometimes repression crushes dissent, whereas at other times it generates increased mobilization. Some suggest that the repression-dissent paradox can be resolved by locating the relationship between repression and dissent within a cycle of protest. It is maintained that repression during an ascending cycle of protest facilitates mobilization, whereas repression during a descending cycle of protest constrains mobilization. However, there are criticisms of this concept, including (1) its inability to make a clear distinction between levels of mobilization and cycles of protest and (2) the fact that actors do not necessarily know what phase of the cycle they are in.

An alternative approach to resolving the repression-dissent paradox is to consider the broader configuration of opportunities in which a challenge occurs (e.g., Osa and Corduneanu-Huci 2003; Schock 1999). For example, in both the Philippines and Burma, violent and indiscriminate repression decreased the legitimacy of the regime and facilitated the mobilization of collective action. Yet in Burma, indiscriminate repression at a later point in time also had the effect of suppressing the movement. How can we account for the apparently paradoxical relationship between repression and dissent in Burma? The relationship must be examined relative to the broader political context, as well as to the characteristics of the challenge.

At an early stage of the people power movement in Burma, during the summer of 1988, violent and often indiscriminate repression had the effect of mobilizing more people to join the movement. Mobilization in response to repression was facilitated by an apparent division within the regime over holding a referendum on multiparty democracy and by the rise of an alternative print media and the workers' takeover of the state newspaper. Later, however, by mid-September 1988, repression had the effect of demobilizing the movement. By mid-September, the regime had reorganized and reunified, it had reimposed censorship, and there were no divisions in the military apparatus. When the state reasserted control over the press and information flows, the movement was demobilized, suggesting that the capacity to sustain a challenging movement in the face of repression depends significantly on the movement's ability to produce and receive accurate information.

Thus, in both the Philippines and Burma, violent and indiscriminate repression facilitated mobilization when it was combined with elite divisions and the flow of alternative information. However, as illustrated in the Burmese case, when violent and indiscriminate repression occurred in combination with a closure of elite divisions and a lack of information flows, its effect was to demobilize the movement. This suggests that the effect of repression on dissent may be at least partly a function of the configuration of opportunities in which it occurs.

In addition to the configurations of opportunities, social movement scholars must also consider the characteristics and actions of challengers when addressing the relationship between repression and dissent. As noted in chapter 2, a major problem with the repression-dissent literature is that challengers, especially those implementing nonviolent action, are generally assumed to be passive objects and powerless in the face of regime repression. As a result, scholars neglect to consider how the characteristics and actions of a challenge affects the repression-dissent relationship. Whether repression crushes dissent or promotes mobilization depends on a variety of conditions other than the level of repression, some of which may be at least within partial control of challenging groups, such as how the challenge is organized, movement strategy, the range of methods and mix of actions implemented, the targets of dissent, and communication within the movement and with third parties.

Violence and Radical Flank Effects

As discussed in chapter 2, the radical flank effect is an important social movement dynamic that, unfortunately, has received scant scholarly attention. A positive radical flank effect occurs when the leverage of "moderate" challengers is strengthened by the presence of a so-called radical wing that has more extreme goals or incorporates violent strategies. The presence of a radical wing makes the moderates' strategies or demands appear more reasonable, and a radical flank may create crises that are resolved to the moderates' advantage. A negative radical flank effect occurs when the activities of a radical wing undermines the leverage of moderates, as the existence of radicals threatens the ability of moderates to invoke third-party support and discredits the entire movement's activities and goals.

All six unarmed insurrections examined in this study were radical in terms of their political demands. That is, they all pursued a fundamental change in the formula for political rule that directly threatened the interests of the ruling elite. Thus, the radical flank concept is more relevant here with regard to strategies than to goals. Although isolated incidences of violence occurred in China, Thailand, and Nepal,[8] no groups were engaged in an armed struggle with the state, and it is unlikely that a radical flank effect was in operation. A radical flank effect could possibly have occurred in South Africa, the Philippines, and Burma, where armed struggles operated contemporaneously with the unarmed insurrections.

In the Philippines, a positive radical flank effect did seem to occur as the growing armed insurgency in the countryside promoted regime defection and increased the willingness of the United States to break with Marcos and support the democratic opposition. Thus, while the New People's Army (NPA) was unable to topple the state through violence, it did promote a context that increased the leverage of the democratic opposition. Burma also had armed insurgents operating at the same time of the unarmed insurrection, namely the ethnic insurgents in the peripheral areas of the country, but their activities do not seem to have had any influence on the trajectory of the pro-democracy struggle. In fact, the military regime seemed grateful that students fled the cities to join the armed insurgents in the jungles, where the comparative advantage of the state was much greater. Thus, a positive radical flank effect does not seem to have occurred in Burma.

Of the six cases examined in this study, the struggle in South Africa was the one in which the role of violence was undoubtedly the most complex. Whereas the armed insurgencies in the Philippines and Burma represented strands of resistance apart from the unarmed insurrections, the armed actions of the African National Congress (ANC) were considered part of and complementary to the struggles being waged, largely through unarmed methods, in the townships. The anti-apartheid struggle adopted the frames and rhetoric forged by the ANC through many years of resistance, and these promoted mobilization throughout South Africa. The armed attacks on state military installations and acts of "armed propaganda" had a symbolic importance and boosted the morale of anti-apartheid activists, and armed activists forged underground networks that were subsequently used to funnel resources to the unarmed insurrections in the townships (Seidman 2001). Thus, although the armed wing of the ANC was never a military threat to the apartheid regime, it did play a significant role in promoting the mobilization of the urban unarmed insurrection.[9]

Although violence never threatened the regime, which held the comparative advantage with regard to the means of violence, violence sometimes played a role in promoting mobilization into campaigns of nonviolent action in the townships. During the course of the South African struggle, instances of coercive mobilization occurred,[10] alleged collaborators were murdered, often through the grisly act of "necklacing" (setting people afire by placing burning tires around their necks); and battles broke out between armed security forces and youths armed with stones, Molotov cocktails, and occasionally guns. To the extent that these promoted mobilization into campaigns of nonviolent action that would not otherwise have occurred, these violent actions increased the power of the anti-apartheid movement. However, any increases in mobilization resulting from violence must be weighed against the loss of support of nonwhites and third parties that might have been forthcoming if these acts of violence had not occurred. Moreover, the energy and resources spent on actions that were not effective in undermining the regime due to the regime's superiority in the methods of violence represented spent energy and resources that could have been channeled into methods more effective in challenging the state. As discussed in chapter 3, segments of the opposition realized the strategic virtue of methods of nonviolent action and also realized that state power was more likely to be undermined through nonviolent action than through violence. While recognizing the symbolic role of violence and violent rhetoric, they attempted to channel the actions of militant youth into more strategically effective campaigns of nonviolent action. Nevertheless, there were times during the course of the anti-apartheid movement when violent and nonviolent action acted in a synergetic manner. Clearly, however, violence by itself was incapable of overturning the apartheid regime, and the anti-apartheid struggle could not have succeeded without broad-based campaigns of nonviolent action.

A brief comparison of the South African struggle in the townships with the Palestinian Intifada—the struggle against Israeli occupation of the West Bank and the Gaza Strip from 1987 to 1990—might shed some additional light on the role of violence accompanying an unarmed insurrection. In both cases, methods of nonviolent action were taken up for pragmatic reasons rather than due to any moral revulsion against violence. Also, in addition to unarmed methods of resistance, both struggles were characterized by instances of coercive mobilization, the murder of alleged collaborators, and the use of mostly nonlethal weapons against the oppressors. In each case, there existed a separate armed wing—the ANC and the Palestinian Liberation Organization (PLO)—that were never military threats to the South African and Israeli regimes, respectively, but did have a symbolic importance and boosted the morale of unarmed activists through their activities. Yet in both cases, the unarmed insurrections emerged somewhat independently from the ANC and the PLO, respectively, and were carried out by the people who directly experienced oppression in their daily lives in the townships and the occupied territories rather than by an armed vanguard.

Despite these similarities, the outcomes of the two unarmed insurrections differed. The crucial difference was that the anti-apartheid movement exploited the South African state's dependence relations to exert leverage against the regime, whereas the Intifada failed to exploit the Israeli regime's dependence relations. As discussed in chapter 3, the challengers in South Africa, largely through methods of nonviolent action, were able to exploit the apartheid regime's dependence upon black labor and upon the acceptance of political reforms by nonwhites, and it was able to activate third parties that used their leverage to pressure the regime for political change. By contrast, the Israeli state was not dependent upon Palestinians in the occupied territories, and the Intifada failed to mobilize the third-party support that would have been necessary to alter the policies of the Israeli regime.[11]

Whereas the South African economy was dependent upon black labor, the Israeli economy was not dependent upon the labor of Palestinians. The leverage of Palestinians who worked in Israel was weak, especially when compared to the leverage of black laborers in South Africa. Moreover, the leverage of Palestinian workers decreased in the late 1980s as an influx of Jewish immigrants from the Soviet Union decreased the number of jobs available to Palestinians in Israel. The dependence relations that were so adroitly exploited by the anti-apartheid movement in South Africa were absent for Palestinians, and in fact, the Palestinians were to a large extent economically dependent on Israel for jobs, goods, and services. Moreover, the economic base of Palestinian society was underdeveloped by the Israeli occupation, and the Israelis created obstacles to prevent the development of indigenous sources of employment in the occupied territories. This prevented the Palestinian economy from developing to a level where it could provide employment for Palestinians. It also limited the impact of any efforts to boycott Israeli-produced goods within the occupied territories, since Israel was the only source of many of the basic necessities of life within the occupied territories. Thus, the probability that an unarmed insurrection would end Israeli occupation and oppression was and is unlikely to the extent that the occupied territories remain economically dependent on Israel and lack the indigenous economic base necessary to sustain such a struggle.

Given these structural relations, the political fates of unarmed insurrections such as the Intifada depend crucially upon the challengers' ability to mobilize the support of third parties with leverage against the target state. One way for the Palestinians to increase their indirect leverage against Israel is to promote political divisions within Israel and cultivate the support of Israeli citizens for the Palestinian cause. Another way of doing this is to mobilize pressure from abroad, particularly from the United States, which has the leverage to vitally affect the options open to Israel. However, the Intifada failed to mobilize the support of crucial third parties, such as Israeli citizens or the U.S. government. Thus, the extent to which violence increased mobilization into the Intifada must be weighed against the potential support that was alienated by violence, from segments of the Palestinian population as well as from third parties.

Thus, while the unarmed insurrection in South Africa can be distinguished from the other five cases examined in this study with regard to the role of violence in the struggle, a comparison of the anti-apartheid movement with the Palestinian Intifada, which was similar to the anti-apartheid struggle in that its campaigns of nonviolent action were sometimes accompanied by violence, suggests that it was the ability of the anti-apartheid struggle to exploit the state's dependence relations and mobilize the support of third parties—largely through methods of nonviolent action rather than through violence—that promoted a political transition. By contrast, in the case of the Palestinian Intifada, the state of Israel was not dependent upon the Palestinians in the occupied territories, and the Intifada failed to mobilize the third-party support that would be necessary to end Israeli occupation and the oppression of Palestinians. Thus, the key variable for the success of an unarmed insurrection is not the amount of violence that accompanies it, but rather the ability to remain resilient in a repressive context and to increase its leverage relative to the state, either by directly severing the state's sources of support or by mobilizing the crucial support of third parties that have leverage against the target state.

More generally, an uncritical view of the power of violence is called into question by the fact that many nondemocratic regimes provoke and welcome violence, as it makes their own repression appear more justifiable and legitimate. Moreover, because states typically have the comparative advantage with regard to the means of violence, they prefer to deal with challengers who confront them on their own terms. The point here is not to suggest that violence is not effective in promoting political change (obviously, in many instances it is), but rather to suggest that the potential of nonviolent action for promoting change in nondemocratic contexts has often been dismissed, overlooked, or underestimated, and that an unarmed insurrection does not have to depend on the existence of a radical flank or the threat of violence in order to succeed. The power of unarmed insurrections, it seems, comes from challenging the state in an alternative manner rather than through the violent methods of the state. Thus, although positive radical flank effects have opened up political space and contributed to the success of some unarmed insurrections, they are not necessary for unarmed insurrections to succeed, and in some cases a negative radical flank effect may occur in which violence undermines the power of the unarmed resistance.

Many have romanticized and idealized the role of violence and armed struggle. It is uncritically assumed that violence is the engine of political transformation and that violence operates behind any successful non-institutional challenge, especially in nondemocratic contexts. Yet it may be the power of disruption and severing the oppressor from its bases of support rather than violence per se that facilitate a successful insurrection. Obviously these can be achieved through violent methods, but they can be achieved through methods of nonviolent action as well. The use of nonviolent methods increased significantly over the course of the twentieth century, especially over its last two decades. As more people recognize the power of nonviolent action and more knowledge is generated about what it is and how it operates, there is reason to believe that nonviolent action will be used with greater frequency and effectiveness to resist oppression.

Responding to and Creating Opportunities

Although most would agree that there is a constantly evolving process by which movements respond to and shape the political context, social movement scholarship has tended to focus on the former to the neglect of the latter. Not only do social movements respond to political opportunities, but they also wield power strategically to overcome constraints, thereby reshaping the political context. The tendency of social movement scholars to focus on how challengers respond to opportunities has thus resulted in an inadequate consideration of how the dynamics of collective action may recast the political context to one that is more favorable to challengers. Divisions among political or military elites, for example, may be the outcome of rather than the precondition for mass mobilization. In the Philippines (and Iran), for example, mutinies in the armed forces occurred only after a widespread protest movement emerged. Similarly, elite divisions and regime defection in South Africa, Nepal, and Thailand (and Poland) emerged or were substantially exacerbated only after the mobilization of a sustained challenge.

Although insights on the inherent leverage of the less powerful and their potential for strategically wielding power to alter political relations can be traced back to the theories of Marx and Weber,[12] contemporary social movement scholarship has tended to neglect these issues. Recent social movement scholarship has emphasized shifts in structural relations that increase the leverage of formerly powerless groups and the ideologies used by these groups to frame their struggles, but the crucial roles of strategies and tactics implemented by challengers to remain resilient in the face of repression, exploit dependence relations, and overcome constraints of the political context have received relatively less attention. In this regard, as argued throughout this study, scholars of social movements may benefit from a careful gleaning of insights from the literature on nonviolent action.

Lessons of Struggle

Speculation after the fact about what those who actively oppose oppression should have done to promote change is not a difficult task. In sharp contrast is the situation of participants in struggles against repressive states, who are constrained by their situations from acting in a manner that in hindsight an outside observer might identify as being advantageous to the struggle. The lack of information and resources, the struggle to live from one day to the next, a lifetime of socialization and indoctrination, and fear all act to constrain action. State violence or the threat of violence makes just about any social movement activity in a nondemocratic context costly and high-risk. How can anyone expect overt political action—not to mention the most efficacious overt political action—from those who lack accurate information and risk the loss of livelihood, imprisonment, torture, or death for their actions? How can a post hoc observer expect people to have acted differently given such constraints?

Nevertheless, in the six cases examined here, people *did* overcome fear, break their habitual patterns of obedience, and risk their lives to struggle against repressive regimes, and there are lessons to be learned from the actions of these courageous people. To examine what they did or did not do and to attempt to learn from their struggles seems like the most appropriate way to honor their courageousness. In fact, in instances where nonviolent action failed to contribute to political change, to learn from their struggles and apply this knowledge to future struggles is one way to ensure that their efforts were not in vain.

The success of unarmed insurrections, like that of armed ones, can never be guaranteed. Nevertheless, this should not prevent scholars from attempting to specify the strategies, actions, technologies, and characteristics of unarmed struggles that may increase the probability of their success.[13] Historically, virtually all unarmed insurrections have been improvised, and although they have produced some notable successes, the probability of success of such actions may increase if past struggles are studied and lessons are drawn from them (Ackerman and Kruegler 1994; Sharp 1973, 1990, chapter 3). Six general lessons from the perspective of the challengers that emerged from the cases in this study are discussed in the following paragraphs. These are based on the assumption that the outcomes of struggles are influenced by aspects of challenges that are subject to human choice and agency, as well as by structural relations outside the recognition or control of individuals. These lessons should be taken not as a "blueprint" or "cookbook" for challenging oppression, but rather as working assumptions based on the six unarmed insurrections examined here that are subject to refinement or refutation based on the analysis of additional cases or more detailed analyses of the cases examined in this study. It is assumed that these lessons apply "all else being equal."

Clear and Limited Goals

According to Peter Ackerman and Christopher Kruegler, one of the principles of strategic nonviolent conflict is to formulate functional objectives (Ackerman and Kruegler 1994, 24–26). That is, the goals of movements should be well chosen, clearly defined, and understood by all parties to the conflict. The goals should be compelling and vital to the interests of the challenging group, and they should attract the widest possible support, both within society and externally. As Ackerman and Kruegler state, "The concept of 'freedom' is inspiring to millions. As an ultimate strategic objective, though, it is not highly functional because it lacks specificity. The legalization of independent trade unions (as in Poland in 1980), on the other hand, is the very model of a clear and functional objective" (Ackerman and Kruegler 1994, 24). Precise goals give direction to the power activated by a movement and inhibit the dispersion of mobilized energies and resources. Moreover, clear goals enable a movement to accurately gauge the extent to which its actions are bringing about the desired change, thus permitting an alteration in its actions if necessary.

The more focused the goals of the challenging movement, the greater the likelihood of success. The four successful movements examined here all had clear goals: a return to multiparty democracy in the Philippines and Nepal, an extension of democratic relations to all races in South Africa, and a more liberal constitution and the removal of an unelected general from office in Thailand. By contrast, the goals of the movement in China were ambiguous and shifting, and there was no clear consensus among the students as to what the goals of the movement were. Goals ranged from the recognition of autonomous student unions to the elimination of government censorship to ending party corruption to the implementation of a democratic system. Of course clear goals by themselves do not ensure success. The anti-regime challenge in Burma had the clear goal of a return to multiparty democracy following Ne Win's proposal of a multiparty referendum, but its lack of organization as well as the political context limited its ability to attain its goal.

Oppositional Consciousness and Temporary Organizations

Whereas totalizing ideologies and permanent vanguard parties seem more suited to the tasks of overthrowing a state through violence and ruling society from above, oppositional consciousness and temporary organizations seem more suited to rolling back authoritarian relations and building more democratic and just relations through nonviolent action from below. Oppositional consciousness is open-ended, nontotalizing, and respectful of diversity, and it facilitates the mobilization of a broad-based opposition. Widespread resistance is significant in that there is a greater distribution of the risks involved in engaging in collective action, it is more difficult for the state to focus its repressive apparatus on a particular group or organization, and campaigns of noncooperation need broad-based support to succeed. Mobilizing through oppositional consciousness has consequences for organizing as well. It rejects permanent, centralized organizations and vanguard parties, opting for united front politics, shifting alliances, and temporary organizations that engage in struggles as situations arise.

The United Democratic Front (UDF) in South Africa, for example, was formed in 1983 to aggregate local struggles and coordinate a national opposition to apartheid. In an effort to avoid ideological debates and mobilize the largest base possible, it adopted an oppositional consciousness. Once it succeeded in forcing the government to negotiate a transition to democracy, it was disbanded. The Campaign for Popular Democracy (CPD) in Thailand provides another example of a temporary organization that incorporated oppositional consciousness in order to mobilize a broad base and then disbanded after its goals were met. The CPD that was formed in 1991 in order to promote the anti-military challenge was actually the CPD's third incarnation. It had originally been formed in 1981 to struggle against the military's attempt to extend certain undemocratic clauses in the 1978 constitution that were to expire in 1982. Once the CPD won the campaign, it dissolved. In 1983 constitutional issues emerged again. Again the CPD was organized to protest clauses in the constitution that permitted civil servants and members of the military to concurrently hold political positions. Once the campaign succeeded, the CPD was again dissolved (Callahan 1998, 127–28).[14]

Multiple Channels of Resistance

Participation in a nondemocratic regime's channels of political participation is not likely to succeed unless combined with noninstitutional pressure. In the Philippines, segments of the opposition participated in Marcos's institutionalized channels, yet they continued to exert noninstitutional pressure as well. In Burma, by contrast, after the military crackdown the opposition focused on the regime-controlled election campaigning leading up to the May 1990 elections without maintaining sufficient noninstitutional pressure against the regime. The opposition won the elections, but was demobilized and unable to force the government to step down as in the Philippines, where campaigns of nonviolent action were implemented concomitantly with participation in elections, and civil disobedience was implemented when Marcos refused to step aside. Alternatively, a challenge can boycott state-imposed channels of political participation altogether, as did the anti-apartheid movement in South Africa, and can mobilize primarily noninstitutional pressure against the regime. The power to disrupt is vital to a challenge, and it should not be given up in exchange for participation in channels controlled by the state.

Incorporation of multiple channels of resistance is reflected in the strategy of social movement unionism adopted in South Africa and the Philippines, where trade unions engaged in noninstitutional political action as well as participating in the regime's institutionalized labor relations. A parallel strategy may be adopted by political parties in which noninstitutional political activity is implemented in addition to or instead of participation in institutionalized channels of political participation. This strategy was implemented by banned or out-of-power political parties such as the ANC in South Africa, UNIDO in the Philippines, the NC and the communist parties in Nepal, and the prodemocracy political parties in Thailand.

Multiple Methods of Nonviolent Action

There are a number of reasons why challengers should attempt to expand their repertoires of nonviolent action. For one, as Peter Ackerman and Christopher Kruegler warned, "Reducing the broad technique of nonviolent action to one or a few familiar methods of conflict is dangerous, but it is often the course that movements based on direct action take. The danger arises from the fact that if either or both parties perceive the conflict to hinge on the success or failure of a limited range of methods, then defeat on a limited front may be misconstrued as total defeat" (Ackerman and Kruegler 1994, 35). The struggle in China, for example, was almost entirely limited to the occupation of Tiananmen Square, and the outcome of the challenge hinged on whether the occupation and hunger strike persuaded the government to give in to some or all of the challengers' demands. Struggles for political change should not depend on a single event, however momentous, but rather should focus on the process of shifting the balance of political power through a range of mutually supporting actions over time.

Second, methods of protest and persuasion or disruptive nonviolent intervention by themselves are rarely sufficient to promote political change. Methods of protest and persuasion may be effective in mobilizing members of the aggrieved population and the support of third parties, but they are less effective in directly undermining state power unless used in tandem with methods of noncooperation. The likelihood of success increases to the extent that challengers can implement broadly supported campaigns of non-cooperation that are aimed at the state's sources of social power. Methods of noncooperation, such as stayaways, strikes, and boycotts in South Africa, *welgang bayan* in the Philippines, and *bandhs* in Nepal, were all crucial in undermining state power and promoting elite divisions. By contrast, the unsuccessful challenge in China depended almost entirely on methods of protest and persuasion and disruptive intervention, which, by themselves, were unable to generate sufficient leverage against the regime.

Third, the sequencing of methods may be important, as it may be necessary to build parallel structures through creative nonviolent inter-vention before engaging in dramatic confrontations with the state. In the Philippines, for example, a parallel government had already been formed before the momentous confrontation with the government at Epifanio de los Santos Avenue. By contrast, the dramatic confrontation with the gov-ernment in Tiananmen Square in China and the 8-8-88 protests in Burma occurred before alternative structures had been sufficiently developed or a situation of dual sovereignty had emerged.

Fourth, different types of methods provide opportunities for different seg-ments of the population to participate. For example, an action implemented in Kathmandu, Nepal, was the citywide blackout during the evening curfew. It permitted the participation of people who were opposed to the regime, but were unwilling to engage in riskier forms of collective action. Implementing a broad range of methods facilitates mobilization by permitting people with different levels of commitment to participate in the struggle.

Multiple Spaces and Places of Resistance

As Peter Ackerman and Christopher Kruegler state, "In almost all cases, wide dispersion of nonviolent sanctions, both geographically [place] and throughout the social and political environment [space] . . . compromise the opponents' ability to respond and diminish their overall control" (Ackerman and Kruegler 1994, 37). Rather than toppling states through force, unarmed struggles suc-ceed by disrupting systems' cycles of social reproduction in multiple spaces (see Foucault 1977, 1980). The more spaces and places challenged, the greater the likelihood of the struggles remaining resilient and undermining state power.[15]

Obviously there is a high degree of risk associated with public protests in nondemocracies. On the one hand, public protest may be necessary to mobilize a challenge and discredit the regime, yet on the other hand, such behavior is an easy target for repression and may result in imprisonment or death for the challengers. Since activists should not expect a government response other than violence, the greater their ability to "stay out of harm's way," the greater their likelihood of sustaining the challenge (Ackerman and DuVall 2000, 497–500; Ackerman and Kruegler 1994). In other words, repression is to be expected, but steps may be taken to limit its reach and impact. The occupation of a single indefensible public place by the Chinese students contributed to the movement's demise, as it was an easy target for repression. By contrast, the "lightning protests" in Nepal and Thailand—whereby protestors gathered at a location, then dispersed upon the approach of authorities, only to reappear at another predetermined place—enabled the challengers to outflank the authorities, avoid the direct brunt of violent repression, remain resilient, and give the impression of being more widespread than they actually were. Moreover, although repression may inhibit public protest demonstrations, it is more problematic for states to use force effectively against broad-based methods of noncooperation, such as general strikes, stayaways, and boycotts, as occurred in South Africa, the Philippines, and Nepal. The occupation of factories by the Solidarity movement in Poland, rather than engagement in protest demonstrations in the street, is another example of challengers effectively utilizing place.

Moreover, activists can create "liberated areas," either spaces or places, outside the control of the state. For example, liberated areas were created in South African townships through the development of autonomous organizations (i.e., the "structures of people power"), and in Nepal the city of Patan was declared a liberated area after citizens constructed barricades to prevent state security forces from entering the city. Similarly, when military repression commenced in Thailand, the opposition created "liberated areas," such as at Ramkhamhaeng University in Bangkok, where protestors constructed barricades and formed a nonviolent "commune," that is, a liberated area outside the control of the military.

Considerations of space and place should underlie decisions about whether methods of concentration or dispersion should be implemented. Methods of concentration, in which a large number of people are concentrated in a public place (e.g., protest demonstrations, sit-ins), provide challengers with the opportunity to build solidarity, highlight grievances, indicate the extent of dissatisfaction, and, if the state responds with repression, expose the fact that the state is based on violence rather than legitimacy.

Methods of concentration may also be effective in promoting a dramatic confrontation with the state when political opportunities are propitious, such as after regime defection or the emergence of a dual sovereignty.

However, if the political elite is not divided, the military is coherent, and the state is prepared to use decisive repression against the movement, methods that minimize the effects of repression must be implemented. Methods of dispersion, in which cooperation is withdrawn, such as strikes and boycotts, do not provide the state with tangible targets for repression and may overextend the state's repressive capacities. Methods of both concentration and dispersal are useful for promoting political change, but their effectiveness depends on the social, political, and geographic context.

Communication and Reference Publics

Communication is vital to the success of unarmed struggles; communication among the challengers, accurate public knowledge about the movement, and international media coverage all increase the likelihood of success (Martin and Varney 2003). According to Peter Ackerman and Christopher Kruegler, "Swift and accurate communications are also necessary to authenticate instructions, to counter enemy propaganda, and generally to inform and bolster the fighting forces. Communications to the world outside the conflict are no less important, with images carried by print and broadcast media playing a key role in interpreting the conflict for outsiders and in motivating third party involvement" (Ackerman and Kruegler 1994, 31). Thus, communication is important within the movement for coordinating and aggregating the struggle, and it is important for events, especially acts of state repression, to be accurately reported to a broader audience due to the importance of reference publics and third parties in unarmed struggles.

For the two unarmed insurrections that occurred in contexts with the highest levels of state censorship, Burma and China, the levels of mobilization were directly related to shifts in the flow of uncensored information within the countries. In Burma, the increased mobilization of the pro-democracy movement was directly related to the emergence of an alternative press and the takeover of the state-run newspaper, whereas the movement's demobilization was related to the suppression of the alternative media and the government's reimposition of control over the state-run newspaper. Similarly, the mobilization and support for the pro-democracy movement in China corresponded to the Chinese journalists' sympathetic coverage of the movement, and its demobilization was related to the reimposition of censorship of domestic news by the state. These cases, especially when compared to that of Poland, where the underground press was crucial in mobilizing the challenge and maintaining its resilience, suggests the importance of developing alternative communication networks that are not centrally controlled (see Burrowes 1996, 200–201; Martin 1993; Martin and Varney 2003).

The power of unarmed insurrections may also be amplified if they receive international media coverage. Favorable media coverage in the home country of a government's chief patron may increase the leverage of a struggle. For example, the coverage of the people power movement in the Philippines by the international media, and especially by the U.S. media, which flocked to the Philippines following the assassination of Benigno Aquino, facilitated the groundswell of support for the movement in the United States and contributed to the U.S. government's eventual severing of its ties with the Marcos regime. By contrast, if unarmed insurrections do not receive favorable media coverage, or receive no coverage at all, in the home country of its chief patron, the likelihood of their success is decreased. The unarmed insurrection in Pakistan in 1983, for example, did not receive much media coverage in the United States, and the United States continued to back the Zia al-Huq regime in Pakistan, contributing to the failure of the unarmed insurrection to promote political change (Zunes 1994, 423). As in the case of the Philippines, international media coverage of the unarmed insurrections also contributed to the mobilization of third-party support in South Africa, Nepal, and Thailand. In China, however, the international coverage of the pro-democracy movement was unable to mobilize significant pressure against the regime, given the relative independence of the Chinese state from external forces.

Conclusion

I hope this study has at least been provocative enough to arouse interested skepticism and critical thinking on the power of nonviolent action as a strategy of resistance outside of democratic contexts. I also hope this study has alerted scholars of social movements and nonviolent action to the potential utility of drawing on each other's theories and literatures. The ongoing effort to develop a comparative framework for understanding the power of nonviolent action in nondemocracies is useful, I think, in that it permits us to move beyond explanations that assume that the outcomes of such action are based entirely on the state's capacity and willingness to use force. Certainly the state's repressive capacities and propensities are important. But the perspective suggested here assumes that it is not the views of the oppressors or their willingness to use repression that solely determine the outcomes of struggles relying on methods of nonviolent action. Characteristics of the challenge are important as well, especially attributes and actions that promote resilience and that generate the withdrawal of support from the state through the networks upon which it depends for its power.

The assumption that nonviolent action works only in democratic or benign regimes or, more generally, the assumption that the outcomes of collective struggles are determined by the political context leads to misleading social scientific explanations. Fortunately, people around the globe have not been stultified by such explanations, but rather have demonstrated that collective action can alter the political context and that people engaged in mass campaigns of nonviolent action are not entirely at the mercy of their oppressors. Certainly there is some outer limit beyond which nonviolent action cannot be mobilized or promote political change, but the outer limit may be much farther out than is typically assumed.

On the other hand, despite the profound political transformations in nondemocracies facilitated by nonviolent action in the last decades of the twentieth century, nonviolent action must not be glorified or viewed as a panacea. Georg Sørensen warns of the dangers of utopianism in peace research, that is, putting forth nonviolence as the brilliant solution to all social problems (Sørensen 1992). Such a view idealizes nonviolence and puts an excessive emphasis on values to the detriment of theory and data. We need an accurate understanding of what nonviolent action is, and we need social scientific analyses of nonviolent action that neither romanticize it, on the one hand, nor dismiss its power and potential, on the other. I hope the analytic framework sketched here will provoke critical thinking and research along these lines. If such research also generates knowledge that people can draw on to break vicious cycles of violence and promote a more just distribution of political, economic, and social power, all the better.

Notes

Introduction

1. Others use the term *unarmed insurrection* in a slightly different way, implying simply that arms are not available but would be used if they were available. In this study I am concerned not with the views regarding violence and nonviolence of the people engaged in struggle (an important topic that deserves study), but rather with the primary methods that people actually implement to promote political change. Thus, other than noting that the struggles examined here were instances of "pragmatic" and "nonidealized" nonviolence, I do not consider the views, ideologies, or rhetoric of those engaged in struggle in this study.

2. See Rigby (1991), who differentiates between the lethal weapons used by states, terrorists, and armed insurgents and the nonlethal weapons that are sometimes used by civilians during the course of unarmed insurrections. With regard to the Palestinian Intifada from 1987–90 he states, "The Intifada can be characterized as an *unarmed* form of resistance, insofar as the tools of confrontation used by the Palestinians have not been *lethal.* Whilst the stones and Molotov cocktails have on occasion caused death, they fall into a different category from some of the weapons used by the Israeli military, notably guns that are designed to maim and kill—a task to which stones are not specially suited" (1).

3. Compare this to McAdam, Tarrow, and Tilly's "transgressive" contention (2001).

4. See also Teixeira (1999) on principled nonviolence.

5. See Smithey and Kurtz (2003) for a more recent call to integrate social movement and nonviolent action approaches to political contention.

6. The people power movement in Thailand emerged in 1991 when Thailand

was run by a military junta, and continued into 1992, when Thailand was technically "democratic," as the military-backed parties formed a ruling coalition after the March 1992 elections. While the country was technically democratic, significant nondemocratic restrictions on the polity existed, such as an appointed senate, an unelected prime minister, and constraints on political organizing; thus the term *semidemocracy* is often used to describe the political system in Thailand during this time period to distinguish it from actual democracies.

7. I also make brief comparisons to unarmed insurrections in Poland (1980–89) and Palestine (1987–90).

1. From "People's War" to "People Power"?

1. This brief account of events in Iran draws on Shivers (1980, 1997).

2. The unarmed insurrection in Iran produced a revolutionary outcome, which is defined as a "transfer of state power from those who held it before the start of multiple sovereignty to a new ruling coalition" (Tilly 1993, 14). Of course the consolidation of the rule of the ayatollahs involved considerable violence and coercion.

3. In Iran, as in a number of other unarmed insurrections, the defection of segments of the military was a direct result of mass campaigns of nonviolent action. In other words, without the mass unarmed insurrections, it is unlikely that the mutinies would have occurred.

4. Of course violent exceptions include the Romanian Revolution in 1989 and the secessionist movement in Chechnya.

5. The unarmed insurrection in El Salvador overlapped with a guerrilla insurgency that was carried out by the Frente Farabundo Martí para la Liberación Nacional (FMLN, or Farabundo Marti National Liberation Front), which formed in 1980.

6. Zunes (1994) identifies twenty-one cases of major unarmed insurrections in the third world that occurred between 1978 and 1994. Since 1994, major unarmed insurrections in the third world have included the uprising against Suharto in Indonesia in 1997–98, the challenge to the Nigerian military in 1998–99, East Timorese resistance to Indonesian occupation in 1999, and the unarmed insurrection that deposed President Estrada in the Philippines in 2001.

7. This section is based on my article "Nonviolent Action and Its Misconceptions: Insights for Social Scientists," *PS: Political Science and Politics* (2003).

8. See also "Correcting Common Misconceptions about Nonviolent Action," by the Albert Einstein Institution (n.d.), *Mahatma Gandhi and His Myths,* by Mark Shepard (2002), and the works of Ackerman and DuVall (2000), Ackerman and Kruegler (1994), Martin (1997), Sharp (1973, 1990, chapter 3, 1999), Zunes (1994, 1999a, 1999b), and Zunes et al. (1999).

9. These, of course, are institutionalized in democracies.

NOTES FOR CHAPTER I

10. See chapter 2 for a discussion of four mechanisms through which nonviolent action promotes political change.

11. Referring to these groups as "terrorist" groups by no means implies support for the targets of their dissent or that the states that they oppose do not also use terrorism.

12. See, for example, the voluminous literature on the relationship between inequality and violent political conflict, such as Boswell and Dixon (1990, 1993), Hibbs (1973), Jenkins and Schock (1992), Lichbach (1989), Muller (1985), Muller and Seligson (1987), Muller and Weede (1990), Paige (1975), and Schock (1996).

13. On identity formation see, for example, Coy and Woehrle (2000), Melucci (1989), Taylor and Whittier (1992), and Touraine (1981). On consciousness raising see, for example, Fisher (1993) and Sarachild (1978). On cultural framing see, for example, Benford and Snow (2000), Snow and Benford (1988, 1992), and Snow et al. (1986). See chapter 2, as well, for a discussion of framing.

14. See Sharp (1973) and Mueller (1999), who argue that exit is a form of contentious political action.

15. For works on resource mobilization see, for example, Jenkins (1983), J. D. McCarthy and Zald (1973, 1977), and Zald and McCarthy (1987). For works on mobilizing structures see, for example, Boudreau (1996), McAdam et al. (1996), Osa (2001), and Tarrow (1998).

16. These are examples of institutional political action in democracies. In nondemocracies there are other forms of institutional political action, for example, democratic centralism in communist regimes. Of course, while I make a distinction between institutional political action and violent political action, we must keep in mind that state institutionalized political relations are ultimately based on violence (Weber 1958).

17. Others have emphasized structural constraints on political freedom in democracies (e.g., Lukes 1974) or the inherent contradictions between states and democratic relations (e.g., Burnheim 1985).

18. See chapter 2 for a discussion of state repression.

19. On the "mythology of violence" see Ackerman and DuVall (2000, chapter 13). On the "myth of redemptive violence" see Wink (1992, chapter 1).

20. See, for example, Gleditsch et al. (2002) and Gurr et al. (2001) for useful catalogues of political violence.

21. These trends are not a straightforward result of the process of decolonization. While many of the Marxist guerrilla insurgencies in Africa and Asia emerged during struggles for national liberation, a number emerged after national independence was achieved (e.g., in the Philippines) or, as in the cases of Nepal and Thailand, in countries that had not been formally colonized, and all of the Marxist guerrilla insurgencies in Latin America emerged after independence was achieved.

Of course one of the first movements for national liberation was the nonviolent struggle in India.

22. Contrary to the assumptions of mainstream social science, state breakdown does not necessarily have to have negative consequences. See the anarchist literature, for example, of Bakunin (1953), Guérin (1970), and Kropotkin (1995).

23. On the role of the United States in developing these methods and exporting them to its client states, see Blum (1995).

24. Of course the newer of these technologies became available only in the late 1980s, and their distribution is highly uneven.

25. See also Anheier et al. (2001) and Glasius et al. (2002).

26. On the growing accountability for human rights atrocities in international law see Ratner and Abrams (2001).

27. For example, Aung San Suu Kyi (1991), Câmara (1972), Chaiwat Satha-Anand (1997), and Soedjatmoko (1987, 1994). Preceding them, of course, was Mohandas Gandhi (1958–94).

28. See also Martin and Varney (2003).

29. Here I refer to terrorism as violent acts undertaken by less powerful groups against civilians for the purpose of promoting political change. Of course state terrorism, that is, terrorism and war implemented by states in an effort to consolidate, perpetuate, or extend their rule, is far more common and pervasive than terrorist activities implemented by challengers. See chapter 2 for a discussion of state repression.

2. Political Process and Nonviolent Action Approaches to Political Contention

1. As illustrated by the Iranian case, unarmed insurrections are not inherently democratic, nor do they necessarily lead to democratic transitions. However, all of the unarmed insurrections in this study were pro-democracy movements and occurred during the third wave of democratization; therefore, it seems appropriate to say a few words on theories of democratization.

2. The classic work in the modernization tradition is Lipset (1981). More recent works include Bollen and Jackman (1985), Crenshaw (1995), Diamond (1992), and Lipset, Kyoung-Ryung, and Torres (1993). On the world polity approach see Meyer et al. (1997). Notable contributions to the transition approach include Di Palma (1990), Higley and Gunther (1992), Mainwaring et al. (1992), O'Donnell et al. (1986), Przeworski (1991), and Shain and Linz (1995). The classic works in the structural tradition are Moore (1966) and Rueschemeyer et al. (1992). Also notable are Paige (1997) and Yashar (1997).

3. The issues of democratic consolidation and stability, which might be better addressed from a structural rather than a movement-oriented approach, are not addressed in this study.

4. See Tarrow's *Power in Movement* (1998) for the definitive review of the social movement literature. Other notable reviews include Jasper (1997, chapter 2)

and Klandermans (1997). Paralleling the development of the political process approach in the United States was the development of new social movement theory in Europe. Political process theorists have tended not to concern themselves with new social movement arguments about large-scale social change and values shifts in the postmodern era, but have incorporated middle-range insights from this body of literature, such as those related to collective identities. For overviews of new social movement theory see Cohen (1985), Offe (1985), Pichardo (1997), and A. Scott (1990). For points of convergence between the new social movement and political process approaches, see Klandermans (1997) and Klandermans et al. (1988).

5. For comparative applications of the political process approach across democracies see, for example, Dalton and Keuchler (1990), Jenkins and Klandermans (1995), Kitschelt (1986), and Kriesi et al. (1995). For applications to the second world see, for example, Oberschall (1996), Osa (1997, 2001), and Zdravomyslova (1996), and for applications to the third world see, for example, Boudreau (1996, 1999, 2002), Brockett (1991, 1993), Eckstein (1989), Gurr (1993), Jenkins and Schock (1992), Noonan (1995), Osa and Corduneanu-Huci (2003), Pagnucco and Smith (1992), Schneider (1995), Schock (1996, 1999), and Zuo and Benford (1995).

6. For an elaboration of frames see, for example, Benford and Snow (2000), Melucci (1989), Snow and Benford (1988, 1992), Snow et al. (1986), and Touraine (1981).

7. See Gamson and Meyer (1996) for a constructive critique of the political opportunity concept.

8. In addition, social movements may be facilitated by regimes as well (Marx 1979). Since the movements examined in this study represented fundamental challenges to the regimes, facilitation is not discussed here.

9. Repression in democracies tends to be more subtle than in nondemocracies. Take, for example, the issue of censorship. In nondemocracies this typically involves the publication of only government-approved information, while in democracies censorship operates through less overt mechanisms such as government propaganda, self-censorship, and limitations on the public sphere posed by the marketplace (see, for example, Herman and Chomsky 1988 and Chomsky 2002).

10. On the positive relationship between repression and dissent see, for example, Brockett (1993), DeNardo (1985), Gartner and Regan (1996), Gurr (1970), Khawaja (1993, 1994, 1995), Olivier (1990, 1991), Snyder and Tilly (1972). On the inverted U-shaped relationship between repression and dissent see, for example, Boswell and Dixon (1990, 1993), Muller (1985), Muller and Seligson (1987), Muller and Weede (1990), and Schock (1996). On the negative relationship between repression and dissent see, for example, Lichbach (1987, 1995). Typically the independent variable in cross-national studies is state repression, measured by counts of negative sanctions and/or the use of force, and the dependent variable is dissent,

measured by counts of protest demonstrations or deaths from contentious politics or by the instantaneous rate of change in collective action.

11. For exceptions see Aditjondro et al. (2000), McAdam (1983, 1999), and Sharp (1973).

12. See also Burstein et al. (1995), Galtung (1989), Gamson (1990), Jenkins (1983), Jenkins and Perrow (1977), Schattschneider (1960), and Tarrow (1998).

13. On the Catholic Church see, for example, Osa (1997), Schock (1999), and Smith (1991). On development and human rights workers see, for example, Brockett (1991), Fisher (1998), Keck and Sikkink (1998), Mahoney and Eguren (1998), and Smith et al. (1997).

14. Of course a major exception is Gamson's *The Strategy of Social Protest* (1990).

15. For example, Domhoff's (2002) and Lukes's (1974) critique of pluralism and Pateman's (1988) critique of consent.

16. In this study I focus primarily on nonviolent action as a method for challenging domestic regimes. There also exists a substantial and related literature on nonviolent civilian-based national defense, for example, Boserup and Mack (1974), King-Hall (1958), Roberts (1968), and Sharp (1985, 1990), and on nonviolent social defense, for example, Anderson and Larmore (1991), Burrowes (1996), and Martin (1984, 1993).

17. Other notable studies on the power of nonviolent action from the same period are Hiller's (1928) and Crook's works on strikes (1931).

18. Of course Gandhi also produced significant writings on the philosophy, theory, and praxis of nonviolent action (1958–94).

19. For encyclopedic overviews of the literature see Kurtz (1999), McCarthy and Sharp (1997), and Powers and Vogele (1997).

20. La Boétie, for example, states, "Resolve to serve no more, and you are at once freed. I do not ask that you place hands upon the tyrant to topple him over, but simply that you support him no longer; then you will behold him, like a great Colossus whose pedestal has been pulled away, fall of his own weight and break into pieces" (1997, 52–53). Weber, for example, writes, "If the state is to exist, the dominated must obey the authority claimed by the powers that be" (1958, 78). And Arendt writes, "When we say of somebody that he is 'in power' we actually refer to his being empowered by a certain number of people to act in their name" (1970, 4).

21. Sharp, unfortunately, refers to his theory of power as "pluralist" (1973). Sharp's view of power, however, is not to be mistaken for the pluralist theory of power, as exemplified by the works of Dahl and others who study competing interest groups in democracies (e.g., Dahl 1961). Sharp's theory of power might be better termed "relational," since it emphasizes the relations between the oppressors and the oppressed. See Galtung (1980), who elaborates a theory of power similar

to that of Sharp, emphasizing that power is a reciprocal relation; Summy (1994), who emphasizes the relations of dependence that bind the ruler and the ruled; and Foucault (1977, 1980), who identifies multiple loci of power throughout oppressive systems.

22. There is a debate among scholars and activists over the appropriateness of classifying sabotage as a method of nonviolent action and over whether or not sabotage should be used in struggles waged primarily through nonviolent action. Sharp discusses why sabotage should be avoided by activists in unarmed struggles, for example, because of the possibility of unintended violence and the alienation of potential support (1973, 608–11). On the other hand, others argue for the utility of nonviolent sabotage, as a type of disruptive nonviolent intervention, in unarmed struggles. Ackerman and Kruegler, for example, maintain that acts of nonviolent sabotage that render the state's resources for repression inoperative may be important in nonviolent struggles (1994, 39–40). See also Martin (1999).

23. Of course, as discussed earlier, rather than preempting a more broad-based movement, accommodation may open the floodgates of dissent, especially in nondemocracies.

24. Interestingly enough, there are parallels in the expected relationship between repression and dissent across social movement and nonviolent action theories. Both theories suggest that repression may have a short-term negative impact on dissent and a long-term positive impact on dissent. According to social movement theories, this is due to the time lapse required for micromobilizational processes to occur (Opp and Roehl 1990; Rasler 1996). According to the nonviolent action approach, this is due to the time lapse required for the "political jiujitsu" dynamic to take effect (Sharp 1973).

25. For an exception see della Porta (1995).

26. Also see Killian (1972). For arguments on a positive radical flank effect in the U.S. women's movement see Freeman (1975, 1987).

27. See also Morris (1984) and Rothschild-Whitt (1979).

28. Andrews (2001) makes a parallel argument with regard to the civil rights movement in the American South. He suggests that the implementation of multiple strategies—disruptive protest (i.e., methods of protest and persuasion, noncooperation, and disruptive nonviolent intervention), routine politics (i.e., institutionalized political action), and independent programs (i.e., creative nonviolent intervention)—increases the leverage of challengers and the likelihood of a successful outcome.

29. As discussed in the introduction, the focus of this study is limited to the trajectories of unarmed insurrections once they have arisen. An explanation of why unarmed insurrections do or do not occur in certain times and places is not considered. This important issue is left open for investigation.

3. People Power Unleashed

1. This brief overview of the history of resistance to political exclusion in South Africa draws on Mufson (1992).

2. The official death toll was sixty-nine, but the actual number is unknown and probably much higher. See Frankel (2001).

3. With the notable exception of the Durban strike wave in 1973.

4. Although the BCM resurfaced in 1978 with the formation of the Azanian Peoples' Organization (AZAPO), many former leaders of the BCM became active in the UDF rather than AZAPO, arguing that black consciousness was a necessary phase in the development of the anti-apartheid struggle, but that changing conditions necessitated a different approach to resistance (Marx 1992; Naidoo 1989).

5. Of course there was an overlap in resources and personnel across the three social movement organizations; leaders of the UDF considered themselves members or supporters of the ANC, and the ANC was generally recognized by the UDF and COSATU as the eventual successor to the National Party.

6. Social movement unionism contrasts sharply with the Leninist strategy for social change. According to Lenin (1970), trade union workers are not capable of pursuing goals beyond economic issues; therefore, to promote political change, they must participate in mass-based centralized political parties led by a revolutionary vanguard. Moreover, Lenin adhered to the idea of "seizing" state power (i.e., through armed methods), while the strategy of social movement unionism is committed to promoting political change through methods of nonviolent action.

7. The notable exception was the vice president of the United States, George Bush, who attended Marcos's inauguration and declared, "We love your adherence to democratic principle and to the democratic process" (Schirmer and Shalom 1987, 168).

8. One group that attempted to do this without much success was the Christians for National Liberation (CNL), whose ideology attempted to combine liberation theology with secular Maoism (Shoesmith 1985, 86–89).

9. According to Lane (1990), "Protest jogs" emerged as a tactic when members of the middle classes combined their recreational interest in jogging with their political interests in removing Marcos from office.

10. PDP-LABAN was formed in 1982, when the Pilipino Democratic Party (PDP) merged with LABAN. In the 1984 elections a number of PDP-LABAN members ran under the UNIDO banner, enhancing the unity of the reformist opposition.

11. The CPP maintained its strategy of election boycotts as well.

12. NAMFREL was originally formed in 1951 with backing from the United States to ensure the "free and fair" election of Ramon Magsaysay, but was later disbanded (Bonner 1987; Shalom 1981). NAMFREL's second incarnation in 1984,

while receiving funds from abroad (e.g., from the U.S. National Endowment for Democracy), remained autonomous from external control and was more of an indigenous grassroots movement than its predecessor, receiving significant backing from the Philippine Catholic Church.

13. *EDSA* is the acronym for Epifanio de los Santos Avenue, which separates Camp Aguinaldo and Camp Crame, the two military bases in Quezon City just outside of Manila.

14. The duration of the unarmed insurrection in South Africa over many years permits the presentation of longitudinal data. Such yearly longitudinal data are not relevant for the other five unarmed insurrections in this study, which occurred over much shorter time spans.

4. People Power Suppressed

1. In July 1989 the official name of Burma was changed by the military regime to Myanmar, the Burmese name for Burma. Since the unarmed insurrection occurred in 1988 and this chapter focuses primarily on events prior to July 1989, I use the name Burma.

2. In a way similar to that in which the U.S. government underestimates or, worse yet, makes no effort to accurately enumerate the number of civilians it murders in other countries (e.g., see Blum 1995; Chomsky 2001), authoritarian regimes such as those in Burma and China underestimate the number of their own civilians that they kill. Thus, there are wide discrepancies between the official estimates and the estimates that scholars report, and even discrepancies among scholars. In this chapter I report numbers of deaths, injuries, and arrests, as well as sizes of protests, based on what seems to be the consensus among area scholars.

3. Guyot (1989, 121) refers to the events as a *"sui coup,"* in which a government run by the military is replaced by the military.

4. Aung Gyi was purged from the political elite in 1963. In May and June of 1988, he wrote open letters that were highly critical of the regime. He was one of the initial leaders of the NLD but subsequently broke with the NLD and formed his own political party.

5. By a free press the challengers did not mean a commercial press that competes for readers and makes a profit from advertising, but rather a press that reports events objectively (Nathan 1989, 24–25).

6. These are pseudonyms. Most student political activists in Burma used pseudonyms as protection against identification and arrest. *Moe Thee Zun* means "June Hailstorm," and *Min Ko Naing* means "Conqueror of Kings."

7. According to Nathan (1989, 24), the students cast themselves not as dissidents but as loyal followers, appealing to the regime to live up to the values encoded in the Chinese constitution. They symbolically undertook the hunger strike in front

of the Mao Mausoleum to highlight its patriotic nature, and it sent the message that the students valued the welfare of the state above their own lives. In doing so, they were drawing on the tradition of Qu Yuan, who in the fourth century BC committed suicide to prove his loyalty to the ruler who had failed to heed his advice.

8. According to Matthews (1993) and Steinberg (1990), approximately 80 percent of the 120,000 Buddhist monks supported the people power movement. See Kurzman (1998) as well.

9. An indication of Burma's isolation and lack of transnational ties compared to the situation in the Philippines, for example, is the membership density per million population of international nongovernmental organizations for each country. For 1989, Burma's score was 6.0 and the Philippines' score was 20.0 (Anheier et al. 2001, 287–90). Another indication of the disparity is the number of social movement organizations listed in the *Human Rights Index* (Human Rights Internet 1994) for each country. The index listed 28 human rights social movement organizations for Burma; however, all of them were located outside of Burma and thus were isolated from the movement within the country. The index listed 209 human rights social movement organizations for the Philippines, of which only 24 were located outside of the country. Although these data are for 1994, they are nevertheless suggestive of the tremendous variation in the transnational ties that existed between the people power movements in Burma and the Philippines in the 1980s.

10. Immediately following the government massacres of Burmese citizens in August and September 1988, Burmese who fled across the border were granted asylum by Thailand. However, after the commander-in-chief of the Thai army, General Chaowalit, met with SLORC officials in Rangoon in December 1988, Thailand reversed its policies and began arresting and deporting Burmese refugees (Amnesty International 1990).

5. Challenging Monarchies and Militaries

1. The *panchayat* system of governance was characterized by a four-tiered partyless system of councils. In practice, the monarchy retained all political power.

2. As mentioned in the introductory chapter, the people power movement in Thailand emerged in 1991, when Thailand was run by a military junta, and continued into 1992, when Thailand was technically "democratic," as the military-backed parties formed a ruling coalition after the March 1992 elections. Nevertheless, significant nondemocratic constraints on the polity existed; thus, the term *semidemocracy* is often used to describe the polity in Thailand during this period to differentiate it from democracies.

3. Apparently the military surreptitiously collected and disposed of a number of bodies of those they killed. Estimates of the number missing or "disappeared" ranges from dozens to hundreds.

4. An opposition politician living in exile in India, Raja Prasad Singh, claimed responsibility for the bombings (Parajulee 2000, 74, n. 214).

5. The following discussion of the people power movement in Nepal is based on Brown (1996, chapter 5), Parajulee (2000, chapter 2), and Raeper and Hoftun (1992).

6. Trajectories of Unarmed Insurrections

1. The framework sketched in this chapter incorporates the concepts of resilience and leverage from the perspective of the challengers. Of course the relational nature of the concepts suggests that they may be incorporated from the perspective of the defenders of the status quo as well. Theories of counterinsurgency, for example, suggest methods for decreasing the resilience of an armed insurgency and undermining its leverage.

2. A rough indicator of the level of integration of a country's citizens into transnational political networks is the number of memberships in international nongovernmental organizations per one million population. For 1990, Burma's score was 6.0, compared to the Philippines' score of 20.0, Nepal's score of 20.0, and Thailand's score of 20.0 (the mean scores for low- and middle-income countries, respectively, were 8.0 and 45.0). The data are from the Union of International Associations, *Yearbook of International Organizations: Guide to Civil Society Networks* (1990), as reported in Anheier et al. (2001, 287–90).

3. For 1990 China had a score of 1.0 with regard to the density of citizen membership in international nongovernmental organizations. See note 2 for an explanation.

4. The discussion of events in Poland is based on Ost (1990).

5. See also Suh (2001), who examines the role of perceived opportunities in the pro-democracy movement in South Korea.

6. Foreign direct investment (inward plus outward foreign direct investment stock as a percentage of GDP) is a rough indicator of a country's integration into the global economy. For 1990, Burma had a score of 0.7 and Thailand a score of 10.1, indicating Burma's greater degree of economic isolation (the mean for Southeast Asia, excluding Singapore, was 11.3). Data from the World Bank, *World Development Indicators* (2001).

7. As indicated in note 2, Burma's citizens were more isolated from transnational political networks than the citizens of Thailand.

8. Prior to and after the people power movement in Nepal, various Maoist communist parties called for an armed overthrow of the state. However, during the course of the movement Maoist communist parties were part of the United Leftist Front (ULF) or the United National People's Movement (UNPM) and participated in the nonviolent people power movement along with the Nepali Congress Party.

They subsequently turned to armed methods after the democratic transition when they felt that their goals could not be met through democratic procedures.

9. The Azanian People's Organization (AZAPO) also existed in South Africa and, like the ANC, supported the use of violence to overthrow the state. It was more radical than the ANC-UDF-COSATU in that it opposed multiracialism and called for a transformation of the capitalist economic system in addition to the end of apartheid. However, the role of AZAPO was too inconsequential in terms of the overall trajectory of the anti-apartheid movement to have contributed to a radical flank effect.

10. As noted in chapter 1, coercive mobilization sometimes characterized campaigns of nonviolent action in South Africa, but it was not inherent to these mobilizations.

11. The discussion of the Palestinian Intifada is based on Rigby (1991).

12. See Marx (2000), especially "The Communist Manifesto," "The Class Struggles in France," and "The Eighteenth Brumaire of Louis Bonaparte," and Weber (1958, 1978), especially "Politics as a Vocation" and "The Distribution of Power within the Political Community: Classes, Status Groups, and Parties."

13. Indeed, Zunes, Kurtz, and Asher note that nonviolent action has not been studied with the same energy and resources as military strategies and armed conflicts, as there are no large academies for nonviolent action that parallel military academies, nor are there government-subsidized infrastructures for the research of nonviolent action that parallel the networks devoted to the study of military strategy and violence. They note, for example, that the U.S. Army Research Bureau's annual research budget exceeds the total social science research budget for all U.S. government agencies combined, which includes the National Science Foundation, the National Institutes of Health, and the United States Institute of Peace (Zunes et al. 1999, 1–5; 5, n. 4).

14. The downside of coalitions forged by broad opposition groups is that once the object of their coordinated effort is attained the constituent groups may begin to struggle with each other. In the Philippines, for example, the more progressive components of the people power movement were marginalized by the traditional democratic politicians after Marcos was deposed, and in Nepal violent conflict erupted between the Nepali Congress government and the communist parties after the monarchy was toppled. This is an important issue concerning people power movements that is beyond the scope of this study.

15. Space and place are significant yet underspecified aspects of social movements. But see Miller (2000), Routledge (1993, 1994), and Sewell (2001).

Works Cited

Ackerman, Peter, and Jack DuVall. 2000. *A Force More Powerful: A Century of Non-violent Conflict.* New York: St. Martin's Press.

Ackerman, Peter, and Christopher Kruegler. 1994. *Strategic Nonviolent Conflict: The Dynamics of People Power in the Twentieth Century.* Westport, CT: Praeger.

Aditjondro, George, David Kowalewski, and Steven Peterson. 2000. "Protest Targeting and Repression: Campaigns against Water Projects in Indonesia." In *Paths to State Repression: Human Rights Violations and Contentious Politics,* ed. Christian Davenport, 109–23. Lanham, MD: Rowman and Littlefield Publishers.

Adler, Glenn, Judy Maller, and Eddie Webster. 1992. "Unions, Direct Action, and Transition in South Africa." In *Peace, Politics, and Violence in the New South Africa,* ed. Norman Etherington, 306–43. London: Hans Zell Publishers.

Adler, Glenn, and Eddie Webster. 1995. "Challenging Transition Theory: The Labor Movement, Radical Reform, and Transition to Democracy in South Africa." *Politics and Society* 23: 75–106.

Albert Einstein Institution. n.d. "Correcting Common Misconceptions about Non-violent Action." Cambridge, MA: Albert Einstein Institution.

Amenta, Edwin, and Michael P. Young. 1999. "Making an Impact: Conceptual and Methodological Implications of the Collective Goods Criterion." In *How Social Movements Matter,* ed. Marco Giugni, Doug McAdam, and Charles Tilly, 22–41. Minneapolis: University of Minnesota Press.

Amnesty International. 1990. *Myanmar: Amnesty International Briefing.* September.

Anderson, Shelley, and Janet Larmore, eds. 1991. *Nonviolent Struggle and Social Defence.* London: War Resisters' International.

Andrews, Kenneth T. 2001. "Social Movement and Policy Implementation: The Civil Rights Movement and the War on Poverty, 1965–1971." *American Sociological Review* 66: 71–95.

Anek Laothamatas. 1991. *From Bureaucratic Polity to Liberal Corporatism: Business Associations and the New Political Economy of Thailand.* Boulder, CO: Westview Press.

Anheier, Helmut, Marlies Glasius, and Mary Kaldor, eds. 2001. *Global Civil Society 2001.* Oxford, England: Oxford University Press.

Aquino, Belinda A. 1987. *Politics of Plunder: The Philippines under Marcos.* Quezon City: Great Books Trading.

Arendt, Hannah. 1970. *On Violence.* New York: Harcourt, Brace, and World.

Aung San Suu Kyi. 1991. *Freedom from Fear and Other Writings,* ed. Michael Aris. London: Viking.

Bakunin, Mikhail. 1953. *The Political Philosophy of Bakunin: Scientific Anarchism,* ed. G. P. Maximoff. New York: Free Press.

Barkan, Steven. 1984. "Legal Control of the Southern Civil Rights Movement." *American Sociological Review* 49: 552–65.

Baskin, J. 1991. *Striking Back: A History of COSATU.* Johannesburg: Ravan Press.

Benford, Robert D., and David Snow. 2000. "Framing Processes and Social Movements: An Overview and Assessment." *Annual Review of Sociology* 26: 611–39.

Bermeo, Nancy. 1997. "Myths of Moderation: Confrontation and Conflict during Democratic Transitions." *Comparative Politics* 29: 305–22.

Biko, Steve. 1978. *Black Consciousness in South Africa,* ed. Millard Arnold. New York, Vintage Books.

Bleiker, Roland. 1993. *Nonviolent Struggle and the Revolution in East Germany.* Cambridge, MA: Albert Einstein Institution.

———. 2000. *Popular Dissent, Human Agency, and Global Politics.* Cambridge, England: Cambridge University Press.

Blum, William. 1995. *Killing Hope: U.S. Military and CIA Interventions since World War II.* Monroe, ME: Common Courage Press.

Bob, Clifford. 2002. "Political Process Theory and Transnational Social Movements: Dialectics of Protest among Nigeria's Ogoni Minority." *Social Problems* 49: 395–415.

Bollen, Kenneth, and Robert Jackman. 1985. "Economic and Noneconomic Determinants of Political Democracy in the 1960s." *Research in Political Sociology* 1: 27–48.

Bond, Douglas G. 1988. "The Nature and Meaning of Nonviolent Direct Action: An Exploratory Study." *Journal of Peace Research* 25: 81–89.

———. 1994. "Nonviolent Action and the Diffusion of Power." In *Justice without*

Violence, ed. Paul Wehr, Heidi Burgess, and Guy Burgess, 59–79. Boulder, CO: Lynne Rienner Publishing.

Bonner, Raymond. 1987. *Waltzing with a Dictator: The Marcoses and the Making of American Policy.* New York: Times Books.

Boserup, Anders, and Andrew Mack. 1974. *War without Weapons: Non-violence in National Defence.* London: Frances Pinter.

Boswell, Terry, and William J. Dixon. 1990. "Dependency and Rebellion: A Cross-National Analysis." *American Sociological Review* 55: 540–59.

———. 1993. "Marx's Theory of Rebellion: A Cross-National Analysis of Class Exploitation, Economic Development, and Violent Revolt." *American Sociological Review* 58: 681–702.

Boudreau, Vincent. 1996. "Northern Theory, Southern Protest: Opportunity Structure Analysis in Cross-National Perspective." *Mobilization* 1: 175–89.

———. 1999. "Diffusing Democracy? People Power in Indonesia and the Philippines." *Bulletin of Concerned Asian Scholars* 31: 3–18.

———. 2002. "State Repression and Democracy in Three Southeast Asian Countries." In *Social Movements: Identity, Culture, and the State,* ed. David S. Meyer et al., 28–46. New York: Oxford University Press.

Bratton, Michael, and Nicolas van de Walle. 1992. "Popular Protest and Political Reform in Africa." *Comparative Politics* 24: 419–42.

———. 1997. *Democratic Experiments in Africa: Regime Transitions in Comparative Perspective.* Cambridge, England: Cambridge University Press.

Brockett, Charles D. 1991. "The Structure of Political Opportunities and Peasant Mobilization in Central America." *Comparative Politics* 23: 253–74.

———. 1993. "A Protest-Cycle Resolution of the Repression / Popular-Protest Paradox." *Social Science History* 17: 457–84.

Brooks, Alan, and Jeremy Brickhill. 1980. *Whirlwind before the Storm.* London: International Defence and Aid Fund for Southern Africa.

Brown, Andrew. 1997. "Locating Working-Class Power." In *Political Change in Thailand: Democracy and Development,* ed. Kevin Hewison, 163–78. New York: Routledge.

Brown, T. Louise. 1996. *The Challenge to Democracy in Nepal: A Political History.* New York: Routledge.

Brysk, Alison. 1994. *The Politics of Human Rights in Argentina: Protest, Change, and Democratization.* Stanford, CA: Stanford University Press.

Burma Watcher. 1989. "Burma in 1989: There Came a Whirlwind." *Asian Survey* 29: 174–80.

Burnheim, John. 1985. *Is Democracy Possible? The Alternative to Electoral Politics.* Berkeley: University of California Press.

Burrowes, Robert J. 1996. *The Strategy of Nonviolent Defense: A Gandhian Approach.* Albany: State University of New York Press.

Burstein, Paul, Rachel L. Einwohner, and Jocelyn A. Hollander. 1995. "The Success of Political Movements: A Bargaining Perspective." In *The Politics of Social Protest: Comparative Perspectives on States and Social Movements,* ed. J. Craig Jenkins and Bert Klandermans, 275–95. Minneapolis: University of Minnesota Press.

Button, James. 1989a. *Blacks and Social Change.* Princeton, NJ: Princeton University Press.

———. 1989b. "The Outcomes of Contemporary Black Protest and Violence." In *Violence in America,* Part 1, ed. Ted Robert Gurr, 286–306. Newbury Hills, CA: Sage Publications.

Calhoun, Craig. 1989. "The Beijing Spring 1989: An Eyewitness Account." *Dissent* 36: 435–47.

Callahan, William A. 1998. *Imagining Democracy: Reading "The Events of May" in Thailand.* Singapore: Institute of Southeast Asian Studies.

Câmara, Dom Helder. 1972. *Revolution through Peace.* New York: Harper Colophon Books.

Case, Clarence Marsh. 1972. *Non-violent Coercion: A Study in Methods of Social Pressure.* New York: Garland.

Chai-Anan Samudavanija. 1995. "Thailand: A Stable Semi-democracy." In *Politics in Developing Countries: Comparing Experiences with Democracy,* ed. Larry Diamond, Juan J. Linz, and Seymour Martin Lipset, 322–67. Boulder, CO: Lynne Rienner Publishing.

———. 1997. "Old Soldiers Never Die, They Are Just Bypassed: The Military, Bureaucracy and Globalisation." In *Political Change in Thailand: Democracy and Development,* ed. Kevin Hewison, 42–57. New York: Routledge.

Chaiwat Satha-Anand. 1997. "Two Plots of Nonviolence Stories: From the Streets of Bangkok to the Forests of Thailand." *Social Alternatives* 16: 12–15.

Chomsky, Noam. 2001. *9-11.* New York: Seven Stories Press.

———. 2002. *Media Control: The Spectacular Achievements of Propaganda,* 2nd ed. New York: Seven Stories Press.

Churchill, Ward, and Jim Vander Wall. 1990. *Agents of Repression: The FBI's Secret Wars against the Black Panther Party and the American Indian Movement.* Boston: South End Press.

Cohen, Jean. 1985. "Strategy or Identity: New Theoretical Paradigms and Contemporary Social Movements." *Social Research* 52: 663–716.

Colburn, Forrest. 1994. *The Vogue of Revolution in Poor Countries.* Princeton, NJ: Princeton University Press.

Colby, David. 1985. "Black Power, White Resistance, and Public Policy." *Journal of Politics* 47: 579–95.

Collier, Ruth Berins, and James Mahoney. 1997. "Adding Collective Actors to Collective Outcomes: Labor and Recent Democratization in South America and South Europe." *Comparative Politics* 29: 285–303.

Conser, Walter H., Ronald M. McCarthy, David J. Toscano, and Gene Sharp, eds. 1986. *Resistance, Politics, and the American Struggle for Independence, 1765–1775.* Boulder, CO: Lynne Rienner Publishers.

Cooney, Robert, and Helen Michalowski, eds. 1987. *The Power of the People: Active Nonviolence in the United States.* Philadelphia: New Society Publishers.

Corr, Anders. 1999. *No Trespassing: Squatting, Rent Strikes, and Land Struggles Worldwide.* Cambridge, MA: South End Press.

Coy, Patrick G., and Lynne M. Woehrle. 2000. *Social Conflicts and Collective Identities.* Lanham, MD: Rowman and Littlefield Publishers.

Crenshaw, Edward M. 1995. "Democracy and Demographic Inheritance: The Influence of Modernity and Proto-Modernity on Political and Civil Rights, 1965–1980." *American Sociological Review* 60: 702–18.

Crook, Wilfred H. 1931. *The General Strike: A Study of Labor's Tragic Weapon in Theory and in Practice.* Chapel Hill: University of North Carolina Press.

Crow, Ralph E., Philip Grant, and Saad E. Ibrahim, eds. 1990. *Arab Nonviolent Struggle in the Middle East.* Boulder, CO: Lynne Rienner Publishing.

Dahl, Robert A. 1961. *Who Governs?* New Haven, CT: Yale University Press.

Dajani, Souad. 1995. *Eyes without a Country: Searching for a Palestinian Strategy for Liberation.* Philadelphia: Temple University Press.

Dalton, Russell J., and Manfred Keuchler, eds. 1990. *Challenging the Political Order: New Social and Political Movements in Western Democracies.* Oxford, England: Oxford University Press.

Davenport, Christian. 2000. "Introduction." In *Paths to State Repression: Human Rights Violations and Contentious Politics,* ed. Christian Davenport, 1–24. Lanham, MD: Rowman and Littlefield Publishers.

Debray, Régis. 1967. *Revolution in the Revolution? Armed Struggle and Political Struggle in Latin America.* New York: Grove Press.

della Porta, Donatella. 1995. *Social Movements, Political Violence, and the State: A Comparative Analysis of Italy and Germany.* Cambridge, England: Cambridge University Press.

DeNardo, James. 1985. *Power in Numbers.* Princeton, NJ: Princeton University Press.

Diamond, Larry. 1992. "Economic Development and Democracy Reconsidered." *American Behavioral Scientist* 35: 450–99.

Diani, Mario. 1995. *Green Networks: A Structural Analysis of the Italian Environmental Movement.* Edinburgh: Edinburgh University Press.

Di Palma, Guiseppe. 1990. *To Craft Democracies: An Essay on Democratic Transitions.* Berkeley: University of California Press.

Dirks, Nicholas B. 1994. "Ritual and Resistance: Subversion as a Social Fact." In *Culture/Power/History: A Reader in Contemporary Social Theory,* ed. Nicholas B. Dirks, Geoff Eley, and Sherry B. Ortner, 483–503. Princeton, N.J.: Princeton University Press.

Dittmer, Lowell. 1990. "China in 1989: The Crisis of Incomplete Reform." *Asian Survey* 33: 25–41.

Dix, Robert H. 1984. "Why Revolutions Succeed and Fail." *Polity* 16: 423–46.

Domhoff, William G. 2002. *Who Rules America? Power and Politics,* 4th ed. Mountain View, CA: Mayfield Publishing Co.

Ebert, Theodor. 1968. "Non-violent Resistance against Communist Regimes?" In *Civilian Resistance as a National Defense: Non-violent Action against Aggression,* ed. Adam Roberts, 173–94. Harrisburg, PA: Stackpole Books.

Eckstein, Susan, ed. 1989. *Power and Popular Protest: Latin American Social Movements.* Berkeley: University of California Press.

Eglitis, Olgerts. 1993. *Nonviolent Action in the Liberation of Latvia.* Cambridge, MA: Albert Einstein Institution.

Elwood, Douglas J. 1986. *Philippine Revolution 1986: Model of Nonviolent Change.* Quezon City: New Day Publishers.

Evans, Sara M., and Harry C. Boyte. 1992. *Free Spaces: The Sources of Democratic Change in America.* Chicago: University of Chicago Press.

Falk, Richard A. 1995. *On Humane Governance: Toward a New Global Politics.* University Park: Pennsylvania State University Press.

Fink, Christina. 2001. *Living Silence: Burma under Military Rule.* London: Zed Books.

Finnemore, Martheanne, and Roux Van der Merwe. 1992. *Introduction to Industrial Relations in South Africa,* 3rd ed. Johannesburg: Lexicon.

Fisher, Jo. 1993. *Out of the Shadows: Women, Resistance, and Politics in South America.* New York: Latin American Bureau.

Fisher, Julie. 1998. *Nongovernments: NGOs and the Political Development of the Third World.* West Hartford, CT: Kumarian Press.

Foran, John. 1994. "The Iranian Revolution of 1977–79: A Challenge for Social Theory." In *A Century of Revolution: Social Movements in Iran,* ed. John Foran, chapter 7. Minneapolis: University of Minnesota Press.

Foreign Broadcast Information Service. 1983–86. *Asia and the Pacific, National Affairs, Daily Reports: The Philippines.* Washington, DC: U.S. Government.

———. 1983–90. *Near East and South Africa, National Affairs, Daily Reports: South Africa.* Washington, DC: U.S. Government.

———. 1988–90. *East Asia, National Affairs, Daily Reports: Burma.* Washington, DC: U.S. Government.

———. 1989. *China, National Affairs, Daily Reports.* Washington, DC: U.S. Government.

———. 1990. *South Asia, National Affairs, Daily Reports: Nepal.* Washington, DC: U.S. Government.

———. 1991–92. *Asia and the Pacific, National Affairs, Daily Reports: Thailand.* Washington, DC: U.S. Government.

Foucault, Michel. 1977. "Revolutionary Action: 'Until Now.'" In *Language, Counter-Memory, Practice,* ed. Donald F. Bouchard, trans. Donald F. Bouchard and Sherry Simon, 218–33. Ithaca, NY: Cornell University Press.

———. 1980. *Power/Knowledge.* New York: Pantheon Books.

Francisco, Ronald A. 1995. "The Relationship between Coercion and Protest: An Empirical Test in Three Coercive States." *Journal of Conflict Resolution* 39: 263–82.

———. 1996. "Coercion and Protest: An Empirical Test in Two Democratic States." *American Journal of Political Science* 40: 1179–1204.

———. 2000. "Why Are Collective Conflicts 'Stable'?" In *Paths to State Repression: Human Rights Violations and Contentious Politics,* ed. Christian Davenport, 149–72. Lanham, MD: Rowman and Littlefield Publishers.

Frankel, Philip H. 2001. *An Ordinary Atrocity: Sharpeville and Its Massacre.* New Haven, CT: Yale University Press.

Freeman, Jo. 1975. *The Politics of Women's Liberation.* New York: Longman.

———. 1987. "Who You Know vs. Who You Represent: Feminist Influence in the Democratic and Republican Parties." In *The Women's Movements of the United States and Western Europe: Feminist Consciousness, Political Opportunity and Public Policy,* ed. Mary Katzenstein and Carol Mueller, 215–44. Philadelphia: Temple University Press.

Friedland, Jonathon. 1992. "Collateral Damage." *Far Eastern Economic Review,* May 28, 12.

Fukuda, Chisako M. 2000. "Peace through Nonviolent Action: The East Timorese Resistance Movement's Strategy for Engagement." *Pacifica Review* 12: 17–31.

Galtung, Johan. 1980. *The True Worlds: A Transnational Perspective.* New York: Free Press.

———. 1989. "Principles of Nonviolent Action: The Great Chain of Nonviolence Hypothesis." In *Nonviolence and Israel/Palestine,* by Johan Galtung, 13–33. Honolulu: University of Hawai'i Press.

Gamson, William A. 1990. *The Strategy of Social Protest,* 2nd ed. Belmont, CA: Wadsworth.

Gamson, William A., Bruce Fireman, and Steven Rytina. 1982. *Encounters with Unjust Authorities.* Homewood, IL: Dorsey Press.

Gamson, William A., and David S. Meyer. 1996. "Framing Political Opportunity."

In *Comparative Perspectives on Social Movements: Political Opportunities, Mobilizing Structures, and Cultural Framing,* ed. Doug McAdam, John D. McCarthy, and Mayer N. Zald, 275–90. Cambridge, England: Cambridge University Press.

Gandhi, Mohandas K. 1958–94. *The Collected Works of Mahatma Gandhi,* 100 vols. New Delhi: Publications Division, Government of India.

Garrow, David. 1978. *Protest in Selma.* New Haven, CT: Yale University Press.

Gartner, Scott Sigmund, and Patrick M. Regan. 1996. "Threat and Repression: The Non-Linear Relationship between Government and Opposition Violence." *Journal of Peace Research* 33: 273–88.

Gerhards, Jürgen, and Dieter Rucht. 1992. "Mesomobilization: Organizing and Framing in Two Protest Campaigns in West Germany." *American Journal of Sociology* 98: 555–96.

Gerlach, Luther P., and Virginia H. Hine. 1970. *People, Power, Change: Movements of Social Transformation.* Indianapolis: Bobbs-Merrill.

Giddens, Anthony. 1990. *The Consequences of Modernity.* Stanford, CA: Stanford University Press.

Girling, John L. S. 1981. *Thailand: Society and Politics.* Ithaca, NY: Cornell University Press.

Giugni, Marco G., Doug McAdam, and Charles Tilly, eds. 1998. *From Contention to Democracy.* Lanham, MD: Rowman and Littlefield Publishers.

———, eds. 1999. *How Social Movements Matter.* Minneapolis: University of Minnesota Press.

Glasius, Marlies, Mary Kaldor, and Helmut Anheier, eds. 2002. *Global Civil Society 2002.* Oxford, England: Oxford University Press.

Gleditsch, Nils Peter, Peter Wallensteen, Mikael, Eriksson, Margareta Sollenberg, and Håvard Strand. 2002. "Armed Conflict 1946–2001: A New Dataset." *Journal of Peace Research* 39: 615–37.

Glick, Brian. 1989. *War at Home: Covert Action against U.S. Activists and What We Can Do about It.* Boston: South End Press.

Goldstone, Jack A., and Charles Tilly. 2001. "Threat (and Opportunity): Popular Action and State Response in the Dynamics of Contentious Action." In *Silence and Voice in the Study of Contentious Politics,* ed. Ronald R. Aminzade, Jack A. Goldstone, Doug McAdam, Elizabeth Perry, William H. Sewell Jr., Sidney Tarrow, and Charles Tilly, chapter 3. Cambridge, England: Cambridge University Press.

Goodwin, Jeff. 2001a. *No Other Way Out: States and Revolutionary Movements, 1945–1991.* Cambridge: Cambridge University Press.

———, ed. 2001b. "Opportunistic Protest? Political Opportunities, Social Movements, and Revolutions." Unpublished book manuscript.

Goodwin, Jeff, and James M. Jasper. 1999. "Caught in a Winding, Snarling Vine: The Structural Bias of Political Process Theory." *Sociological Forum* 14: 27–54.

Goodwin, Jeff, and Theda Skocpol. 1989. "Explaining Revolutions in the Contemporary Third World." *Politics and Society* 17: 489–509.

Gould, Roger. 1995. *Insurgent Identities: Class, Community, and Protest in Paris from 1848 to the Commune.* Chicago: University of Chicago Press.

Gramsci, Antonio. 1971. *Selections from the Prison Notebooks,* ed. and trans. Quintin Hoare and Geoffrey Nowell Smith. London: Lawrence and Wishart.

Gregg, Richard B. 1966. *The Power of Nonviolence.* New York: Schocken Books.

Guérin, Daniel. 1970. *Anarchism: From Theory to Practice.* New York: Monthly Review Press.

Gupta, Dipak, Harinder Singh, and Tom Sprague. 1993. "Government Coercion of Dissidents: Deterrence or Provocation?" *Journal of Conflict Resolution* 37: 301–39.

Gurr, Ted Robert. 1970. *Why Men Rebel.* Princeton, NJ: Princeton University Press.

———. 1986. "Persisting Patterns of Repression and Rebellion: Foundations for a General Theory of Political Coercion." In *Persistent Patterns and Emergent Structures in a Waning Century,* ed. Margaret P. Karns, 149–68. New York: Praeger Publishers.

———. 1993. *Minorities at Risk: A Global View of Ethnopolitical Conflicts.* Washington, DC: U.S. Institute of Peace.

Gurr, Ted Robert, Monty G. Marshall, and Deepa Khosla. 2001. *Peace and Conflict 2001: A Global Survey of Armed Conflicts, Self-Determination Movements, and Democracy.* College Park: Center for International Development and Conflict Management, University of Maryland.

Guyot, James F. 1989. "Burma in 1988: *Perestroika* with a Military Face." In *Southeast Asian Affairs 1989,* by James F. Guyot, 107–33. Singapore: Institute of Southeast Asian Studies.

———. 1991. "Myanmar in 1990: The Unconsummated Elections." *Asian Survey* 31: 205–11.

Guyot, James F., and John Badgley. 1990. "Myanmar in 1989: *Tatmadaw V.*" *Asian Survey* 30: 187–95.

Haines, Herbert H. 1984. "Black Radicalization and the Funding of Civil Rights, 1957–1970." *Social Problems* 32: 31–43.

———. 1988. *Black Radicals and the Civil Rights Mainstream, 1954–1970.* Knoxville: University of Tennessee Press.

Harmel, Barbara. 1997. "African National Congress of South Africa." In *Protest, Power, and Change: An Encyclopedia of Nonviolent Action from ACT-UP to Women's Suffrage,* ed. Roger S. Powers and William B. Vogele, 14–16. New York: Garland Publishing.

Harvey, David. 1989. *The Condition of Post Modernity: An Inquiry into the Origins of Cultural Change.* Cambridge, MA: Blackwell Publishers.

Havel, Vaclav, et al. 1985. *The Power of the Powerless: Citizens against the State in Central-Eastern Europe,* ed. John Keane. Armonk, NY: M. E. Sharpe.

Held, David. 1995. *Democracy and the Global Order.* Stanford, CA: Stanford University Press.

Herman, Edward S., and Noam Chomsky. 1988. *Manufacturing Consent: The Political Economy of the Mass Media.* New York: Pantheon Books.

Hewison, Kevin. 1993. "Of Regimes, State, and Pluralities: Thai Politics Enters the 1990s." In *Southeast Asia in the 1990s: Authoritarianism, Democracy and Capitalism,* ed. Kevin Hewison, Richard Robison, and Garry Rodan, 161–89. Sydney: Allen and Unwin.

———. 1996. "Political Oppositions and Regime Change in Thailand." In *Political Oppositions in Industrializing Asia,* ed. Garry Rodan, 72–94. New York: Routledge.

———. 1997. "The Monarchy and Democratisation." In *Political Change in Thailand: Democracy and Development,* ed. Kevin Hewison, 58–74. New York: Routledge.

Hewison, Kevin, and Garry Rodan. 1996. "The Ebb and Flow of Civil Society and the Decline of the Left in Southeast Asia." In *Political Oppositions in Industrializing Asia,* ed. Garry Rodan, 40–71. New York: Routledge.

Hibbs, Douglas A., Jr. 1973. *Mass Political Violence: A Cross-National Causal Analysis.* New York: Wiley.

Higley, John, and Richard Gunther, eds. 1992. *Elites and Democratic Consolidation in Latin America and Southern Europe.* Cambridge, England: Cambridge University Press.

Hiller, E. T. 1928. *The Strike: A Study in Collective Action.* Chicago: University of Chicago Press.

Hirschman, Albert O. 1993. "Exit, Voice, and the Fate of the German Democratic Republic: An Essay in Conceptual History." *World Politics* 45: 173–202.

Hirschsohn, Philip. 1998. "From Grassroots Democracy to National Mobilization: COSATU as a Model of Social Movement Unionism." *Economic and Industrial Democracy* 19: 633–66.

Holmes, Robert L., ed. 1990. *Nonviolence in Theory and Practice.* Belmont, CA: Wadsworth Publishing.

Hufbauer, Gary Clyde, Jeffrey J. Schott, and Kimberly Ann Elliott. 1990. *Economic Sanctions Reconsidered: History and Current Policy,* 2nd ed. Washington, DC: Institute for International Economics

Human Rights Internet. 1994. *Master List: A Listing of Organizations Concerned with Human Rights and Social Justice Worldwide,* supplement to vol. 15 of the *Human Rights Internet Reporter.* Ottawa: Human Rights Internet.

Huntington, Samuel P. 1991. *The Third Wave: Democratization in the Late Twentieth Century.* Norman: University of Oklahoma Press.

Hutchcroft, Paul D. 1991. "Oligarchs and Cronies in the Philippine State: The Politics of Patrimonial Plunder." *World Politics* 43: 414–50.

Ileto, Reynaldo C. 1985. "The Past in the Present Crisis." In *The Philippines after Marcos,* ed. R. J. May and Francisco Nemenzo, 7–16. New York: St. Martin's Press.

Innes, Duncan. 1992. "Labor Relations in the De Klerk Era." *South Africa Review* 6: 338–51.

Jackson, Peter A. 1997. "Withering Centre, Flourishing Margins: Buddhism's Changing Political Roles." In *Political Change in Thailand: Democracy and Development,* ed. Kevin Hewison, 75–93. New York: Routledge.

Jasper, James M. 1997. *The Art of Moral Protest: Culture, Biography, and Creativity in Social Movements.* Chicago: University of Chicago Press.

Jenkins, J. Craig. 1983. "Resource Mobilization Theory and the Study of Social Movements." *Annual Review of Sociology* 9: 527–53.

———. 1985. *The Politics of Insurgency: The Farm Worker Movement in the 1960s.* New York: Columbia University Press.

Jenkins, J. Craig, and Barbara Brents. 1989. "Social Protest, Hegemonic Competition, and Social Reform." *American Sociological Review* 54: 891–910.

Jenkins, J. Craig, and Craig M. Eckert. 1986. "Channeling Black Insurgency: Elite Patronage and Professional Social Movement Organizations in the Development of the Black Movement." *American Sociological Review* 51: 812–29.

Jenkins, J. Craig, and Bert Klandermans, eds. 1995. *The Politics of Social Protest: Comparative Perspectives on States and Social Movements.* Minneapolis: University of Minnesota Press.

Jenkins, J. Craig, and Charles Perrow. 1977. "Insurgency of the Powerless." *American Sociological Review* 42: 249–68.

Jenkins, J. Craig, and Kurt Schock. 1992. "Global Structures and Political Processes in the Study of Domestic Political Conflict." *Annual Review of Sociology* 18: 161–85.

Keck, Margaret E., and Kathryn Sikkink. 1998. *Activists beyond Borders: Advocacy Networks in International Politics.* Ithaca, NY: Cornell University Press.

Khawaja, Marwan. 1993. "Repression and Popular Collective Action: Evidence from the West Bank." *Sociological Forum* 8: 47–71.

———. 1994. "Resource Mobilization, Hardship, and Popular Collective Action in the West Bank." *Social Forces* 73: 191–220.

————. 1995. "The Dynamics of Local Collective Action in the West Bank: A Test of Rival Explanations." *Economic Development and Cultural Change* 44: 147–79.

Killian, Lewis M. 1972. "The Significance of Extremism in the Black Revolution." *Social Problems* 20: 41–48.

King-Hall, Stephen. 1958. *Defence in the Nuclear Age.* London: Victor Gollancz.

Kitschelt, Herbert. 1986. "Political Opportunity Structures and Political Protest: Anti-Nuclear Movements in Four Democracies." *British Journal of Political Science* 16: 57–85.

Klandermans, Bert. 1997. *The Social Psychology of Protest.* Cambridge, MA: Blackwell Publishers.

Klandermans, Bert, Hanspeter Kriesi, and Sidney Tarrow, eds. 1988. *From Structure to Action: Comparing Movement Participation across Cultures.* Greenwich, CT: JAI.

Kreager, Philip. 1991. "Aung San Suu Kyi and the Peaceful Struggle for Human Rights in Burma." In *Freedom from Fear and Other Writings,* by Aung San Suu Kyi, ed. Michael Aris, 284–325. London: Viking.

Kriesi, Hanspeter, Ruud Koopmans, Jan Willem Duyvendak, and Marco G. Guigni. 1995. *The Politics of New Social Movements in Western Europe: A Comparative Analysis.* Minneapolis: University of Minnesota Press.

Kropotkin, Peter. 1995. *The Conquest of Bread and Other Writings,* ed. Marshall S. Shatz. Cambridge, England: Cambridge University Press.

Kurtz, Lester R., ed. 1999. *Encyclopedia of Violence, Peace, and Conflict.* San Diego: Academic Press.

Kurzman, Charles. 1996. "Structural Opportunity and Perceived Opportunity in Social-Movement Theory: The Iranian Revolution of 1979." *American Sociological Review* 61: 153–70.

————. 1998. "Organizational Opportunity and Social Movement Mobilization: A Comparative Analysis of Four Religious Movements." *Mobilization* 3: 23–49.

La Boétie, Étienne de. 1997. *The Politics of Obedience: The Discourse of Voluntary Servitude.* Montreal: Black Rose Books.

Lakey, George. 1973. *Strategy for a Living Revolution.* New York: Grossman.

Lambert, Rob, and Eddie Webster. 1988. "The Re-emergence of Political Unionism in Contemporary South Africa?" In *Popular Struggles in South Africa,* ed. William Cobbett and Robin Cohen, 20–41. Trenton, NJ: Africa World Press.

Lane, Max R. 1990. *The Urban Mass Movement in the Philippines, 1983–87.* Singapore: Institute of Southeast Asian Studies.

Lenin, V. I. 1970. "What Is to Be Done? Vexatious Questions of Our Movement." In *V. I. Lenin's What Is to Be Done?* ed. S. V. Utechin, trans. S. V. and Patricia Utechin, 37–192. Oxford, England: Clarendon Press.

Lichbach, Mark Irving. 1987. "Deterrence or Escalation? The Puzzle of Aggregate Studies of Repression and Dissent." *Journal of Conflict Resolution* 31: 266–97.

———. 1989. "An Evaluation of 'Does Economic Inequality Breed Political Conflict?' Studies." *World Politics* 41: 431–70.

———. 1995. *The Rebel's Dilemma.* Ann Arbor: University of Michigan Press.

———. 1998. "Contending Theories of Contentious Politics and the Structure-Action Problem of Social Order." *Annual Review of Political Science* 1: 401–24.

Likhit Dhiravegin. 1992. *Demi Democracy: The Evolution of the Thai Political System.* Singapore: Times Academic Press.

Lintner, Bertil. 1990. *Outrage: Burma's Struggle for Democracy,* 2nd ed. London: White Lotus.

———. 1994. *Burma in Revolt: Opium and Insurgency since 1948.* Boulder, CO: Westview Press.

Lipset, Seymour Martin. 1981. *Political Man: The Social Bases of Politics,* 2nd ed. Baltimore: Johns Hopkins University Press.

Lipset, Seymour Martin, Kyoung-Ryung Seong, and John Charles Torres. 1993. "A Comparative Analysis of the Social Requisites of Democracy." *International Social Science Journal* 45: 154–75.

Lipsitz, Lewis, and Herbert M. Kritzer. 1975. "Unconventional Approaches to Conflict Resolution: Erikson and Sharp on Nonviolence." *Journal of Conflict Resolution* 19: 713–33.

Lipsky, Michael. 1968. "Protest as a Political Resource." *American Political Science Review* 62: 1144–58.

Lodge, Tom. 1988. "State of Exile: The African National Congress of South Africa, 1976–86." In *State, Resistance, and Change in South Africa,* ed. Philip Frankel, Noam Pines, and Mark Swilling, 229–58. London: Croom Helm.

———. 1992. "Rebellion: The Turning of the Tide." In *All, Here, and Now: Black Politics in South Africa in the 1980s,* ed. Tom Lodge and Bill Nasson, 21–204. London: Hurst and Company.

Lopez, George, and Michael Stohl, eds. 1989. *Dependence, Development, and State Repression.* New York: Greenwood Press.

Lukes, Steven. 1974. *Power: A Radical View.* New York: Macmillan.

Lyng, Stephen G., and Lester R. Kurtz. 1985. "Bureaucratic Insurgency: The Vatican and the Crisis of Modernism." *Social Forces* 63: 901–22.

MacQueen, Graeme, ed. 1992. *Unarmed Forces: Nonviolent Action in Central America and the Middle East.* Toronto: Science for Peace / S. Stevens.

Mahony, Liam, and Luis Enrique Eguren. 1997. *Unarmed Bodyguards: International Accompaniment for the Protection of Human Rights.* West Hartford, CT: Kumarian Press.

Mainwaring, Scott, Guillermo O'Donnell, and Arturo Valenzuela, eds. 1992. *Issues in Democratic Consolidation.* Notre Dame, IN: University of Notre Dame Press.

Mann, Michael. 1986. *The Sources of Social Power: A History of Power from the Beginning to A.D. 1760,* vol. 1. Cambridge, England: Cambridge University Press.

Maree, Johann. 1985. "The Emergence, Struggles, and Achievements of Black Trade Unions in South Africa from 1973 to 1984." *Labour, Capital, and Society* 18: 278–303.

Markoff, John. 1996. *Waves of Democracy: Social Movements and Political Change.* Thousand Oaks, CA: Pine Forge Press.

———. 1997. "Peasants Help Destroy an Old Regime and Defy a New One: Some Lessons from (and for) the Study of Social Movements." *American Journal of Sociology* 102: 1113–42.

Martin, Brian. 1984. *Uprooting War.* London: Freedom Press.

———. 1989. "Gene Sharp's Theory of Power." *Journal of Peace Research* 26: 213–22.

———. 1993. *Social Defence, Social Change.* London: Freedom Press.

———. 1996. "Communication Technology and Nonviolent Action." *Media Development* 43: 3–9.

———. 1997. "Critique of Violent Rationales." *Pacifica Review* 9: 83–91.

———. 1999. "Technology, Violence, and Peace." In *Encyclopedia of Violence, Peace, and Conflict,* vol. 3, ed. Lester R. Kurtz, 447–59. San Diego: Academic Press.

———. 2001. *Nonviolence versus Capitalism.* London: War Resisters' International.

Martin, Brian, and Wendy Varney. 2003. *Nonviolence Speaks: Communicating against Repression.* Cresskill, NJ: Hampton Press.

Martin, Brian, Wendy Varney, and Adrian Vickers. 2001. "Political Jiu-Jitsu against Indonesian Repression: Studying Lower Profile Nonviolent Resistance." *Pacifica Review* 13: 143–56.

Marwell, Gerald, and Pam Oliver. 1993. *The Critical Mass in Collective Action: A Micro-Social Theory.* Cambridge, England: Cambridge University Press.

Marx, Anthony W. 1992. *Lessons of Struggle: South African Internal Opposition, 1960–1990.* Oxford, England: Oxford University Press.

Marx, Gary T. 1974. "Thoughts on a Neglected Category of Social Movement Participant: The Agent Provocateur and Informant." *American Journal of Sociology* 80: 402–42.

———. 1979. "External Efforts to Damage or Facilitate Social Movements: Some Patterns, Explanations, Outcomes, and Complications." In *The Dynamics of Social Movements: Resource Mobilization, Social Control, and Tactics,* ed. Mayer N. Zald and John D. McCarthy, 94–125. Cambridge, MA: Wintrhop Publications.

Marx, Karl. 2000. *Karl Marx: Selected Writings,* 2nd. ed., ed. David McLellan. Oxford, England: Oxford University Press.

Mason, T. David, and Dale A. Krame. 1989. "The Political Economy of Death

Squads: Toward a Theory of the Impact of State-Sanctioned Terror." *International Studies Quarterly* 33: 175–98.

Masotti, Louis H., Jeffrey K. Hadden, Kenneth F. Seminatore, and Jerome R. Corsi. 1969. *A Time to Burn? An Evaluation of the Present Crisis in Race Relations.* Chicago: Rand-McNally.

Matthews, Bruce. 1993. "Buddhism under a Military Regime: The Iron Heel in Burma." *Asian Survey* 33: 408–23.

Maung, Mya. 1990. "The Burma Road from the Union of Burma to Myanmar." *Asian Survey* 30: 602–24.

———. 1991. *The Burma Road to Poverty.* New York: Praeger.

———. 1992. *Totalitarianism in Burma: Prospects for Economic Development.* New York: Paragon House.

McAdam, Doug. 1983. "Tactical Innovation and the Pace of Insurgency." *American Sociological Review* 48: 735–54.

———. 1988. *Freedom Summer.* Oxford: Oxford University Press.

———. 1996. "Conceptual Origins, Current Problems, Future Directions. " In *Comparative Perspectives on Social Movements: Political Opportunities, Mobilizing Structures, and Cultural Framing,* ed. Doug McAdam, John D. McCarthy, and Mayer N. Zald, 23–40. Cambridge, England: Cambridge University Press.

———. 1999. *Political Process and the Development of Black Insurgency, 1930–1970,* 2nd ed. Chicago: University of Chicago Press.

McAdam, Doug, John D. McCarthy, and Mayer N. Zald. 1988. "Social Movements." In *Handbook of Sociology,* ed. Neil Smelser, 695–738. Newbury Park, CA: Sage.

———, eds. 1996. *Comparative Perspectives on Social Movements: Political Opportunities, Mobilizing Structures, and Cultural Framing.* Cambridge, England: Cambridge University Press.

McAdam, Doug, Sidney Tarrow, and Charles Tilly. 2001. *Dynamics of Contention.* Cambridge, England: Cambridge University Press.

McCarthy, John D., and Mark Wolfson. 1992. "Consensus Movements, Conflict Movements and the Cooptation of Civic and State Infrastructures." In *Frontiers in Social Movement Theory,* ed. Aldon D. Morris and Carol McClurg Mueller, 273–97. New Haven, CT: Yale University Press.

McCarthy, John D., and Mayer N. Zald. 1973. *The Trend of Social Movements in America: Professionalization and Resource Mobilization.* Morristown, NJ: General Learning Press.

———. 1977. "Resource Mobilization and Social Movements: A Partial Theory." *American Journal of Sociology* 82: 1212–41.

McCarthy, Ronald M. 1990. "The Techniques of Nonviolent Action: Some Principles of Its Nature, Use, and Effects." In *Arab Nonviolent Struggle in the Middle*

East, ed. Ralph E. Crow, Philip Grant, and Saad E. Ibrahim, 107–20. Boulder, CO: Lynne Rienner Publishing.

———. 1997. "Methods of Nonviolent Action." In *Protest, Power, and Change: An Encyclopedia of Nonviolent Action from ACT-UP to Women's Suffrage,* ed. Roger S. Powers and William B. Vogele, 319–28. New York: Garland Publishing.

McCarthy, Ronald M., and Christopher Kruegler. 1993. *Toward Research and Theory Building in the Study of Nonviolent Action.* Boston: Albert Einstein Institution.

McCarthy, Ronald M., and Gene Sharp. 1997. *Nonviolent Action: A Research Guide.* New York: Garland Publishing.

McGuinness, Kate. 1993. "Gene Sharp's Theory of Power: A Feminist Critique of Consent." *Journal of Peace Research* 30: 101–15.

McManus, Phillip, and Gerald Schlabach. 1991. *Relentless Persistence: Nonviolent Action in Latin America.* Philadelphia: New Society Press.

Meisner, Maurice J. 1999. *Mao's China and After: A History of the People's Republic,* 3rd ed. New York: Free Press.

Melucci, Alberto. 1989. *Nomads of the Present: Social Movements and Individual Needs in Contemporary Society,* ed. John Keane and Paul Mier. Philadelphia: Temple University Press.

Meyer, John W., John Boli, George M. Thomas, and Francisco O. Ramirez. 1997. "World Society and the Nation-State." *American Journal of Sociology* 103: 144–81.

Miller, Byron. 2000. *Geography and Social Movements: Comparing Antinuclear Activism in the Boston Area.* Minneapolis: University of Minnesota Press.

Moksha, Yitri. 1989. "The Crisis in Burma: Back from the Heart of Darkness?" *Asian Survey* 29: 543–58.

Moore, Barrington Jr. 1966. *Social Origins of Dictatorship and Democracy: Lord and Peasant in the Making of the Modern World.* Boston: Beacon Press.

———. 1978. *Injustice: The Social Basis of Obedience and Revolt.* White Plains, NY: M. E. Sharpe.

Moore, Will H. 1995. "Repression and Dissent: Substitution, Context, and Timing." *American Journal of Political Science* 42: 851–73.

Morell, David, and Chai-Anan Samudavanija. 1981. *Political Conflict in Thailand: Reform, Reaction, Revolution.* Cambridge, MA: Oelgesclager, Gunn, and Hain.

Morobe, Murphy. 1987. "Towards a People's Democracy: The UDF View." *Review of African Political Economy* 14: 81–87.

Morris, Aldon D. 1984. *The Origins of the Civil Rights Movement: Black Communities Organizing for Change.* New York: Free Press.

Mozia, Timothy U. 1991. "Appendix A: Chronology of Arms Embargoes against South Africa" and "Appendix B: Chronology of Economic Embargoes against South Africa." In *Effective Sanctions on South Africa: The Cutting Edge of Eco-*

nomic Intervention, ed. George W. Shepard Jr., 97–125. Westport, CT: Greenwood Press.

Mueller, Carol McClurg. 1978. "Riot Violence and Protest Outcomes." *Journal of Political and Military Sociology* 6: 49–63.

———. 1999. "Escape from the GDR, 1961–1989: Hybrid Exit Repertoires in a Disintegrating Regime." *American Journal of Sociology* 105: 697–735.

Mufson, Steven. 1992. "Introduction: The Roots of Insurrection." In *All, Here, and Now: Black Politics in South Africa in the 1980s,* ed. Tom Lodge and Bill Nasson, 3–17. London: Hurst and Company.

Muller, Edward N. 1985. "Income Inequality, Regime Repressiveness, and Political Violence." *American Sociological Review* 50: 47–61.

Muller, Edward N., and Mitchell A. Seligson. 1987. "Inequality and Insurgency." *American Political Science Review* 81: 425–51.

Muller, Edward N., and Erich Weede. 1990. "Cross-National Variation in Political Violence: A Rational Action Approach." *Journal of Conflict Resolution* 34: 624–51.

Muse, Benjamin. 1968. *The American Negro Revolution: From Nonviolence to Black Power.* Bloomington: Indiana University Press.

Naidoo, Kumi. 1989. "Internal Resistance in South Africa: The Political Movements." In *South Africa: No Turning Back,* ed. Shaun Johnson, 172–205. Bloomington: Indiana University Press.

Nathan, Andrew J. 1989. "Chinese Democracy in 1989: Continuity and Change." *Problems of Communism* 38: 16–29.

National Manpower Commission. 1986–89. *Annual Reports.* Pretoria: Republic of South Africa.

Noonan, Rita. 1995. "Women against the State: Political Opportunities and Collective Action Frames in Chile's Transition to Democracy." *Sociological Forum* 10: 81–111.

Oberschall, Anthony. 1996. "Opportunities and Framing in the East European Revolts of 1989." In *Comparative Perspectives on Social Movements: Political Opportunities, Mobilizing Structures, and Cultural Framing,* ed. Doug McAdam, John D. McCarthy, and Mayer N. Zald, 93–121. Cambridge, England: Cambridge University Press.

O'Donnell, Guillermo, Philippe C. Schmitter, and Laurence Whitehead. 1986. *Transitions from Authoritarian Rule: Comparative Perspectives.* Baltimore: Johns Hopkins University Press.

Offe, Claus. 1985. "New Social Movements: Changing Boundaries of the Political." *Social Research* 52: 817–68.

Olivier, Johan L. 1990. "Causes of Ethnic Collective Action in the Pretoria-Witwatersrand Triangle, 1970 to 1984." *South African Sociological Review* 2: 89–108.

———. 1991. "State Repression and Collective Action in South Africa, 1970–1984." *South African Journal of Sociology* 22: 109–17.

Opp, Karl-Dieter, and Wolfgang Roehl. 1990. "Repression, Micromobilization, and Political Protest." *Social Forces* 69: 521–47.

Osa, Maryjane. 1997. "Creating Solidarity: The Religious Foundations of the Polish Social Movement." *East European Politics and Societies* 11: 64–91.

———. 2001. "Mobilizing Structures and Cycles of Protest: Post-Stalinist Contention in Poland, 1954–1959." *Mobilization* 6: 140–61.

Osa, Maryjane, and Cristina Corduneanu-Huci. 2003. "Running Uphill: Political Opportunity in Non-Democracies." *Comparative Sociology* 2: 605–29.

Ost, David. 1990. *Solidarity and the Politics of Antipolitics: Opposition and Reform in Poland since 1968.* Philadelphia: Temple University Press.

Overholt, William. 1986. "The Rise and Fall of Ferdinand Marcos." *Asian Survey* 26: 1137–63.

Pagnucco, Ronald, and Jackie Smith. 1992. "Political Process and the 1989 Chinese Student Movement." *Studies in Conflict and Terrorism* 15: 169–84.

Paige, Jeffery M. 1975. *Agrarian Revolution: Social Movements and Export Agriculture in the Underdeveloped World.* New York: Free Press.

———. 1997. *Coffee and Power: Revolution and the Rise of Democracy in Central America.* Cambridge, MA: Harvard University Press.

Parajulee, Ramjee P. 2000. *The Democratic Transition in Nepal.* Lanham, MD: Rowman and Littlefield.

Parkman, Patricia. 1988. *Nonviolent Insurrection in El Salvador: The Fall of Maximiliano Hernández Martínez.* Tucson: University of Arizona Press.

———. 1991. *Insurrectionary Civic Strikes in Latin America, 1931–1961.* Cambridge, MA: Albert Einstein Institution.

Pasuk Phongpaichit and Chris Baker. 1997. *Thailand: Economy and Politics.* Oxford, England: Oxford University Press.

Pateman, Carole. 1988. *The Sexual Contract.* London: Polity Press.

Pichardo, Nelson A. 1997. "New Social Movements: A Critical Review." *Annual Review of Sociology* 23: 411–30.

Piven, Frances Fox, and Richard A. Cloward. 1979a. "Electoral Instability, Civil Disorder, and Relief Rises." *American Political Science Review* 73: 1012–19.

———. 1979b. *Poor People's Movements: Why They Succeed, How They Fail.* New York: Vintage Books.

Powell, Walter W. 1990. "Neither Market nor Hierarchy: Network Forms of Organization." *Research in Organizational Behavior* 12: 295–336.

Powers, Roger S., and William B. Vogele, eds. 1997. *Protest, Power, and Change: An Encyclopedia of Nonviolent Action from ACT-UP to Women's Suffrage.* New York: Garland Publishing.

Powledge, Fred. 1967. *Black Power, White Resistance: Notes on the New Civil War.* Cleveland: World Publishing.

Price, Robert M. 1991. *The Apartheid State in Crisis: Political Transformation in South Africa, 1975–1990.* Oxford, England: Oxford University Press.

Prudhisan Jumbala. 1992. *Nation-Building and Democratization in Thailand: A Political History.* Bangkok: Chulalongkorn University, Social Research Institute.

Prudhisan Jumbala, and Maneerat Mitprasat. 1997. "Non-governmental Development Organisations: Empowerment and Environment." In *Political Change in Thailand: Democracy and Development,* ed. Kevin Hewison, 195–216. New York: Routledge.

Przeworski, Adam. 1991. *Democracy and the Market: Political and Economic Reforms in Eastern Europe and Latin America.* Cambridge, England: Cambridge University Press.

Raeper, William, and Martin Hoftun. 1992. *Spring Awakening: An Account of the 1990 Revolution in Nepal.* New Delhi: Viking.

Rasler, Karen. 1996. "Concessions, Repression, and Political Protest in the Iranian Revolution." *American Sociological Review* 61: 132–52.

Ratner, Steven R., and Jason S. Abrams. 2001. *Accountability for Human Rights Atrocities in International Law: Beyond the Nuremberg Legacy.* Oxford, England: Oxford University Press.

Rigby, Andrew. 1991. *Living the Intifada.* London: Zed Books.

Roberts, Adam, ed. 1968. *Civilian Resistance as a National Defense: Non-violent Action against Aggression.* Harrisburg, PA: Stockpole Books.

———. 1991. *Civil Resistance in the East European and Soviet Revolutions.* Cambridge, MA: Albert Einstein Institution.

Robinson, William I. 1996. *Promoting Polyarchy: Globalization, US Intervention, and Hegemony.* Cambridge, England: Cambridge University Press.

Rothschild-Whitt, Joyce. 1979. "The Collectivist Organization: An Alternative to Rational- Bureaucratic Models." *American Sociological Review* 44: 509–27.

Routledge, Paul. 1993. *Terrains of Resistance: Nonviolent Social Movements and the Contestation of Place in India.* Westport, CT: Praeger.

———. 1994. "Backstreets, Barricades, and Blackouts: Urban Terrains of Resistance in Nepal." *Environment and Planning D: Society and Space* 12: 559–78.

Rueschemeyer, Dietrich, Evelyn Huber Stephens, and John D. Stephens. 1992. *Capitalist Development and Democracy.* Chicago: University of Chicago Press.

Rummel, R. J. 1994. *Death by Government.* New Brunswick, NJ: Transaction Publishers.

Saich, Tony. 1990. "The Rise and Fall of the Beijing People's Movement." *Australian Journal of Chinese Affairs* 24: 180–208.

Saiyud Kerdphol. 1986. *The Struggle for Thailand: Counter-Insurgency 1965–1985.* Bangkok: S. Research Centre.

Sarachild, Kathie. 1978. "Consciousness Raising: A Radical Weapon." In *Feminist Revolution,* ed. Kathie Sarachild, 144–50. New York: Random House.

Schattschneider, E. E. 1960. *The Semisovereign People.* New York: Holt.

Schirmer, Daniel B., and Stephen Rosskamm Shalom, eds. 1987. *The Philippines Reader: A History of Colonialism, Neocolonialism, Dictatorship, and Resistance.* Boston: South End Press.

Schneider, Cathy Lisa. 1995. *Shantytown Protest in Pinochet's Chile.* Philadelphia: Temple University Press.

Schock, Kurt. 1996. "A Conjunctural Model of Political Conflict: The Impact of Political Opportunities on the Relationship between Economic Inequality and Violent Political Conflict." *Journal of Conflict Resolution* 40: 98–133.

———. 1999. "People Power and Political Opportunities: Social Movement Mobilization and Outcomes in the Philippines and Burma." *Social Problems* 46: 355–75.

———. 2003. "Nonviolent Action and Its Misconceptions: Insights for Social Scientists." *PS: Political Science and Politics* 36: 705–12.

Schoeman, Elna. 1988. *South African Sanctions Directory, 1946–1988.* Johannesburg: South African Institute of International Affairs.

Schumaker, Paul. 1975. "Policy Responsiveness to Protest Group Demands." *Journal of Politics* 37: 488–521.

Schwartz, Michael. 1976. *Radical Protest and Social Structure.* New York: Academic Press.

Scipes, Kim. 1992. "Understanding the New Labor Movement in the 'Third World': The Emergence of Social Movement Unionism." *Critical Sociology* 19: 81–101.

———. 1996. *KMU: Building Genuine Trade Unionism in the Philippines, 1980–1994.* Quezon City: New Day Publishers.

Scoble, Harry M., and Laurie S. Wiseberg. 1974. "Human Rights and Amnesty International." *Annals of the American Academy* 413: 11–26.

Scott, Alan. 1990. *Ideology and the New Social Movements.* London: Unwin Hyman.

Scott, James C. 1985. *Weapons of the Weak: Everyday Forms of Peasant Resistance.* New Haven, CT: Yale University Press.

———. 1989. "Everyday Forms of Resistance." In *Everyday Forms of Peasant Resistance,* ed. Forrest D. Colburn, 3–33. New York: M. E. Sharpe.

———. 1990. *Domination and the Arts of Resistance: Hidden Transcripts.* New Haven, CT: Yale University Press.

Scott, James C., and Benedict J. Tria Kerkvliet, eds. 1986. *Everyday Forms of Peasant Resistance in South-East Asia.* Totowa, NJ: Frank Cass.

Seekings, Jeremy. 2000. *The UDF: A History of the United Democratic Front in South Africa, 1983–1991.* Athens: Ohio University Press.

Seidman, Gay W. 1994. *Manufacturing Militancy: Workers' Movements in Brazil and South Africa, 1970–85.* Berkeley: University of California Press.

———. 2001. "Guerrillas in Their Midst: Armed Struggle in the South African Anti-Apartheid Movement." *Mobilization* 6: 111–27.

Sewell, William H., Jr. 2001. "Space in Contentious Politics." In *Silence and Voice in the Study of Contentious Politics,* ed. Ronald R. Aminzade, Jack A. Goldstone, Doug McAdam, Elizabeth Perry, William H. Sewell Jr., Sidney Tarrow, and Charles Tilly, chapter 3. Cambridge, England: Cambridge University Press.

Shain, Yossi, and Juan J. Linz. 1995. *Between States: Interim Governments and Democratic Transitions.* Cambridge, England: Cambridge University Press.

Shalom, Stephen Rosskamm. 1981. *The United States and the Philippines: A Study of Neocolonialism.* Philadelphia: Institute for the Study of Human Issues.

Sharp, Gene. 1973. *The Politics of Nonviolent Action.* Boston: Porter Sargent Publishers.

———. 1985. *Making Europe Unconquerable: The Potential of Civilian-Based Deterrence and Defense.* Cambridge, MA: Ballinger.

———. 1990. *Civilian-Based Defense: A Post-Military Weapons System.* Princeton, NJ: Princeton University Press.

———. 1999. "Nonviolent Action." In *Encyclopedia of Violence, Peace, and Conflict,* vol. 2, ed. Lester R. Kurtz, 567–74. San Diego: Academic Press.

Sharp, Gene, and Bruce Jenkins. 1989. "Nonviolent Struggle in China: An Eyewitness Account." *Nonviolent Sanctions* 1: 3–7.

Shepard, Mark. 2002. *Mahatma Gandhi and His Myths.* Los Angeles: Shepard Publications.

Shivers, Lynne. 1980. "Inside the Iranian Revolution." In *Tell the American People: Perspectives on the Iranian Revolution,* ed. David H. Albert, 58–80. Philadelphia: Movement for a New Society.

———. 1997. "Iranian Revolution, 1963–1979." In *Protest, Power, and Change: An Encyclopedia of Nonviolent Action from ACT-UP to Women's Suffrage,* ed. Roger S. Powers and William B. Vogele, 263–66. New York: Garland Publishing.

Shoesmith, Dennis. 1985. "The Church." In *The Philippines after Marcos,* ed. R. J. May and Francisco Nemenzo, 70–89. New York: St. Martin's Press.

Shridharani, Krishnalal. 1972. *War without Violence: A Study of Gandhi's Method and Its Accomplishments.* London: Victor Gollancz.

Silverstein, Josef. 1977. *Burma: Military Rule and the Politics of Stagnation.* Ithaca, NY: Cornell University Press.

Smith, Christian. 1991. *The Emergence of Liberation Theology.* Chicago: University of Chicago Press.

Smith, Jackie. 1992. "The 1989 Chinese Student Movement: Lessons for Non-violent Activists." *Peace and Change* 17: 82–102.

———. 1997. "Characteristics of the Modern Transnational Social Movement Sector." In *Transnational Social Movements and Global Politics: Solidarity beyond the State,* ed. Jackie Smith, Charles Chatfield, and Ron Pagnucco, 42–58. Syracuse, NY: Syracuse University Press.

———. 1998. "Global Civil Society?" *American Behavioral Scientist* 42: 93–107.

Smith, Jackie, Charles Chatfield, and Ron Pagnucco, eds. 1997. *Transnational Social Movements and World Politics: Solidarity beyond the State.* Syracuse, NY: Syracuse University Press.

Smith, Jackie, Ron Pagnucco, and Charles Chatfield. 1997. "Social Movements and World Politics: A Theoretical Framework. In *Transnational Social Movements and Global Politics: Solidarity beyond the State,* ed. Jackie Smith, Charles Chatfield, and Ron Pagnucco, 59–77. Syracuse, NY: Syracuse University Press.

Smith, Martin. 1991. *Burma: Insurgency and the Politics of Ethnicity.* London: Zed Books.

Smithey, Lee, and Lester R. Kurtz. 1999. "'We Have Bare Hands': Nonviolent Social Movements in the Soviet Bloc." In *Nonviolent Social Movements: A Geographical Perspective,* ed. Stephen Zunes, Lester R. Kurtz, and Sarah Beth Asher, 96–124. Malden, MA: Blackwell Publishers.

———. 2003. "Parading Persuasions: Nonviolent Collective Action as Discourse in Northern Ireland." *Social Movements, Conflicts, and Change* 24: 319–59.

Smuts, Dene, and Shauna Westcott, eds. 1991. *The Purple Shall Govern: A South African A to Z of Nonviolent Action.* Oxford, England: Oxford University Press.

Snow, David A., and Robert D. Benford. 1988. "Ideology, Frame Resonance, and Participant Mobilization." *International Social Movement Research* 1: 197–217.

———. 1992. "Master Frames and Cycles of Protest." In *Frontiers in Social Movement Theory,* ed. Aldon D. Morris and Carol McClurg Mueller, 133–55. New Haven, CT: Yale University Press.

Snow, David A., E. Burke Rochford Jr., Steven K. Worden, and Robert D. Benford. 1986. "Frame Alignment Processes, Micromobilization, and Movement Participation." *American Sociological Review* 5: 464–81.

Snyder, David, and Charles Tilly. 1972. "Hardship and Collective Violence in France, 1830–1960." *American Sociological Review* 37: 520–32.

Soedjatmoko. 1987. "Violence in the Third World." In *The Quest for Peace: Transcending Collective Violence and War among Societies, Cultures, and States,* ed. Raimo Väyrynen, 290–300. Newbury Park, CA: Sage Publications.

———. 1994. *Transforming Humanity: The Visionary Writings of Soedjatmoko,* ed. Kathleen Newland and Kamal Chandrakirana Soedjatmoko. West Hartford, CT: Kumarian Press.

Somsak Kosaisuk. 1993. *Labour against Dictatorship.* Bangkok: Friedrich Ebert Stiftung.

Sørensen, Georg. 1992. "Utopianism in Peace Research: The Gandhian Heritage." *Journal of Peace Research* 29: 135–44.

Steinberg, David I. 1982. *Burma: A Socialist Nation of Southeast Asia.* Boulder, CO: Westview Press.

———. 1990. *The Future of Burma: Crisis and Choice in Myanmar.* Lanham, MD: University Press of America.

Stohl, Michael, and George Lopez, eds. 1983. *The State as Terrorist: The Dynamics of Government Violence and Repression.* Westport, CT: Greenwood Press.

Strand, David. 1989. "Protest in Beijing: Civil Society and Public Sphere in China." *Problems of Communism* 39: 1–19.

Suh, Doowon. 2001. "How Do Political Opportunities Matter for Social Movements? Political Opportunity, Misframing, Pseudosuccess, and Pseudofailure." *Sociological Quarterly* 42: 437–60.

Summy, Ralph. 1993. "Democracy and Nonviolence." *Social Alternatives* 12: 15–19.

———. 1994. "Nonviolence and the Case of the Extremely Ruthless Opponent." *Pacifica Review* 6: 1–29.

Surin Maisrikrod. 1993. "Thailand 1992: Repression and Return to Democracy." In *Southeast Asian Affairs 1993,* by Surin Maisrikrod, 327–49 Singapore: Institute of Southeast Asian Studies.

Suthy Prasartset. 1995. "The Rise of NGOs as Critical Social Movement in Thailand." In *Thai NGOs: The Continuing Struggle for Democracy,* by Suthy Prasartset, 97–134. Bangkok: Thai NGO Support Project.

Swilling, Mark. 1988. "The United Democratic Front and Township Revolt." In *Popular Struggles in South Africa,* ed. William Cobbett and Robin Cohen, 90–113. Trenton, NJ: Africa World Press.

Tarrow, Sidney. 1991. "Struggle, Politics, and Reform: Collective Action, Social Movements and Cycles of Protest." Western Societies Paper no. 21. Ithaca, NY: Cornell Studies in International Affairs.

———. 1995. "Mass Mobilization and Elite Exchange: Democratization Episodes in Italy and Spain." *Democratization* 2: 221–45.

———. 1998. *Power in Movement: Social Movements and Contentious Politics,* 2nd ed. Cambridge, England: Cambridge University Press.

Taylor, J. L. 1993. "Buddhist Revitalisation, Modernisation, and Social Change in Contemporary Thailand." *Sojourn* 8: 62–91.

Taylor, Robert H. 1987. *The State in Burma.* Honolulu: University of Hawai'i Press.

———. 1991. "Change in Burma: Political Demands and Military Power." *Asian Affairs* 22: 131–41.

Taylor, Verta, and Nancy Whittier. 1992. "Collective Identity in Social Movement Communities: Lesbian Feminist Mobilization." In *Frontiers of Social Movement Theory*, ed. Aldon D. Morris and Carol McClurg Mueller, 104–29. New Haven, CT: Yale University Press.

Teixeira, Bryan. 1999. "Nonviolence Theory and Practice." In *Encyclopedia of Violence, Peace, and Conflict*, vol. 2, ed. Lester R. Kurtz, 555–65. San Diego: Academic Press.

Thaxton, Ralph A., Jr. 1997. "Everyday Forms of Resistance." In *Protest, Power, and Change: An Encyclopedia of Nonviolent Action from ACT-UP to Women's Suffrage*, ed. Roger S. Powers and William B. Vogele, 173–75. New York: Garland Publishing.

Thompson, Mark R. 1995. *The Anti-Marcos Struggle: Personalistic Rule and Democratic Transition in the Philippines*. New Haven, CT: Yale University Press.

Thomson, Curtis N. 1994. "Thailand's May 1992 Uprising: Factors in the Democratic Reform." *Asian Profile* 22: 487–500.

Tianjian Shi. 1990. "The Democratic Movement in China in 1989: Dynamics and Failure." *Asian Survey* 30: 1186–1205.

Tilly, Charles. 1978. *From Mobilization to Revolution*. Englewood Cliffs, NJ: Prentice-Hall.

———. 1985. "War Making and State Making as Organized Crime." In *Bringing the State Back In,* ed. Peter B. Evans, Dietrich Rueschemeyer, and Theda Skocpol, 169–91. Cambridge, England: Cambridge University Press.

———. 1992. *Coercion, Capital, and European States, AD 990–1992*. Cambridge, MA: Blackwell Publishers.

———. 1993. *European Revolutions, 1492–1992*. Cambridge, MA: Blackwell Publishers.

———. 1995a. *Popular Contention in Great Britain, 1758–1834*. Cambridge, MA: Harvard University Press.

———. 1995b. "To Explain Political Processes." *American Journal of Sociology* 100: 1594–1610.

———. 1997. "Means and Ends of Comparison in Macrosociology." *Comparative Social Research* 16: 43–53.

———. 2001. "Mechanisms in Political Processes." *Annual Review of Political Science* 4: 21–41.

Timberman, David G. 1991. *A Changeless Land: Continuity and Change in Philippine Politics*. Armonk, NY: M. E. Sharpe.

Tin Maung Maung Than. 1988. "The *Sangha* and *Sasana* in Socialist Burma." *Sojourn* 3: 26–61.

Tocqueville, Alexis de. 1998. *The Old Regime and the Revolution,* ed. Françoise

Furet and Françoise Mélonio, trans. Alan S. Kahan. Chicago: University of Chicago Press.

Touraine, Alain. 1981. *The Voice and the Eye: An Analysis of Social Movements,* trans. Alan Duff. Cambridge, England: Cambridge University Press.

Trotsky, Leon. 1980. *The History of the Russian Revolution,* trans. Max Eastman. New York: Monad Press.

Uhlig, Mark A. 1986. "The African National Congress: Waiting for the Day." In *Apartheid in Crisis,* ed. Mark A. Uhlig, 149–75. New York: Vintage Books.

United Nations. 1991. *World Development Report* 4, no. 4 (July).

Walder, Andrew G. 1989. "The Political Sociology of the Beijing Upheaval of 1989." *Problems of Communism* 38: 30–40

Weber, Max. 1958. "Politics as a Vocation." In *From Max Weber: Essays in Sociology,* ed. and trans. H. H. Gerth and C. Wright Mills, chapter 4. Oxford, England: Oxford University Press.

———. 1978. *Economy and Society: An Outline of Interpretive Sociology,* 2 vols., ed. Guenther Roth and Claus Wittich. Berkeley: University of Califiornia Press.

Webster, Eddie. 1988. "The Rise of Social Movement Unionism: The Two Faces of the Black Trade Union Movement in South Africa." In *State, Resistance, and Change in South Africa,* ed. Philip Frankel, Noam Pines, and Mark Swilling, 174–96. London: Croom Helm.

Wehr, Paul, Heidi Burgess, and Guy Burgess, eds. 1994. *Justice without Violence.* Boulder, CO: Lynne Rienner Publishing.

Wink, Walter. 1987. *Violence and Nonviolence in South Africa: Jesus' Third Way.* Philadelphia: New Society Publishers.

———. 1992. *Engaging the Powers: Discernment and Resistance in a World of Domination.* Minneapolis: Fortress Press.

Wolfsfeld, Gadi. 1997. *Media and Political Conflict: News from the Middle East.* Cambridge, England: Cambridge University Press.

Wood, Elisabeth Jean. 2000. *Forging Democracy from Below: Insurgent Transitions in South Africa and El Salvador.* Cambridge, England: Cambridge University Press.

World Bank. 1991. *World Development Report.* Washington, DC: World Bank.

———. 1997. *World Development Indicators.* Washington, DC: World Bank.

———. 2001. *World Development Indicators.* Washington, DC: World Bank.

Wurfel, David. 1988. *Filipino Politics: Development and Decay.* Ithaca, NY: Cornell University Press.

Yashar, Deborah J. 1997. *Demanding Democracy: Reform and Reaction in Costa Rica and Guatemala, 1870s–1950s.* Stanford, CA: Stanford University Press.

Zald, Mayer N., and John D. McCarthy, eds. 1987. *Social Movements in an Organizational Society.* New Brunswick, NJ: Transaction Books.

Zdravomyslova, Elena. 1996. "Opportunities and Framing in the Transition to Democracy: The Case of Russia." In *Comparative Perspectives on Social Movements: Political Opportunities, Mobilizing Structures, and Cultural Framing,* ed. Doug McAdam, John D. McCarthy, and Mayer N. Zald, 122–37. Cambridge, England: Cambridge University Press.

Zhao, Dingxin. 2001. *The Power of Tiananmen: State-Society Relations and the 1989 Beijing Student Movement.* Chicago: University of Chicago Press.

Zielonka, Jan. 1986. "Strengths and Weaknesses of Nonviolent Action: The Polish Case." *Orbis* 30: 91–110.

Zunes, Stephen. 1994. "Unarmed Insurrections against Authoritarian Governments in the Third World: A New Kind of Revolution?" *Third World Quarterly* 15: 403–26.

———. 1999a. "The Origins of People Power in the Philippines." In *Nonviolent Social Movements: A Geographical Perspective,* ed. Stephen Zunes, Lester R. Kurtz, and Sarah Beth Asher, 129–57. Malden, MA: Blackwell Publishers.

———. 1999b. "The Role of Non-violent Action in the Downfall of Apartheid." *Journal of Modern African Studies* 37: 137–69.

Zunes, Stephen, and Lester R. Kurtz. 1999. "Conclusion." In *Nonviolent Social Movements: A Geographical Perspective,* ed. Stephen Zunes, Lester R. Kurtz, and Sarah Beth Asher, 302–22. Malden, MA: Blackwell Publishers.

Zunes, Stephen, Lester R. Kurtz, and Sarah Beth Asher, eds. 1999. *Nonviolent Social Movements: A Geographical Perspective.* Malden, MA: Blackwell Publishers.

Zuo, Jiping, and Robert D. Benford. 1995. "Mobilization Processes and the 1989 Chinese Democracy Movement." *Sociological Quarterly* 36: 131–56.

Index

KURT SCHOCK is associate professor of sociology and a member of the graduate faculty in global affairs at Rutgers University.